"WELCOME TO THE BIG TEN"

Penn State's Inaugural Football Season

KIP RICHEAL

SAGAMORE PUBLISHING
Champaign, IL

Production Manager: Susan M. McKinney
Cover design: Michelle R. Dressen and Amy Todd
Proofreader: Phyllis L. Bannon

ISBN: 1-57167-000-9
Library of Congress Catalog Card Number: 94-67276

Printed in the United States

This book is dedicated to my niece, Jolene Richeal.
Thanks for keeping me on my toes.
I hope you will always be my biggest fan.

CONTENTS

ACKNOWLEDGMENTS

Writing a book about Penn State football has extra significance for me because I spent four tremendous years working with a great group of people as a student equipment manager for the Nittany Lions. Not only did I get my college degree from Penn State, which was my life-long goal, I also got to be a part of the national championship team in 1982—Penn State's first ever in nearly 100 years of existence. No one can ever take away that experience from me, no matter what happens during the rest of my life.

If you're a Penn Stater, you probably already understand my meaning, and I hope this book will give you a little more insight as to what these dedicated players and coaches went through, not only during the memorable 1993 season, but the preparation that went into joining the Big Ten, including the dismal 1992 season—Penn State's last as an independent. It is a cliche, but the Nittany Lions—from head coach Joe Paterno on down— had to take a good, long look in the mirror after 1992's 7-5 finish and decide whether they were a team worthy of competing in a conference as traditional and prestigious as the Big Ten.

Anyone who's ever seen Paterno roam the sideline during a Penn State game should know he came away from '92 with an empty feeling. There was genuine concern and the rightful questions of integrity, heart, guts, lack of determination, and the will to win among the entire team were all brought to the surface as the '93 season approached. You don't really have to be a Penn Stater to figure out what an uphill battle the Nittany Lions were facing.

Whether you're a fan of Penn State, Michigan, Ohio State, or any other Big Ten team, or even if you just like college football, regardless of the school or conference it represents, I hope you will get the same enjoyment out of reading this book that I got in writing it.

A book like this does not write itself. And in a fact-based setting such as college football, the author doesn't play out the season in his mind. There are many groups and individuals who have assisted me in some form or fashion through the course of this book. I owe them many thanks, for without them, none of this would have been possible. They include:

—First and foremost, my mother and father, Helen and Milton Richeal, who suffered with me through some tough Penn State losses, but also enjoyed the many victories.

—Thanks to Joe Bannon, Jr., Peter Bannon, Jude Lancaster, Susan McKinney, Kathy Dressel, Michelle Dressen, Amy Todd, and the rest of the great crew at Sagamore Publishing. Your patience and assistance is deeply appreciated.

—Mr. L. Budd Thalman, Associate Athletic Director for Communications at Penn State, and the outstanding Sports Information staff that works with him. Budd answered every question I had for him and provided me with any bit of information that proved useful.

—Head coach Joe Paterno, who didn't have to let me follow the team around along the sidelines; or on the buses; or in the locker rooms; or in the meeting rooms, but he did because he always encouraged me to reach for opportunity while you have the chance. My relationship with Penn State football is very special and unique, and without Coach Paterno, it would not be possible.

—Assistant coaches Jerry Sandusky, Fran Ganter, Dick Anderson, Tom Bradley, Craig Cirbus, Bill Kenney, Kenny Jackson, Joe Sarra, and Greg Schiano, and Assistant Strength coach Kevin O'Dea. Thanks for letting me hang around the meeting rooms.

—Thanks to all the players who took the time to interview with me throughout the season and never seemed to mind the endless questions that often go into such a project. Special thanks to defensive end Tyoka Jackson for his writing contribution as well.

—Athletic Director Jim Tarman, who also supported my efforts in his last year before retirement; Assistant A.D., Frank

Rocco, who set me up with places to stay on the road; Administrative Assistant, Jim "Ace" Williams; Administrative Aide, Cheryl Norman, and staff assistants, Mel Capobianco, Marcy Collitte, Mike Franzetta, Patty Shawley.

—Head equipment manager Tim Shope and his assistant Brad Caldwell, and all the student managers who busted their butts through every game and every practice to keep the team running smoothly throughout the season.

—Team physician, Dr. Harry Weller; Director of Athletic Medicine, Dr. Wayne Sebastianelli; Head trainers, George Salvaterra and Charles Thompson; compliance coordinator, John Bove; and ticket manager Bud Meredith.

—Thanks to Blue White Illustrated, an outstanding magazine for and about Penn State athletics, and its owner, Phil Grosz, who allowed me access to his office's tremendous photo collection and loaned me most of the photographs in this book. Also special thanks to the rest of the staff at BWI: Mark Brennan, Matt Herb, Dale Grdinic, Stacey Schrenkel and Neil Rudel, and photographers Harvey Levin and Mark Selders.

—Sharon Dixon and the staff at State College Best Western Inn; Bill Lee III, Director of Golf at Toftrees Golf Course, State College; and Gary Cording, a bus driver for Tri-State Tours. I thank him for not leaving me stranded at Cedar Rapids Airport in Iowa.

—Special thanks also to friends and relatives who assisted me throughout the season: My brothers Larry, John, Lance, Jeff, Milt Jr., and Jim; nephew Keith Richeal and niece Racquel Richeal; Joe Young, Jim Riggio, Patti Gerard and Jennifer Saccani; and friends from my place of full-time employment who traded shifts with me numerous times throughout the season so that I could attend the Penn State football games I wrote about: Becky Brunnell, Steve Brutout, Jean Cason-Wynter, Mark Churchfield, Cindy Farbo, Steve Ford, Mary Lynn Fratangeli, Danny Gunn, Joanne Harris, Diane McCallan, Lisa McClure, Bob Monzi, Ed Petronchak, Mary Portman, Jim Powell, Jana Ribeau, Sharon Taylor, Vonnie Vaughn and Jim Yule.

FOREWORD

When I think back to the events of 1990 that culminated in Penn State's invitation to become a member of the Big Ten Conference, I'm reminded of the reaction of Lady Lion basketball coach Rene Portland, who said she felt like she had just been appointed to a new job without the inconvenience of moving.

For everyone associated with Penn State athletics, membership in the Big Ten represented a new frontier. After more than 100 years as a football independent, we were about to enter a conference we knew very little about.

I am the first to admit that we approached our Big Ten affiliation with some apprehension. I knew little about the personnel on the various conference teams. We had no "feel" for the instincts of the Big Ten coaches and how they might respond in critical game situations. We were ignorant of the intensity of conference games and the week-in, week-out grind of a league schedule.

In short, we had a lot to learn about being a member of a conference.

There isn't any question that the 1993 football season was revealing for Penn State coaches, student-athletes, and fans. As with any new experience, there were moments of high excitement and, at the other extreme, deep disappointment. Such swings are typical of almost any football season, but on this shakedown cruise through the Big Ten, they were understandably intensified.

We'll always remember scoring on our initial offensive play in the Big Ten and going on to a win over Minnesota. The sting of our first conference loss in our inaugural game against Michigan, before the largest crowd ever in Beaver Stadium, also is prominent in our recollections of last season.

On our first time around the block, we found Big Ten football a challenging experience. Every conference opponent played us tough. It was a war every week. There are no shortcuts to success in the Big Ten. It's a solid conference from top to bottom. As we learned last fall, being the best in the Big Ten requires a substantial commitment.

While there may have been some early misgivings about Penn State's historic decision to align with the Big Ten Conference, we think reflection will endorse it as a bold initiative that will be of enormous benefit to both the University and the Conference. It certainly triggered changes that have altered the face of college athletics.

The 1993 season was something special. It is memorable as one of those moments in time when our direction was launched on a new and uncharted course. Penn State's initial journey through the Big Ten is an excursion that chronicles the Nittany Lions' first steps on the conference landscape.

Penn State and the Big Ten represents the marriage of a program that always has aspired to success within the rules with a conference that shares with same traditional values. It is an association that was long overdue and that we hope will long endure.

Joseph V. Paterno

INTRODUCTION

There may never be another person who could sit down and write a better perception of Penn State football than Kip Richeal. I have known Kip since he was a student manager at Penn State and have witnessed in him the feeling that there is truth in the notion that the harder you work for something, the more meaning the results seem to have.

Kip took something from his experience with our football team. He learned the lesson of hard work and dedication, and poured those efforts into everything he has done, from getting his degree to developing his passion for writing. He has been with us through the emotional highs of great victories and also at our darkest moments following devastating defeat. He knows our strengths and weaknesses; he is a part of the heart and soul of the Nittany Lion tradition.

Out of respect for Kip, the Penn State football family has opened its doors to this special person and has supported him as he presents this in-depth look at our inaugural season in the Big Ten. It is my hope, along with every other member of this proud family, that you will enjoy and relive the many significant moments.

Jerry Sandusky
Defensive Coordinator

1

Not Just
Another Season

In the shadows of Mount Nittany, about as close to the geographical center of Pennsylvania as one can get, there lies an acre or two of fresh green grass. Nothing really new or stirring, considering the vast agricultural richness that surrounds this normally quiet and peaceful stretch of country. At 5 a.m., the balanced population of Centre County's farmers are already hard at work, harvesting their crops and tending to the business that is their livelihood.

It is early August, and the acre or two of wide open grass is also being nurtured. White markings are painted over the green ever so carefully, line after line; yard after yard. Much of the neatly cropped lawn will become mulch in just a few short days, with bits of sod strewn here and there within the confines of this 100-yard masterpiece. There is artificial grass as well, and an enormous shelter to guard the inhabitants of this land from the cold and sometimes dreary weather that is often a fixture of autumn in this otherwise breathtaking setting.

It is only a short while until a large group of young men will embark on the dawn of a new era. They will be asked to rise at the first sign of light to face the challenge that no similar group from this region has ever encountered. And they will be led by a legend. A man who has survived his profession — and conquered it — longer than anyone would have ever thought possible.

Joseph Vincent Paterno had anticipated this moment for a very long time. Longer than the nearly four years that had passed since the Penn State Nittany Lion athletic program had been extended an invitation to join one of the most revered conferences in all of intercollegiate athletics.

It seemed, from the beginning, to be a match made in heaven.

Over the years, the Big Ten Conference has strived for nothing less than perfection from its members. Whether the venue is the athletic field or the class room, excellence has always been the key component.

When the Big Ten first entertained thoughts of expansion, its governing body believed only a university like those in its own conference should be considered for invitation. Penn State had spent the first 100 years or so of its football existence as an independent. During that time, the program grew to be one of the most respected in the country and had developed some of the finest athletes to ever set foot in the National Football League. Over 100 players moved on to professional football after experiencing the Penn State way of life.

Aside from athletics, Penn State has also never wavered in its commitment to academics. Paterno, Penn State's head football coach for the past 27 years, makes it clear to every incoming freshman that he is expected to make the grades in the classroom, or he will not make the run through the tunnel of Beaver Stadium with his teammates on some glorious Saturday afternoon in autumn, when football is the focal point of life in State College, Pennsylvania.

Paterno takes tremendous pride in the student-athlete concept, which helps explain his 19 first-team Academic All-Americans, 10 Hall of Fame Scholar Athletes and 14 NCAA Postgraduate Scholarship winners through 1992. It is his belief that the words "college" and "football" should go hand in hand and when they don't, well, even All-American athletes have felt Paterno's wrath on the field with suspensions and even dismissals from the team when taking a lazy attitude toward hitting the books. Sadly, that player's misfortune is often another player's valuable lesson.

Through 1993, Stanley O. Ikenberry was the current president at the University of Illinois and also chaired the board of directors for the Big Ten Conference. Before he accepted his post at Illinois, Ikenberry served as vice president at Penn State. He knew all about the tradition; the glory; the respect that went with being a Penn Stater.

And he knew Paterno.

With that in mind and with conference expansion on the horizon, Ikenberry and the other board members voted to extend the Big Ten's 11th conference membership invitation to the Pennsylvania State University.

"I was surprised at how quickly things developed," Paterno said during a break in his team's 1993 spring practice sessions that would prepare the Nittany Lions for their first official venture into Big Ten country. "When we were originally contacted [Penn State Athletic Director] Jim Tarman called me and said we were in the Big Ten. I said, 'Yeah right,' and he said it was true, that he really wasn't kidding. He told me they didn't have all the formal approvals, but everyone said they wanted to do it."

Well, almost everyone.

While the board of directors and conference presidents showed enthusiasm at the thought of adding Penn State to its already prestigious conference, athletic directors and coaches quietly frowned on the idea. The Big Ten had always been made up of schools from the midwest. Geographically, Columbus, Ohio was the farthest east any school had to travel for a conference game. State College would result in roughly another 350 miles of travel due east.

Bobby Knight, the outspoken, but highly respected head basketball coach at Indiana University, probably issued the harshest statements about the Big Ten's newest prospective member when he questioned the location of State College and said its local airport didn't have a runway long enough to land even a small commuter. As he continued to describe the great farm land central Pennsylvania has to offer, everyone realized that Knight is often rather candid in a humorous sort of way, and his words on this particular occasion were accepted as rather tongue-in-cheek. But still, when The General speaks, people usually listen.

"I think the presidents all felt we'd be a good addition to the conference because they were pleased with our reputation," Paterno said. "They looked at our record and saw that we had no problems, no NCAA violations or probations. They just felt our institution would be a good match for their conference."

Ikenberry all but said as much when he extended the formal invitation to Penn State's hierarchy on December 18, 1989.

"We are delighted with the prospect that Penn State will join the conference," Ikenberry said as he represented the conference's Council of Presidents. "From an academic standpoint, Penn State is comparable in quality and character to our member universities. The Penn State tradition of integrity in athletics would enable our conference to become an even stronger leader in the movement to reform intercollegiate athletics. This would be a natural and positive expansion."

Tarman also spoke positively of the university's decision: "As we plot the future direction of Penn State athletics, joining the Big Ten Conference represents the kind of bold, positive step that will bring new energy and commitment to our total program."

A decision like this took much consideration not just for Penn State's football team but the rest of its broad-based athletic system. Men's basketball had just achieved notoriety by landing legitimate talent in its program and was on the verge of supremacy in the tough, but underrated Atlantic 10 Conference. Penn State was a force in the conference and would eventually appear in two straight NCAA tournaments as an A-10 representative.

Women's basketball was already a force and had been for several years. Coach Rene Portland had become accustomed to leading her team to conference championships and top-ten finishes year after year. Women's field hockey and men's soccer are constant forces in intercollegiate athletics at Penn State. So are the men's and women's volleyball programs and Penn State's wrestling program has become one of the nation's elite.

But all sports at Penn State had to take a good hard look at the tremendous decision that faced Jim Tarman, Paterno and other athletic figures within the university. While consideration for all of Penn State's athletic teams was being taken, the decision would largely be based on what was best for the football team.

Why? Because other sports' survival at Penn State depended on the football program. Everything the football team did, every success it ever had and every dollar of revenue it ever generated would ultimately prove fruitful for other sports on campus. As an independent over the years, a national television appearance for the football team meant upwards of $100,000 or more in revenue for Penn State to distribute to its overall athletic program. A postseason bowl appearance was always beneficial, while a New Year's Day bowl game meant millions to the university.

As an independent, this was revenue Penn State needed only to share with itself. That is all well and good if your program stays up to date, which Penn State was still perfectly capable of doing. The Nittany Lions reaped generous rewards for their appearances in the 1983 Sugar Bowl, the 1986 Orange Bowl and the 1987 Fiesta Bowl. All three of those games pitted No. 1 in the country versus No. 2, and Penn State captured the national championship on two of those occasions.

But soon after its much talked about Fiesta Bowl upset over the University of Miami (FL), Penn State's football program seemed never to be quite the same. The Nittany Lions finished 8-4 in 1987 and appeared to go through the motions in a 35-10 Citrus Bowl loss to Clemson. Things would reach an all-time low in 1988 when one of college football's long-standing records would come to a crashing halt.

Penn State had not suffered a losing season since 1938, when the Nittany Lions endured a 3-4-1 record. It came close a couple of times, like the back-to-back 5-5 records of 1965 and 1966, which were Rip Engle's last year as head coach and Joe Paterno's first. Penn State won the national championship with an 11-1 record in 1982, but started the '83 campaign, 0-3. Things looked bleak for a winning season, but the Nittany Lions righted their ship and finished the rest of the season 8-1.

For 49 years, the Penn State football program somehow found the will to win when the cards were stacked against it and built a legacy that will be hard to match by any school in the future. But in 1988, the numbers in the loss column finally outweighed the other side. A season-ending loss to arch-rival University of Pittsburgh put the stamp on a 5-6 season and left many Penn State fans scratching their heads, wondering what had become of their precious football team in just two short years.

These were the thoughts that drifted through executive minds at Penn State as well. The last big payday for Penn State came in its previous Fiesta Bowl appearance and without a bowl to attend in 1988, a severe dent in the university's athletic budget was suddenly felt. It was not a drastic situation, but smaller sports within the university were probably not going to benefit as much as they had in the past. There was a bit of talk concerning the future of certain smaller sports at Penn State, but nothing that would come to fruition.

Independence was the key word at Penn State since 1887. All of a sudden, however, it was a word that 100 years later, needed to be studied more seriously. Were the Nittany Lions ready to give up their independence?

"We were having a hard time maintaining the kind of program we were accustomed to," Paterno said. "Parity was coming on strong, and we weren't a school that was going to just go out and win a national championship every three or four years. Parity cut back on scholarships and with that parity continuing, you had to have something for the fans once your team loses a game or two."

With the prospect of joining a conference, Penn State could benefit not only from its own success, but also the success of others within its conference. For instance, a percentage of the revenue from every national television appearance made by a conference member is shared equally by all other member universities. The same also holds true for bowl appearances. That means even Northwestern University, the long-time cellar dweller of the Big Ten Conference in football shares in the revenue of the Big Ten champion's Rose Bowl appearance. This concept would certainly benefit Penn State's other intercollegiate sports and help ensure their survival in the future.

This talk of joining a conference wasn't the first time Penn State had entertained such a notion. Joe Paterno performed dual roles as head coach and athletic director in the early 1980s and at that time he proposed the idea of an eastern conference to several schools, including Pitt, West Virginia, Syracuse, Temple and Rutgers.

"We needed a conference with a little more exposure than the Atlantic 10," Paterno said. "I would like to have seen an all-sports conference similar to the ACC, but things fell through when Pitt joined the Big East in basketball. With them gone, I didn't see it being as successful and I didn't want some sports to be in one conference and some in another."

So Penn State remained an independent in football while most of its other sports programs continued to participate in the Atlantic 10.

Penn State's membership in the Big Ten Conference became official on June 4, 1990, when it was formally accepted by all the member universities. After a century of independence, Penn State had placed itself firmly into one of the most respected and prestigious conferences in intercollegiate athletics. Academics would remain a high standard and as the Nittany Lions would soon discover, competition in athletics would reach levels of intensity most of the school's sports programs — including football — had never experienced.

Once the dust had settled on Penn State's move, however, it seemed a trend was soon developing. Soon after the Big Ten made its bold assertion to add Penn State as its 11th member, other conferences followed suit. Some expanded, others realigned. Still other institutions packed their bags and moved from one conference to another, such as Florida State, which also said goodbye to independence and hello to the Atlantic Coast Conference.

The Big East turned on to football as well as basketball and added Miami to its fold, which gave it instant credibility on the gridiron. Other notable football independents such as Louisville found themselves looking for a new home even at the end of the 1993 season and it seemed independence was becoming a thing of the past. The only independent that would seem firm in remaining that way was Notre Dame and with its own NBC television contract plus its tremendous national following, the Fighting Irish seemed to be one of the only schools that didn't need a conference to survive.

There have been many realignments and adjustments over the years in college sports. Finances play a huge factor and so do the projected rivalries. But the first real feedback around the country seemed to happen when Penn State made its decision to join the Big Ten. College football fans around the country were stunned by the news. Some were torn by tradition, others were perhaps delighted by the fact their team would no longer be mere prey on the Nittany Lions feeding schedule.

Joe Paterno had suddenly become a tyrant to eastern football fans because his team's move would ultimately bring some of the east's fiercest rivalries to an end. Penn State-Syracuse; Penn State-West Virginia; Penn State-Boston College. And most of all, Penn State-Pitt. The game had been played 92 times since 1893 with the Nittany Lions holding a slight 47-41-4 advantage in the overall series.

University of Pittsburgh fans were outraged that Paterno had the gall to exclude the Panthers from his regular season schedule beginning with the 1993 season. But Paterno reasoned that Penn State had to remain loyal to those who were at one time loyal to it, such as Temple and Rutgers, who supported Paterno's idea of an all-sports conference in the early '80s.

"I think it mattered more to Pitt fans than the Penn State fans, because Penn State had really come to dominate the series," said Phil Grosz, owner of *Blue White Illustrated*, a weekly publication that deals exclusively with Penn State athletics. "People have written to our publication this past season and said, 'You know, what we miss most about being an independent is playing Alabama, Notre Dame, Nebraska.' Their letters are reminiscent of the big games of the 1980s, the ones that provided the most drama year after year. The only drama with the games against Pitt, West Virginia or Boston College were the few times those schools had a chance to beat Penn State."

Pitt football remained an independent until the Big East put together eight teams for the 1991 season — some of which did not participate in Big East basketball. Syracuse and Boston College did the same as Pitt while West Virginia remained in the Atlantic 10 in basketball with Rutgers and Temple. Those three programs also kept their independence until the Big East turned to football. This was the kind of unbalanced system Paterno had referred to and why he did not want to see Penn State enter into such a system.

Joe Paterno felt the sores from the other university's rejections in 1982 and as he looks back on it, he can only imagine the power an eastern football conference might have generated in today's competitive market that conference play inhabits.

"I think it would've been a tremendous conference," he said. "You already had a lot of the rivalries, not just with us, but with the other schools, Pitt-West Virginia; West Virginia-Syracuse. I think if the conference was around that we had proposed back then, we would not have lost as many of the kids we recruited from the east to a lot of other schools around the country. The eastern region would have been even more of a hotbed for recruiting."

The way the Big East is set up now, Pitt, Miami, Boston College and Syracuse are the only member institutions that participate in both football and basketball in the conference. West Virginia, Rutgers and Temple are members of the Atlantic 10 in basketball, while the fourth football school in the Big East mix, Virginia Tech, participates in the Metro Conference in every sport *but* football. This system was set up in 1991, but at the end of the 1993 football season, those four schools decided they wanted full membership in the Big East Conference.

The Big East was suddenly facing a dilemma, because if it said no to such a proposal, those schools could have moved elsewhere and the Big East would have lost its football setup almost as quickly as it began. Rutgers was holding a considerable amount of leverage, because it has on numerous occasions been discussed as a further addition to the Big Ten, which was also looking toward midwestern expansion by possibly inviting Nebraska and Missouri into its fold.

Rutgers would add the New York recruiting market to the Big Ten, which in turn would cripple an already struggling Big East. With that in mind, the Big East would almost *have* to consider inviting Rutgers and the other three football-only schools into the conference as basketball members.

No one is certain where that would leave Georgetown, Connecticut, Providence, St. John's, Seton Hall and Villanova — the other basketball members in the conference — but according to Big East commissioner Mike Tranghese, the conference was in the midst of reviewing a study conducted by Rutgers over the previous six months concerning the feasibility of a 14-team conference for all sports. That doesn't sit well with the basketball-only schools because it would mean the profits would have to be split 14 ways instead of 10.

"They're basically doing now what we wanted to do ten years ago," Paterno said. "When it fell through at the time, we remained an independent, but we weren't going to rule out the possibility of someday belonging to a conference."

Which could lead one to believe that Paterno feels he owes no apologies to the University of Pittsburgh or any of the other schools that rejected his proposal at the time.

"It's something I definitely would like to have seen," Paterno said. "It's too bad not everyone was in agreement, but that's the way things go sometimes. Sure, we'll miss the rivalries with Pitt and West Virginia and some of the other schools, but one thing I hope our kids will get out of [joining the Big Ten] is that there are a lot of other rivalries just waiting to get started."

The outcry was especially strong over the removal of Pitt from the Nittany Lions' schedule. It had become a tradition, and usually it was the last game of the regular season for both teams. Many times, the outcome of the game decided the winner of the Lambert Trophy, which symbolized the best team in the east. The game was also a tremendous recruiting factor for both schools, because a kid who was wavering between the two often settled with the winner.

It wasn't just the Panther contingent who voiced their disapproval when the word got out that tradition was about to come to an end. Penn State fans and alumni everywhere filled the sports talk show airwaves wondering how Paterno could make such a foolish decision. Penn State fans despised Pitt and Pitt fans loathed Penn State. It was one of those cases where records didn't matter. The two teams always came prepared for a war and fans seemed never to be disappointed once the biggest game of their season was complete.

Through it all, however, Paterno hung tough and urged Penn State fans to trust in the university's decision. They would see soon enough that Penn State football was not going to lose its credibility. For every Pitt, Syracuse and West Virginia to dislike, there was soon to be a Michigan, Ohio State or Michigan State on the horizon. And the animosity could certainly grow just as strong.

2

1992 Fallout

The "lame duck" label is often associated with politicians who are finishing out their last term in office, whether their departure is due to retirement or defeat in election.

In sports, the title is often pinned on a coach who has been all but handed his pink slip but is asked to finish out the season anyway, as though it were a gesture of good faith on the part of ownership or management.

Such a label is most often looked upon with disfavor. Earning respect is mostly an exercise in futility. It is rare to see an entire *team* viewed in the lame-duck sense, but that is exactly how the Penn State Nittany Lions appeared as they headed into the 1992 season — their final season as an independent.

This year would be unique; different than any other. To a man, the players would attest to that. It would be their final opportunity to prove their worth as an independent. It would take perfection to achieve the goal that every major college player strives for.

College football had gotten to the point where one loss could just about erase any team's chance at a national championship. In 1982, Penn State won its first ever title despite one early-season loss to Alabama. It took an 11-0 regular season and a 14-10 Fiesta Bowl victory over Miami, (Fla.) to capture the 1986 crown.

Those two seasons were the Lions' only claim to college football supremacy in their over-100-year history. In 1992 they were set to have their last matchups — at least for a while — with annual foes Boston College, West Virginia and the University of Pittsburgh. Add to that a home game against Miami and road trips to Brigham Young and Notre Dame and thoughts of a national championship would have seemed even more difficult to comprehend.

With Penn State being Penn State, however, challenges were a way of life, and these players were going into the season with nothing less than perfection on their minds.

The Nittany Lions were coming off an impressive 11-2 showing in 1991, which included a 42-17 Fiesta Bowl victory over Tennessee and a No. 3 national ranking behind co-champions Washington and Miami (FL). They had lost some tremendous talent from the '91 team including quarterback Tony Sacca, who had broken most of Penn State's major passing records as a rare (under Joe Paterno) four-year starter; the inside linebacking duo of Mark D'Onofrio and Keith Goganous; and exceptional secondary performers Leonard Humphries and Darren Perry, who earned 1991 All-American honors.

Despite the personnel losses, Paterno liked his crew as he headed into the 1992 season. "They're good football players," he said in his preseason media address. "They're going to play the way you like to see kids play.

"How good we can be will depend on how quickly our players, particularly the young ones, learn to handle the pressure and whether we can keep them healthy long enough to make the necessary progress. If all that happens, I think we'll have a good year."

Penn State may have lost a few of its key individuals from the 1991 squad, but there was definitely quality talent returning in '92. Among the returners were quarterbacks John Sacca (Tony's brother) and Kerry Collins. The two would enter a competition that would have its twists and turns right through the middle of the 1993 season. Regardless of who took the snaps, the quarterback would be guarded by an offensive line that had seen players move to all sorts of positions in the previous spring workouts but seemed ready to mesh for the regular season.

Junior redshirt tailback Richie Anderson, who scored 10 touchdowns in 1991 was back for more, while the Nittany Lion defense was looking forward to an exciting combination of defensive linemen in juniors Lou Benfatti and Tyoka Jackson.

The Lions were certainly not without their great players in 1991, but one in particular was not only a great player, but a tremendous athlete. Senior wide receiver O.J. McDuffie was described in the 1992 Penn State football yearbook as "a throw-back to the days of the triple-threat halfback." He was named by his grandmother for Hall of Fame running back O.J. Simpson, although she only chose the initials, preferring to stay away from Simpson's real first name, Orenthal.

As was soon discovered at Penn State, McDuffie not only shared a first name with one of pro football's greatest, he also shared his zest for the game, his desire, and a knack for coming through in the biggest of games.

*In the 1991 Kickoff Classic against defending national champion Georgia Tech, McDuffie caught a pair of third-quarter touchdown passes — including one that was tipped several times and caught flat on his back — to thwart any Yellow Jacket comeback hopes in the Nittany Lions' impressive victory.

*Later that season, Penn State faced No. 1 Notre Dame at home. The Lions pulled off the upset thanks in large part to McDuffie's three touchdowns, one of which was a 37-yard run on a reverse that sent the Irish defense reeling.

*Penn State was playing its final game of the season. Tennessee was the opponent in the Fiesta Bowl, where the Nittany Lions had achieved a few of their more impressive bowl victories. The Volunteers led 17-7 midway through the third quarter, but McDuffie got his teammates rolling by returning a punt 39 yards, which set up the first of Penn State's five consecutive touchdowns. McDuffie's heroics led to a 42-17 win, an 11-2 record and a No. 3 national ranking in the polls. He also came away with Fiesta Bowl MVP honors with 149 all-purpose yards.

There was a tremendous air of optimism that surrounded the Penn State football program as camp broke for the 1992 season. With the returning talent ready to go a step or two higher in the rankings, it would only seem fitting for the players to embrace the new season and attack each opponent with a vengeance. Unlike seasons before, however, the Nittany Lions knew where they were headed at the end of the season regardless of their record, regardless of their standing and most importantly perhaps, regardless of their feelings.

Selecting a national champion in Division I-A college football has never been an exact science. In fact, the whole problem with this level of play is the fact that every year, young men's blood and sweat and hopes and dreams are left to a mere selection. In most cases, only one or two teams actually get the opportunity to *play* for the national championship. A No. 1 or No. 2 ranking at bowl time helps a team get that chance, but Nos. 3, 4, 5, etc. are most often left in the cold without the chance to say, "Hey, what about us?"

The debate has raged on for the last several years. So many people who have an interest in college football — the fans, some members of the media, even coaches and other university officials — would like to see a national championship playoff of some sort. The traditionalists say it can't be done. Their argument is either that a playoff would lengthen an already long season, or it would cut into the popularity of the annual bowl season. They say the importance of major bowls would be minimalized greatly, while some other bowls would most certainly be discontinued altogether.

Those in favor of playoffs, however, argue that the minor bowls could serve as quarterfinal games in the first two weeks of December for the top 16 teams in the final regular season rankings with the four major New Year's Day bowls — Cotton, Rose, Orange and Sugar — alternating yearly as semifinals and a final that would be played on New Year's Day. All other divisions of college football have a playoff to decide their champion and there seem to be no problems on those levels when it comes to some teams playing 15-game seasons.

Playoff advocates also cite the importance and popularity of March Madness, which is the name given to the NCAA basketball tournament. Talk about a frenzy. Everyone from the casual basketball fan, to the diehard, to Dick Vitale looks forward to the three-week hysteria that decides a champion from a field of 64 teams. Those players go through at least 30 games to reach the tournament and are on the road for almost half the season. But they still find time to study without the premise that their season is too long.

Joe Paterno has supported a college football playoff format almost since the day he took over as coach at Penn State. In the late 1960s, the Nittany Lions fielded back-to-back undefeated teams, but received little consideration for the national championship. Very little respect was shown toward eastern football at the time and many of the so-called experts cited Penn State's "soft" schedule, even though the Nittany Lions scored impressive Orange Bowl victories over Big-Eight opponents Kansas in 1969, (15-14) and Missouri in 1970, (10-3).

As the 1992 season approached, Division I-A college football was still without a playoff system, but the NCAA believed it had the answer at least to finding a definite No. 1 by forming what would be known as the coalition poll. It involved a point system that would combine the totals of the two major polling systems currently in effect — the Associated Press poll and the coaches poll. Most of the time the coaches and writers agreed at season's end on a national champion, but there were some seasons, most recently in '91, where opinions slightly differed. The nation ended up with co-champions as Miami, (FL) finished first in one poll, while the University of Washington topped the other, thus sharing the national championship.

The coalition poll would ultimately guarantee a No. 1 versus No. 2 matchup at the end of each season with the Sugar, Orange and Cotton Bowls all somehow having a say in where the game would be played. This was to be the first year of the new system and undoubtedly, some kinks were about to unfold.

Because of the coalition, bowls were scrambling for the hottest ticket possible and teams were looking earlier than usual to put their name on any bowl list that was possible. Tradition won out in the Rose Bowl, which had for many years pitted the Pacific-10 champion against the Big Ten champ. Things would stay that way so there was no chance for any outside bidding, but on the down side of the new system, the Rose Bowl would seem to have little chance of ever featuring a national championship game.

You have to figure the bowl picture is getting just a bit out of hand when your school's media guide for the upcoming season announces exactly when and where your favorite university will be playing come New Year's Day.

That was the case at Penn State as page 50 of the 1992 football yearbook displayed the Blockbuster Bowl logo and a headline proclaiming, **"Penn State Will Play in Blockbuster Bowl New Year's Day — CBS-TV to Televise Game Nation-**

ally." It wasn't a case of extra sensory perception that foretold the Nittany Lions' postseason whereabouts. Just the first blow delivered from the onslaught of the new bowl coalition.

The decision was made on May 20, 1992 and it was a unique situation, to be sure. Penn State athletic director Jim Tarman even admitted as much. But he also added that it was "not inappropriate given circumstances which forced Penn State to assume an aggressive and accelerated posture toward the postseason."

Perhaps Tarman's meaning was based on the fact that because of the new coalition, every team that belonged to a conference had a shot at a major bowl bid. Those that didn't would find the postseason road a bit more difficult. With a decent record, Notre Dame wouldn't have any trouble finding a place to play on New Year's Day because, well, because it was Notre Dame.

Penn State characteristically, has always been a major draw come bowl time as well, but with the Nittany Lions playing their last season as an independent, the big wigs at Penn State felt they might not receive enough attention at the end of the season. The minor bowls were bound to roll out their collective red carpets for Penn State, but the pay day would not suffice for a team that had visions of a 9-2 or 10-1 season.

The Blockbuster Bowl fit Penn State's portfolio nicely because it was supposed to be an up-and-coming bowl game. The payout was about $2 million to each team and it would guarantee the Lions a New Year's Day bowl game. Penn State had also played in the very first Blockbuster Bowl just two years earlier, where it dropped a 24-17 decision to Florida State in front of a sellout crowd of 74,102 at the newly constructed Joe Robbie Stadium in Fort Lauderdale. Therefore, it would not be playing in unfamiliar surroundings.

"We are happy to make this arrangement with the Blockbuster Bowl and look forward to a return trip to the Fort Lauderdale/Miami area," Tarman said at the formal announcement. "We especially like the fact we will be playing on New Year's Day and the involvement of CBS Television in the national coverage of the game."

Tarman made certain to thank everyone possible for Penn State's early travel plans as he called the three-year-old Joe Robbie Stadium "an outstanding facility, perhaps the best for a postseason game," and praised the corporate representatives from Blockbuster Video and Raycom for their "organization and staging of the game" and the volunteers who made Penn State's last Blockbuster Bowl appearance such a pleasant one.

Even Penn State president Dr. Joab Thomas got into the act.

"We obviously are pleased to return to the Blockbuster Bowl," Thomas said. "When we visited in 1990 we were impressed with the warmth of our reception by the South Florida community. We're happy as well that Joe Robbie Stadium is within easy reach for many of our thousands of Penn State alumni."

In a sense, Penn State had succeeded before even a down of the 1992 season had been played. As was required for all postseason participants, Penn State would have to win at least six games against Division I-A opponents to qualify for the game, but that seemed to be an issue that was never in doubt. It was a lucrative deal for the university and what seemed to be most important at the time, it guaranteed that Penn State would not be shut out of the major postseason bowl action and that should have made everyone concerned happy.

But did it?

"It's an awkward situation," Penn State assistant coach Tom Bradley said. "It's tough from a coaching standpoint because I think the administration has a whole different philosophy. They figure it's a great bowl with a nice payoff and we got what we were looking for. But the players come into the season knowing exactly what they're playing for. Their goal is still the national championship, but what happens if they lose one game along the way? You get so fired up for the whole bundle, if you lose one game you have to redefine your goals. That was something I think all the coaches looked at a little bit."

"As a coach [in that situation] losing one game is something that crosses your mind for a minute and then you just forget about it," Penn State defensive coordinator Jerry Sandusky said. "You have to take things one game at a time. Actually I wasn't disappointed at the time because I felt we had plenty of incentive. Our schedule was tough enough that if we won all of our games, the Blockbuster Bowl certainly had a chance to be in the national championship spotlight."

At the time, however, at least one of the players felt a little uncertain about Penn State's naming a postseason bowl destination so soon.

"It was hard because everything was locked in and we felt like we were being excluded," senior linebacker and 1992 cocaptain Brett Wright said. "We knew we were going into the Big Ten and it was our last season as an independent, but we were kind of upset we weren't included in any of the stuff dealing with the bowl alliance. Being an independent, it's always a pot shot on where you're going [to a bowl game]. It all depends on your record and we felt we had to be decisive with our wins to have a chance at a national championship."

A national championship was the right goal and the 1992 Nittany Lions were confident they could get there whether it was through the Blockbuster Bowl or a rumble in the street. All they wanted was a chance to be heard, a chance to be recognized and an opportunity to play the best.

Penn State began its quest at Cincinnati on September 5 in a game that was a far cry from the 81-0 shellacking the Nittany Lions handed the Bearcats at Penn State's Beaver Stadium the season before. Cincinnati was a much-improved football team and showed it by returning the opening kickoff 69 yards, which set up a five-yard run and a 7-0 Cincinnati lead.

Junior fullback Brian O'Neal tied it for the Nittany Lions a short time later on a five-yard run, but Penn State struggled into the third quarter before it finally took the lead.

The preseason hoopla centered mostly around Penn State's quarterback situation. It was to be a battle between junior quarterbacks John Sacca and Kerry Collins, but when the season opened in Cincinnati, neither player would figure in the game's final outcome. Sacca went down in the second quarter with a shoulder injury, while Collins was out indefinitely with a broken index finger on his passing hand, which he reportedly hurt while playing volleyball at a family picnic during the summer.

Wally Richardson, a true freshman, stepped in for Sacca and marched the Nittany Lions to three second-half scoring drives as Penn State hung on for a 24-20 victory. The Lions relied on their running game as they rolled up 243 yards on the ground to just 44 passing. Richie Anderson led all carriers with 83 yards on 18 carries and a touchdown, while O'Neal added 46 yards and two TDs on 14 carries.

Richardson got his first career start the following weekend in Penn State's home opener against Temple and made the most of it by hitting on 10-of-19 passes for 164 yards and a touchdown in the Lions' 49-8 laugher. Richardson also rushed for a touchdown as the Nittany Lions scored 33 second-half points to break open what was a close game for Temple.

Penn State was again led by the junior tailback Anderson, who had 103 of the Lions' 387 rushing yards, while senior O.J. McDuffie reached the 100-yard plateau in receiving for the third time in his brilliant career with 118 yards on only six receptions.

John Sacca was back in the starting lineup for the Nittany Lions in Week 3 as an undermanned Eastern Michigan team came to University Park and fell behind 28-0 before it barely knew what state it was in. Sacca closed the 28-point first-quarter barrage for Penn State by hitting McDuffie for a 17-yard score, while Anderson sandwiched two rushing touchdowns around junior Shelley Hammonds' 32-yard interception return for a score.

Sacca was an impressive 10-of-17 for 153 yards and two TDs (the first two of his career), while Ki-Jana Carter, a tailback with freshman eligibility, came off the bench in the second half and rushed for a game-high 73 yards and two touchdowns on just six carries.

The Penn State defense forced five turnovers and frustrated Eastern Michigan quarterbacks into a collective 5-for-23 performance and three interceptions. It also snuffed a potential scoring threat near the end of the first half by pushing Eastern Michigan back from a first down at the Lions' 10-yard line to a fourth down at the 34. Eastern Michigan wasn't exactly an indicator of what was to come in the Big Ten, but Penn State didn't want to waste any opportunity to show that its defense would be a force to be reckoned with.

The Nittany Lion defense wasn't so much tested the following week as it was worked. Penn State faced Maryland, which featured the popular, but not always successful run-and-shoot offense. The Terrapins ran 89 plays on offense and amassed 518 yards, but the Lions prevailed behind the running of Richie Anderson, 49-13.

Anderson reached the 100-yard mark for the third time in '92 as he gained 138 yards on 20 carries. He also scored four times, including three on the ground, while Sacca threw for 195 yards and two TDs.

Maryland actually struck first in the second quarter as it capitalized on a Sacca fumble to take a 3-0 lead. Sacca quickly atoned for his mistake by hitting McDuffie for a 29-yard score in the ensuing series to give Penn State, which was playing its third straight home game, a 7-3 lead. Anderson scored his first touchdown on a six-yard run the next time the Lions got the ball and followed with a 26-yard reception from Sacca to give his team a 21-3 lead at halftime.

Penn State cruised to a 4-0 record in the second half behind Anderson touchdown runs of 25 and 22 yards that capped one of the best games of his career.

The Nittany Lions made their second road trip of the season the following weekend by traveling to Giants Stadium in East Rutherford, N.J., to take on the Scarlet Knights of Rutgers, another eastern foe that coach Joe Paterno preferred to keep on the schedule out of loyalty.

Rutgers used an eight-man defensive front to try and stop the pounding Penn State running game. The move appeared successful as Anderson, the Lions' leading rusher through the first four games, was held to his lowest output of the season — 16 yards on 12 carries — and was forced to sit out most of the second half with a sore knee.

Penn State rushed for a season-low 142 yards as a team, but Sacca came up big when it counted by becoming just the third Nittany Lion quarterback ever to throw for at least 300 yards in a game. His 303-yard, three touchdown performance helped the Lions score 31 second-half points on their way to a 38-24 victory.

O.J. McDuffie raised his season total to five touchdown receptions by handling two of Sacca's 21 completions in the end zone. McDuffie caught a career-best eight passes for 129 yards, which was just three yards short of his all-time high.

Defensive tackle Lou Benfatti spoke up for the defense with eight tackles, six of which were unassisted and two for losses. Reggie Givens, Rich McKenzie and Willie Smith registered quarterback sacks as the defense held Rutgers to just 68 total rushing yards.

It was almost the halfway point of the season and Penn State was right where it wanted to be. It was 5-0 (a mark that would be remembered during the 1993 season also) and still in charge of its own fate. If this were professional football, the preseason would be over and the real schedule would be about to start. Penn State was undefeated and set to host the Miami Hurricanes, who were coming to University Park with a 4-0 record, a Heisman Trophy candidate at quarterback and a lot of national attention.

The national spotlight was on Penn State for the entire week leading up to the game against Miami. It was a rematch of sorts for the Nittany Lions, who were beaten by the Hurricanes in 1991, 26-20. In that game the Lions made numerous mistakes and felt they beat themselves more than Miami beat them on the field.

The concentration was intense all week in practice as each player knew it would take an outstanding effort to maintain their lofty goal of a perfect season. Mistakes could not be afforded against a Miami team that exploded with confidence and strutted its stuff on every occasion in order to back up its No. 2 national ranking.

Penn State was riding an 11-game winning streak (its last loss was to Miami the season before) and a record crowd of 96,704 packed Beaver Stadium to watch the nationally televised showdown. It was Joe Paterno, who was in the middle of his 27th season at Penn State, against Dennis Erickson, who came into the game with a 37-3 record in his fourth season as head coach at Miami.

The Hurricanes struck first on a 10-yard touchdown run in the first quarter and added a Mike Prewitt field goal in the second to take a 10-0 lead into the locker room at halftime.

Penn State finally got on the scoreboard to start the second half thanks to Richie Anderson's 10-yard touchdown run, but the first of several key miscues developed for the Lions soon after. Penn State had the ball deep in its own territory when quarterback John Sacca dropped back to look for an open receiver. What he found was an all-out Miami blitz, and in his haste to throw the ball away, Sacca threw it right into the arms of Hurricane defensive end Darren Krein, who returned it 28 yards for a Miami touchdown. It was the first interception thrown by a Penn State quarterback in 148 attempts for the season.

The score was 17-7 now, but Penn State still had the fourth quarter to work with. Sacca took advantage of the time by driving the Nittany Lions to the end zone on the next series. His 14-yard touchdown strike to O.J. McDuffie drew the Lions to within 17-14, but two more possessions resulted in a punt and an interception as Miami won for the first time since 1979 at Beaver Stadium.

"When two good football teams play, that's what happens," a solemn Paterno said afterward. "They [Miami] played a perfect game. They didn't have a turnover. We got the penalties, had a field goal blocked and missed another field goal. We played hard, but it's tough to beat a team that's good at doing those things."

Mistakes were what cost Penn State a win the season before at Miami. The Lions went into this game knowing they couldn't commit the brutal errors that had hurt them the year before, but that's exactly what happened. The Penn State defense did its job for the most part. Miami came in averaging 393.8 yards per game in total offense, but the Nittany Lion defense held it to a season-low 218 yards.

Miami quarterback Gino Toretta would go on to capture the Heisman Trophy in 1992, but he was below average on this sunny October afternoon as Penn State defenders held him to just 80 yards on 11-for-31 passing. Toretta passed for only 22 yards in the second half and completed just three of 16, while Miami's longest gain all afternoon went for only 16 yards.

Penn State, on the other hand, outgained Miami (370-218) and had more first downs (21-16), but was penalized nine times for 77 yards to just two for 24 yards against Miami. The Nittany Lions also wasted two scoring opportunities inside the Hurricanes' 15-yard line as kicker Craig Fayak missed a 20-yard field goal and Anderson was stopped short on a fourth-and-one situation by Miami's Michael Barrow.

The last time Penn State had beaten Miami was for the national championship in the highly publicized 1987 Fiesta Bowl. In the eyes of many, that was also the last time Penn State had won in a situation that was labeled "the big game." Writers were becoming critical of Paterno and his play calling and were ready to put him out to pasture in the same vein that was once put on professional coaching legends such as Tom Landry, Chuck Noll and Don Shula in recent years.

To be sure, all hopes for a national championship had faded for Penn State with the loss to Miami, and it seemed as though now was the time to realize what everyone was made of in 1992. After all, one more win and the Lions would have their postseason bowl bid all locked up. Right? You would have had to pardon the Penn State players if they didn't immediately jump for joy at such a prospect. At that moment, they weren't thinking about the Blockbuster Bowl, the Rose Bowl or any bowl. All they could think about was another stupid loss to Miami. Boston College was next on the Lions' schedule, but even three days before the Eagles were to visit State College, the question in the locker room continued to be, *"How did we lose that game to Miami?"*

The quotes continued in the newspapers right into Friday, the day before Penn State's season continued against Boston College. "We shouldn't have lost to Miami," one player would say. "The mistakes were what killed us. We had 'em and we blew it," another groaned.

Those thoughts and signs of remorse from too many players would prove to carry just a bit too far.

"Boston College had a good team and I didn't want to take anything away from them," Paterno said. "But we lost a game we should never have lost."

It took until halftime of the Boston College game for Penn State to finally realize its situation and put Miami in the past. Unfortunately, the Nittany Lions had dug themselves a hole they would find impossible to climb out of. In the past, BC was, for the most part, one of those teams Penn State fans looked forward to disposing of quickly.

The year before, Boston College quarterback Glenn Foley was intercepted five times by the Nittany Lion defense, but this October day in 1992 was Foley's chance for redemption. The junior quarterback threw for 344 yards and four touchdowns as the Golden Eagles pulled off the unlikeliest of upsets, 35-32.

It was Homecoming at Beaver Stadium and the 96,000-plus in attendance looked for the Lions to regroup after the disappointing loss to Miami. For a while Penn State seemed on the verge of erasing the memories of the Hurricane that swept through State College the week before. The Nittany Lions led 10-

7 with a little over four minutes remaining in the first half. While it's hard to believe that four minutes could virtually wipe out an entire season, that was exactly what happened.

Penn State was about to get the ball back when it was penalized for roughing the punter. Foley, who had struggled to that point, hit flanker Ivan Boyd for a 48-yard touchdown reception and the Eagles were ahead 14-10.

Penn State went three-and-out on its next possession and Foley drove Boston College 79 yards on 4-of-5 passing. The seven-play drive culminated with a 16-yard scoring pass to tight end Pete Mitchell and the Eagles were up 21-10.

There was very little time left until halftime, but Boston College still was not quite finished. The Golden Eagles gained possession again after a careless Penn State turnover and instead of taking satisfaction with an 11-point halftime lead on the road and falling on the ball, Foley threw a quick 29-yard strike to Mitchell in the end zone. There was one second left on the clock and stunned silence in Beaver Stadium as Boston College had whipped up an improbable 28-10 lead over Penn State.

"Foley's a great quarterback," Penn State defensive coordinator Jerry Sandusky said. "It was unfortunate, but yeah, it seemed like we were thinking about the week before in that first half and by the time we got back into it we were too late."

After Foley threw his fourth touchdown pass in the third quarter to give the Golden Eagles a 35-10 cushion, Penn State finally caught fire. O.J. McDuffie was again the catalyst as he moved the Lions to the BC 10-yard line on a 43-yard flanker reverse. Two plays later Richie Anderson scored from the one-yard line and it was 35-16 after a failed two-point conversion.

Quarterback John Sacca drove the Lions 80 yards in their next series and hit McDuffie, who finished with 11 catches for 212 yards, for a seven-yard touchdown. Backup tailback Mike Archie caught the two-point conversion pass and it was a 35-24 game.

Sacca was injured during Penn State's next series and Kerry Collins was called into action for the first time after sitting out the season with a broken index finger on his throwing hand. Collins completed three long passes to the BC two-yard line and Anderson punched it in from there. Collins hit McDuffie for the two-point conversion and the Lions were down 35-32 with 1:39 to play.

Penn State created an opportunity to either tie or win the game as Kyle Brady recovered kicker V.J. Muscillo's onside kick at the Penn State 46-yard line. On first down, however, Collins overthrew McDuffie down the left sideline and Boston College defensive back Joe Karma intercepted to finally clinch his team's second victory in 21 tries against Penn State.

The fire seemed absent again the next weekend as Penn State traveled to West Virginia for the final game of another backyard rivalry. The Nittany Lions held a slim 19-16 halftime lead and extended it to 26-16 early in the third quarter.

West Virginia mounted a rally, however, in front of a raucous home crowd and tied the game on kicker Mike Vanderjagt's 41-yard field goal with barely two minutes gone in the fourth quarter.

Penn State appeared to be letting another game slip away when running back J.T. Morris fumbled the ensuing kickoff. West Virginia moved to the Lions' one-yard line in four plays, but Penn State linebacker Reggie Givens made the play of the game when he recovered a Mountaineer fumble on third-and-goal.

With the crowd silenced just a bit, Penn State went to work. After trading punts, the Nittany Lions began the deciding drive with 5:40 remaining in the game.

Kerry Collins, making his first start at quarterback, was sensational during the drive as he threw for 50 yards and guided the Nittany Lions through three critical moments. The first came on a third-and-nine from deep in Penn State territory when Collins hit McDuffie for a 10-yard gain and a first down.

Penn State then faced third-and-seven from its own 25, but Collins pumped short, then hit flanker Justin Williams down the right sideline for a 40-yard gain. Three running plays netted nine yards and the Lions were faced with a fourth-and-one.

Joe Paterno disdained the Lions' field goal opportunity and made the decision to go for it. Collins stretched his 6-foot-5 frame just enough over the line for the first down and fullback Brian O'Neal then atoned for an earlier fumble by dashing 21 yards to the West Virginia three-yard line. Richie Anderson carried it in from there for his third touchdown of the game and 16th of the season to give Penn State a seven-point lead.

Penn State used four minutes and 48 seconds during its impressive 12-play drive and made sure West Virginia would not muster a miraculous finish in its final 52 seconds when linebacker Phil Yeboah-Kodie intercepted Mountaineer quarterback Jake Kelchner's sideline pass and returned it 23 yards for a touchdown. The insurance score sealed Penn State's 40-26 victory and finished a rivalry that saw the Nittany Lions win 48 out of the 59 games between the two teams.

The Penn State Nittany Lions were 6-2 with their win over West Virginia and seemed to be poised to right their ship and salvage a still respectable season. The bowl bid had been officially earned — albeit a month early — and now the team could concentrate on the rest of its schedule.

But in reality, knowing its postseason plans in the middle of October might have been the very reason Penn State's season would suddenly go completely and inexcusably flat.

Next up for the Nittany Lions was a trip to Provo, Utah for a date with Brigham Young. Penn State was 2-0 lifetime against the Cougars and had won both games in relatively convincing fashion. The picturesque mountains were a sight to behold, but for Penn State, the scene was about to become an all-too-familiar nightmare.

Brigham Young was known for its passing attack. Plain and simple. Jim McMahon, Steve Young and Ty Detmer are just a sample of the list of quarterbacks who have engineered coach LaVell Edwards high-powered offense over the years. Furthermore, the Cougars had never sported more than a passive running game. This was evidenced in the 1991 meeting between Penn State and Brigham Young when the Nittany Lion defense held the Cougars to zero rushing yards.

Even so, Joe Paterno had preached all week that Brigham Young — even though it was ranked No. 2 in passing in the nation — had the best running game he had ever seen in Cougar uniforms. Once again the coach was right. Brigham Young quarterback Ryan Hancock threw only 19 passes in the cold, snowy weather while his running backs rushed for 241 yards, which was the best any team had done all season against the Penn State defense.

Kalin Hall became the third back to rush for more than 100 yards (117) against Penn State for the season and began BYU's scoring assault with a five-yard first-quarter run to give the Cougars a 7-3 lead. BYU didn't stifle its passing game, it merely equalized it. Hancock completed 13 of his passes for 220 yards and smoked the Nittany Lions with three second-quarter touchdown passes to give his team an insurmountable 27-3 halftime lead.

Quarterback Kerry Collins set Penn State passing records for attempts (54) and completions (28), but mostly because he had to. His 317 passing yards were the second best in team history, but when the Nittany Lions needed the yards in scoring situations, its offense was producing very little. Collins threw a five-yard touchdown pass to O.J. McDuffie, who had his usually effective day with 124 all-purpose yards, and tailback Richie Anderson, who was the leading scorer in the nation at the time, scored from the one-yard line in the fourth quarter to make the final score somewhat respectable.

But the Lions' 30-17 setback once again left everyone involved scratching their heads, wondering what had become of such a promising team just a few weeks earlier. Penn State twice moved inside the BYU 10-yard line when the game was still within reach, but came away empty on both occasions. It was the third loss in four games for the Nittany Lions, and it was clearly the first sign that some of those involved had lost interest in the season.

"It seemed as though a lot of the players had lost touch with the mental aspect of the game," said Phil Grosz, owner of *Blue-White Illustrated*. "After the loss [to Miami], Penn State didn't have a lot to play for. If Penn State were to play BYU under normal circumstances, even at BYU, Penn State would win nine out of ten times. They were totally unfocused, and if you don't have that, I don't care who you're playing, you're going to have a difficult time."

Coaches take a different approach in dealing with the losses and, understandably so, they hardly ever come right out and say publicly that their team, for whatever reason, lost its competitive edge. Joe Paterno knew his team was lost in some dark cavern at the time, but no member of the Nittany Lion team felt it was a time to forget about pride and call it a lost season.

Penn State needed to rise to some occasion, and its next challenge was certain to deliver that opportunity. Still another rivalry — not quite as long standing, but cherished nonetheless — was coming to an end in famed Notre Dame Stadium. Penn

State had won eight of its 11 meetings against ND in the current series, including the last two in a row. Even a high school team would step its game up a notch if it played a game in front of the risen arms of Touchdown Jesus overlooking one of this immortal stadium's end zones.

The Nittany Lions may have been struggling, but on this day they had their focus. It was a blustery day with off and on snow squalls covering the field with a white coating for most of the afternoon. The Fighting Irish were coming off a convincing 54-7 victory over Boston College the previous week and were heavy favorites to defeat Penn State. The Lions appeared deserving of this lack of respect because of the embarrassing defeats they endured over the past few weeks, but they shrugged everything off and displayed the pride that is most commonly expected of them.

This was classic football. None of the astro-turf or sterile dome atmosphere or fancy footwear that has commercialized the game to painstaking heights. It was Notre Dame, with its basic gold pants and helmets and dark blue jerseys, against Penn State, who by now had become synonymous with the word "generic" in the eyes of the nation's sports media, in their all white pants, jerseys and helmets. Both teams were as traditional as the game gets, right down to their black, high-top shoes and a finish that would fit a Hollywood script.

Notre Dame opened with a 3-0 lead on kicker Craig Hentrich's 26-yard field goal, but Penn State responded with Richie Anderson's 18th touchdown of the year, a one-yard run that gave the Nittany Lions a 6-3 lead. Kicker V.J. Muscillo had his extra point blocked and as the result so often goes, the miss would prove costly to the Lions.

Two more Hentrich field goals gave the Fighting Irish a 9-6 lead through three quarters and once again the Penn State offense seemed to be struggling with itself. Quarterback Kerry Collins completed only seven of 28 passes for 131 yards and the Notre Dame defense held Penn State to its third-lowest rushing total of the season with 107 yards.

As much as Penn State's offense was being held in check, however, its defense stood tall against the Fighting Irish and their All-American quarterback, Rick Mirer. Sophomore Brian Gelzheiser had spent most of the season backing up outside linebacker Reggie Givens, a position he wasn't much accustomed to, but when inside linebacker and co-captain Brett Wright went down with an injury against Brigham Young, Gelzheiser moved back to his more comfortable position and led the Nittany Lions with a game-high 15 tackles. Givens also stepped up with a career-high 11 tackles as Notre Dame found it would not be as easy as the oddsmakers had predicted.

Notre Dame drove to the Penn State 34-yard line early in the fourth quarter, but Penn State safety Lee Rubin turned the momentum in his team's favor by knocking down a Hentrich pass out of punt formation. The Nittany Lions went on one of their lengthy ball-control drives that covered 17 plays and culminated in a 22-yard Muscillo field goal and a 9-9 tie. Collins kept the drive alive by hitting tight end Troy Drayton for 22 yards and a first down at the Notre Dame one. But two runs and a pass netted a loss of two yards and prompted Paterno to go for the field goal.

Much like it did against West Virginia, Penn State capitalized on an opponent's turnover when Gelzheiser recovered a Notre Dame fumble at the Irish 44-yard line. Penn State again kept the ball on the ground as it ran four straight plays. Collins then changed up and hit receiver O.J. McDuffie for 15 yards and a first down at the Notre Dame 13. Fullback Brian O'Neal scored on the very next play as he burst through the middle for the touchdown that gave the Nittany Lions a 16-9 advantage.

Mirer had four minutes and 25 seconds to work with and Penn State knew all too well of the mystique of Notre Dame Stadium and the leprechauns that seemingly come out of nowhere to snare a Fighting Irish victory from the jaws of defeat. Mirer had established himself as Notre Dame's all-time leader in total offense and touchdown passes and with the coolness of a Joe Montana, another famous Notre Dame quarterback, he went to work against a Nittany Lion defense that had been unrelenting to that point.

With the combination of Mirer's passing and fullback Jerome Bettis' running, the Irish moved from their own 36-yard line to the Penn State nine with a little over a minute to play. Mirer and tailback Reggie Brooks were stopped on consecutive running plays and after a third-down incompletion, Penn State's defense — which had given up 91 points in its three previous games —

was faced with stopping Notre Dame on fourth-and-goal at the Lions' three-yard line.

Mirer dropped back to pass and with the veteran prowess that was expected of him, he calmly found Bettis on a delay pattern in the back of the end zone for the touchdown. Penn State now found itself clinging to a one-point lead with 20 seconds remaining and it was decision time for Notre Dame Coach Lou Holtz.

Both head coaches in this game had been involved in similar situations before. Joe Paterno has spent his entire coaching life going for the win in such circumstances. And Holtz has usually lived and died by the same sword. On this day Holtz wasn't going to settle for a tie. Penn State had played too hard to be caught in a deadlock. Notre Dame had battled back so gallantly in the closing minutes. Neither team deserved to lose, but one definitely deserved to win. No matter who it was, Holtz was going to make sure there was a clear-cut winner.

Hentrich, the kicker, stayed on the sidelines for Notre Dame and Mirer took the play from the coaches. Penn State's defense braced itself for the final play, a situation it had faced countless times over the years and one that had been practiced probably a thousand times in each player's lifetime. In 1987 Penn State stopped a similar Notre Dame rally by stuffing a two-point conversion in the closing seconds to preserve a 21-20 victory at Beaver Stadium. Five years later a different Notre Dame quarterback faced a different Nittany Lion defense, but the results weren't as favorable for the Penn State fans.

Mirer threw for a modest 164 yards on the day and completed 12 of 23 passes. His last pass, however, the one that didn't count in the final statistics, was his most important. The senior quarterback dropped back for Notre Dame's final play and immediately felt the pressure of Penn State's defensive line rush. Mirer left the pocket and rolled to his right as if he was going to tuck the ball under his arm and run for the end zone. Just as quickly he pulled up and tossed a prayer that was answered in the corner of the end zone by Brooks.

Of all the wins and losses Penn State endured during the 1992 season, its 17-16 setback at Notre Dame was the most heart-wrenching. "It was probably the best game we played all year defensively," Penn State defensive end Tyoka Jackson said. "We played hard and even though things had gone kind of down hill earlier, we showed we weren't quitters in that one. We just came up short."

Lou Holtz shook his head at mid-field as he shook hands with Joe Paterno. It was a sign of respect that two noteworthy coaches could acknowledge the other's courage and ability. Holtz knew his team had faced a Penn State team that was better than what the experts had said and what it had shown a week earlier at Brigham Young. Penn State had one more game to play on its regular-season schedule. One more rivalry to complete before it moved to the Big Ten Conference. This was the cross-state rivalry that seemingly no football fan in Pennsylvania wanted to see come to an end.

Penn State had won 47 of the previous 92 games played against Pitt and was a heavy favorite to end this rivalry on a positive note despite its fall from a 5-0 beginning. The University of Pittsburgh football program was in disarray and its visit to State College sure didn't seem to be the answer. The Panthers had won only three of their first 11 games and coach Paul Hackett was almost assuredly on his way out.

Pitt had not fielded a contending football team since the national championship days of Johnny Majors in 1976 and the following years under Jackie Sherrill. Pitt fans growled for the rivalry with Penn State to continue, but the game itself each season had become somewhat of a laugher in recent years. Penn State had won five out of the last seven games by such scores as 31-0 in 1985, 34-14 in 1986 and 32-20 in 1991. Even though Penn State also took the appearance of a confused team in 1992, there were very few believers that Pitt could pull off some sort of upset. Hackett, the latest answer to Pitt's woeful slumber, was about to serve his last game as the team's head coach. To that point, the Panthers had built a mere 13-20-1 record under his roughly three years of leadership.

The Nittany Lions scored first as fullback Brian O'Neal started the best day of his career with a three-yard touchdown run to give his team a 7-0 lead. O'Neal scored again early in the second quarter, this time on an 11-yard dash up the middle, and Penn State was up 14-0.

One thing Pittsburgh had going for it was the passing of four-year starter Alex Van Pelt, who rewrote several of the Panthers' passing records that had been set by All-American Dan Marino in the early '80s. Van Pelt came into the game ranked fourth in the nation in total offense and he finished with 149 yards to gain the No. 4 position on the NCAA career passing yardage chart.

Van Pelt led the Panthers to a second-quarter score with a 71-yard drive in eight plays that was highlighted by his one-yard TD pass to tight end Rob Coons. Penn State's Tyoka Jackson broke through the line to block the extra point and safety Lee Rubin took advantage of the NCAA's two-point conversion rule that says an opposing player can return a botched conversion the length of the field and receive two points for the defense. Rubin scooped up the blocked kick at the Nittany Lions' 18 and re-turned it 82 yards to put Penn State ahead 16-7.

O'Neal (105 yards rushing) and tailback Richie Anderson (129) became the first pair of Penn State running backs to crack 100 yards in the same game since Leroy Thompson and Gary Brown accomplished the feat in 1990. Penn State gained 374 yards on the ground and averaged 7.2 yards per carry against a tired Pitt defense. O'Neal added touchdown runs of four and three yards to become the first runner to score four touchdowns in a game since Thompson did it against Rutgers in 1990.

Anderson built his total around a 64-yard touchdown run, while O.J. McDuffie capped his brilliant regular season career with 192 all-purpose yards, including 112 yards on eight recep-tions. The fifth-year senior broke four Penn State records as he established season marks in receptions, touchdown catches and all-purpose yards, to go along with a career record for pass receptions.

The backup tailback trio of Ki-Jana Carter, Mike Archie and Stephen Pitts provided a bit of a preview for the backfield competition in 1993 as they combined for 115 additional yards and two touchdowns. Pitts scored on a 22-yard run from scrim-mage and Archie returned a punt 62 yards — the longest return of the season for the Lions — as Penn State breezed to a 57-13 victory over Pitt.

Brian Gelzheiser started his second consecutive game at inside linebacker and turned in another great performance with

10 tackles, as did senior Ivory Gethers. Penn State outgained Pitt, 534-381, as quarterback Kerry Collins threw for an additional 143 yards on 11-for-20 passing. Van Pelt finished his brilliant Pitt career with a 10-for-25 performance, one touchdown and one interception.

In one sense, Penn State could look toward its January 1 Blockbuster Bowl commitment with confidence and momentum. It took a convincing win over arch-rival Pitt and a well-played, but gut-wrenching loss to Notre Dame before that to bring out that confidence. But the Nittany Lions were also faced with a ton of questions, the biggest being perhaps, "WHAT HAPPENED?"

While those last two games could be taken with a grain of confidence, they could also be taken with a grain of salt. After all, Pitt was not the same Pitt that had provided the stiff challenges of the 1970s and early '80s. And no matter how well the Nittany Lions played, the final result against Notre Dame was still a loss.

Penn State had gone from a 5-0 team with serious national championship hopes to a team in serious disorder that had seemingly lost all interest in what it was playing for week after week. The Nittany Lions lost four of their last six regular season games, two to teams they should never have lost to and two to teams they could just as easily have beaten had a couple of breaks fallen their way.

The last of the former rivalries was concluded on November 21 when the Nittany Lions disposed of Pitt in a somewhat orderly fashion. Penn State was now six weeks away from a game its players knew they would be playing back in May, but never seemed to take much pleasure in reaching. Even Joe Paterno had to wonder if the Blockbuster Bowl would bring out the best in his squad for a successful conclusion to 1992, or if it was merely the final chapter of an unusual story that simply said, "Let's get this thing over with."

3

The "Lackluster" Bowl

It was January 1, 1993, a beautifully sunny day, and a future Big Ten team was playing against a Pac-10 representative, but two things were absolutely certain. The city was not Pasadena and the setting was not the Rose Bowl. Penn State would have to wait at least a year before that could happen, and while Stanford was eligible from the Pac-10, it missed going to the "grandaddy of 'em all" by one game.

For Penn State, the surroundings were familiar. It had played in the first Blockbuster Bowl only two years before, where it lost to Florida State, 24-17. The Blockbuster committee liked Penn State because of its tremendous fan base throughout the country, and the Nittany Lions would almost certainly draw fans to the spacious and still new Joe Robbie Stadium in Fort Lauderdale.

The attraction would hopefully grow even more because not only did the Blockbuster Bowl have Penn State and its time-honored tradition, its other participant was Stanford University, a well-respected academic and athletic institution from northern California. And talk about coaching matchups. This one may have been the best of all the bowl games in 1992.

It was Joe Paterno, the legend from Penn State who had won 247 games in his 27 seasons as head coach, against Bill Walsh, the genius whose mind is considered by many to be an instant play book.

Walsh was the former head coach at Stanford before taking over as head coach of the San Francisco 49ers in 1978. He built a dynasty at San Francisco with probably the greatest quarterback of all time in Joe Montana guiding his complex, but highly effective offense. Walsh led the 49ers to three of their four Super Bowl titles in the 1980s, a decade the 49ers reigned over in the same manner that the 1970s were ruled by the Pittsburgh Steelers and the '60s belonged to the Green Bay Packers.

After the 49ers won their third Super Bowl title in 1988, Walsh decided to step up from the sidelines and into the broadcast booth, where he became NBC's No. 1 color analyst alongside play-by-play man Dick Enberg. He analyzed other team's X's and O's for two years, but soon the coaching itch came back to him as it did for so many other ex-coaches in recent years.

Walsh really didn't have a yearning to get back into the NFL, but when Dennis Green — a former Walsh disciple in San Francisco — left Stanford to coach the NFL's Minnesota Vikings, Walsh accepted the challenge of becoming the Cardinal head coach once again.

Stanford, as noted, had always been held in high regard because of its strong academic tradition. The two schools were very similar in that matter, but Penn State's football success was much more documented over the years than that of the Cardinal. Walsh brought with him the same offense he had employed at San Francisco, but Stanford fans were reminded quite often that Joe Montana didn't come with the package.

Just like he did with the 49ers, Walsh scripted the first 25 plays or so of his offensive game plan and ran those plays regardless of the situation. The man responsible for playing the part of Montana was quarterback Steve Stenstrom, and his efforts throughout the season gave all Stanford fans a reason for hope as the Cardinal ran to a 9-2 regular season record and a top-ten finish in the final polls. One loss stood out in particular as Stanford fell to Washington, 41-7, thus enabling the Huskies to represent the Pac-10 in the Rose Bowl.

So, here was Stanford in the Blockbuster Bowl, ready to face Penn State, a school filled with tradition, but currently wrought with uncertainty. The only thing Penn State could be sure of as game day approached was that its football team would be taking the field as an independent for the last time.

There were a lot of distractions involved in a Joe Paterno-Bill Walsh matchup. The two coaches would be the first to say they didn't want it to be a game that focused on their personal coaching philosophies, or the way they approached each game. It was a game for the kids, a reward for their hard work and dedicated efforts throughout the season.

But the media played up the coaching matchup anyway. And they did it in the biggest way. Almost from the outset, newspapers throughout the country ran either photographs or caricatures of Paterno and Walsh and labeled them "The Legend versus The Genius." Meanwhile Walsh would almost assuredly point out that Paterno didn't gain his legendary status without some genius of his own, and Paterno would instantly agree that Walsh had become something of a legend in his own right. Neither coach was comfortable with the labels put on them for the game, while players from both sides seemed to shrug off the hype.

Both coaches did their best to build up the other team as Walsh shuddered at the thought of facing a team as "big and powerful as Penn State" in his first bowl test in quite some time, while Paterno called Stanford, "the best team in the Pac-10." The legend's words would prove, perhaps, to be quite true as Stanford showed in its first possession that it had come to play a football game, and had come to play it well.

No one knew which Penn State football team would show up against the Cardinal. Naturally, the coaches hoped the Nittany Lions that started out 5-0 and played so formidably against West Virginia, Pitt and even Notre Dame down the stretch would suit up. But frankly, most expected the team that tripped all over itself in the loss to Miami and never quite got up against the likes of Boston College and Brigham Young.

Bowl games are meant to be pleasant experiences for both teams, win or lose. For Penn State, the Blockbuster Bowl eventually proved to be the final game on its 1992 schedule, even though technically it was the first day of 1993. Suspense is often the main ingredient in a bowl recipe; this one had none. Stanford saw to that and so too, perhaps, did Penn State.

There was no desire, no emotion, no fire. As it turned out, the flame went out in the Nittany Lions' season when they lost their opportunity for a national championship way back in

October against Miami. On any given day, any football team can be beaten. Upsets everywhere have proven that theory in the past to be true. On any given day; any *realistic* day, Penn State should beat Stanford by two touchdowns. Maybe the Nittany Lion faithful who bothered to show up in South Florida expected too much.

Penn State came into the game with a string of four straight wins over Pac-10 teams in postseason games, but Stanford refused to become the fifth. Stenstrom threw for 210 yards and two touchdowns as the Cardinal defeated the Nittany Lions with relative ease, 24-3.

Walsh's game plan went into effect from the opening kickoff and Stenstrom guided his team 71 yards in eight plays. Senior tight end Ryan Wetnight had caught only seven passes over the last four games for Stanford, but Stenstrom hit him three times in the opening drive for a total of 45 yards, the last three of which came on the game's first touchdown.

Penn State answered quickly with a drive of its own as quarterback Kerry Collins hit wideout O.J. McDuffie on passes of 21 and 26 yards to move the Lions to the Stanford 15-yard line. Penn State couldn't muster another first down and it had to settle for V.J. Muscillo's 33-yard field goal.

The offense seemed to stall on both sides through much of the first half, but Stanford began a key scoring march late in the second quarter as it started a drive at its own 35-yard line with 5:45 remaining in the half. Penn State's defense had pretty much bottled Stanford's running game through much of the afternoon, but senior fullback Ellery Roberts got outside of the containment and rumbled 34 yards to the Penn State 28.

Wetnight, who caught five passes on the afternoon for 71 yards, took a 17-yard completion to the Penn State 11-yard line and on third-and-four, fullback J.J. Lasley carried on a reverse pivot and found the end zone to give the Cardinal a 14-3 lead at the break. Penn State held a 181-158 advantage in total offense and totaled almost three more minutes than Stanford in time of possession, but it couldn't dent the scoreboard when it had the opportunities.

The next most featured attraction in the Blockbuster Bowl besides the head coaching matchups was the All-American status of two key players. For Penn State, it was McDuffie, who set a school record for all-purpose yardage with 1,831 for the season. It broke down to 63 receptions for 977 yards and nine touchdowns; seven rushes for 133 yards; 30 punt returns for 398 yards; and 14 kickoff returns for 323 yards. His touchdown total was second to Richie Anderson's 19 and his rushing total was sixth best on the team.

Stanford had its own All-American in tailback Glyn Milburn, who was held to just 19 yards rushing by Penn State's defense, but was still a major force in Stanford's 10-2 season as he ranked No. 2 in the nation in all-purpose yardage, while McDuffie ranked No. 6. While Penn State did contain Milburn out of the backfield, it did not fare as well in the open field as Milburn caught four passes for 54 yards and a touchdown to lend his talents elsewhere.

Penn State got 138 all-purpose yards from McDuffie, including a game-high 111 on six pass receptions, but it could do little else offensively as Stanford's defense came up big when it had to. Stanford, meanwhile, scored 10 insurance points midway through the third quarter on a 28-yard field goal by freshman kicker Eric Abrams and a 40-yard TD pass from Stenstrom to Milburn.

The Nittany Lions were denied any further scoring despite five more opportunities with the ball. The deepest Penn State could penetrate was to the Stanford 31-yard line, but the Cardinal defense refused to break. Paterno tried everything he could think of to get his offense fired up, including reverses, trick plays, and two changes at quarterback. When Kerry Collins couldn't get the Lions going, Paterno turned the reins over to John Sacca. When he went 0-for-2 in one short series, it was freshman Wally Richardson's turn to run the offense. Richardson completed just 1-of-8 for 11 yards and Penn State could muster just 82 yards total offense in the second half.

"We didn't do some things that maybe we should have done," Paterno offered afterward. "I have to sum it all up and figure out how we start eliminating some of the reasons we were not more competitive. Even when I get all of those things straightened out, we still might have lost. They may be better than we are and have had a better day than we did. You have those days."

Whether Stanford was a better football team than Penn State or not could be debated for a long time. On this New Year's

Day, Stanford culminated the season by showing it was a rejuvenated football team in its first year under Walsh and it was every bit deserving of its 10-2 finish. It was the best record at Stanford since 1940, and the Cardinal ranked No. 9 in all three of the final national polls for 1992.

By finishing 7-5, Penn State posted its worst record since 1988 when it ended 5-6. The Lions finished No. 24 in the CNN/ *USA Today* and United Press International rankings, and all five of their losses were to teams that played in bowl games, including three (Miami, Notre Dame and Stanford) in the Top 10.

Paterno appeared disheveled as he spoke of his team's disappointing finish. The bowl game was his opportunity to tie the late Bear Bryant for all-time bowl wins with 15 and many wondered after the loss if Paterno would ever get — or want — another opportunity to reach that goal.

There was a lot of soul searching to be done in the place all Penn Staters know as Happy Valley. Some starters would be leaving due to graduation, but Penn State was still a fairly young team as it looked to 1993. The last thing Paterno or any of his coaches wanted, or needed, was a repeat of 1992. January 1 marked the beginning of a new year in 1993, but after his team lost in such a poor, uninspired fashion to a revved-up Stanford team, Paterno looked at that day as an end to what was admittedly one of his poorest seasons as a head coach.

"We've got to become mentally tougher," he said just a few days after the Blockbuster Bowl loss. "That includes myself and my staff. We have to realize that just because we're Penn State, it doesn't mean we're going to automatically win. We have to get back to playing like we're underdogs."

Questions needed to be answered. Hearts had to be turned inside out. Everyone from the coaching staff, to the players, to the medical staff and equipment crew needed to reach deep inside themselves to see if they were ready to face the challenge that would begin on January 2, 1993. A lot of things went wrong in 1992. Too many things. It was time to straighten them out and Paterno couldn't wait a minute longer.

4

How to Right the Wrongs

In reality, spring football practices are never an exciting prospect for players at any collegiate level. The prospect of live practices with live hitting and scrimmages with no end in sight are all that can be looked forward to. Instead of a glamorous bowl game as the final reward for the player's efforts, they get to participate in an annual rite known as the Blue-White game, which is a game for the fans featuring Penn State versus Penn State.

Spring workouts are a time for the basics. This is an opportunity for the coaching staff to do what it does best — teach. The disaster of 1992 was long past, and the problems, disappointments and unhappiness were hopefully ironed out. Joe Paterno took a good, long look at his program and himself and decided the best thing to do was talk it out.

Before anyone could look ahead, however, everyone had to take one last painful look back. Where exactly did the Penn State slide begin? Many feel the air was let out of the proverbial balloon when the Lions lost a game they definitely gave away to Miami. That loss ended all hopes for a national championship and coupled with the knowledge that one more win secured their New Year's Day bowl plans, many of the players wondered what else there was to play for.

"The [team's] morale really went down after the loss to Miami," punter V.J. Muscillo said. "It was unfortunate that we put all our marbles into one basket like that. We looked at it as though if we beat Miami, we'd have a great shot at the title. If we lost, that would be about it. It seemed more like our goal for the whole season was just to beat Miami and not getting to the bowl game."

"It's funny," Penn State defensive end Tyoka Jackson said. "When you're in that situation, you don't really notice the reasons of why things went wrong. But looking back, it seems like we really did dwell on that loss to Miami. And we let it affect us for the rest of the season."

"The [1992] season started with such promise," kicker Craig Fayak said. "When we lost to Miami, it seemed as though everyone took it pretty hard. We were still down and Boston College simply came in here and beat us. From there, the attitude [in the locker room] was hard to describe. It seemed like everyone was just thinking, 'Okay, let's just win a couple more games and go to the Blockbuster Bowl.'"

Fans took the loss to Miami fairly hard as well. There are those that support their favorite teams in the proper ways — with sportsmanship and consolation — and there are those that are just plain ridiculous. Those are the people known as fair-weather fans. While it's true that everyone supports a winner, fair-weather fans are nowhere to be found when their team suffers a loss.

Craig Fayak knows all about those kind of fans, and he realizes that his position will often draw their ire quicker than say, a lineman or running back. "Let's face it," he said. "A lot of wins and losses come down to the kicker's foot and if he doesn't come through, the fans are going to find a way to let him know about it."

Against Miami, Fayak missed two field goals, one a chip shot from 20 yards. Those six points meant the difference in a Penn State victory, but so did many other things. There was the Miami interception return for a touchdown and several offensive series that sputtered into nothing. Several fans, however, remembered the dastardly kicker and his errant right foot and told him so with prank calls and death threats throughout the following week.

"In a sense, it's hard to believe that people would take the time to do things like that, but that's the way it goes sometimes," Fayak said, as if to shrug the whole thing off. "My family and friends stood by me and I realized that not all fans were like that. Penn State fans are good, and I got a lot of letters that said I should hang in there and things would be OK."

What the fans didn't know as Penn State and Miami slugged it out on the field was that Fayak was kicking through the pain of a sore back and with every swing of his leg, he felt the twinge of a severely damaged muscle that hampered his follow through and would eventually keep him out for the rest of the season.

It was the competitive nature of the game that willed Fayak to stick it out against Miami. He stretched until he could stretch no more on the Penn State sideline, but when he trotted onto the field, the pain was too excruciating for him to get a full extension into his kicks. Common sense should tell anyone to sit down if they're hurting, but tell that to a young man who has the hopes of 96,000-plus pinned on his shoulders.

When it was over and Penn State's national championship hopes had melted to nothing, Fayak felt the heat of the loss. He heard it from the fans — the fair-weather fans — and deep down, he had become his own worst critic.

"Yeah, to an extent, I believed what the fans were saying," he said. "It was tough, but at the time I was actually feeling as though it was my fault. Everybody has to step up and do their job, and on that day I didn't do mine. The season started with such promise and I was kicking so well. I wish I knew what happened."

No one in Penn State's locker room blamed Craig Fayak for the loss to Miami, but everyone seemed to agree it was the turning point of the season. When you become a Penn State football player, you automatically learn that losses are just not a part of the locker room vocabulary. That is a trait that every coach loves to see, but what the players seemed to get away from after their first setback of the season was the way to handle a loss when it does come around. A Penn State football player also knows to accept a loss the next day, then forget it and go on to the next game. This was something that Penn State admittedly had trouble doing.

"The loss to Miami had the greatest effect on us," quarterback Kerry Collins said. "After that, it seemed like we had nothing else to play for. And that was the general talk in the locker room."

"There was a lot of pressure to go undefeated," Penn State's Associated Press All-American wideout O.J. McDuffie said. "We looked to get a good start, which we did, but we looked so forward to the Miami game that the concentration wasn't there in the beginning. We were so geared up and we thought so much about beating Miami that we suffered a tremendous letdown when we lost.

"Not to take anything away from Boston College, they were a very good team. But we were never up for them. And ultimately, we lost because of that."

"We had a tough time of it that [Boston College] week," Nittany Lion center E.J. Sandusky said. "BC always plays us tough and we weren't mentally prepared for them. I guess we learned that kind of disappointment can happen when you set your sights so high."

Some felt that when things started to go sour in Penn State's 1992 season, neither the coaches nor the players showed much communication to turn things around. That seemed to give an even stronger indication that at times, Penn State was merely playing out the string and wishing its season to be over.

"Everyone was in kind of a state of shock," Sandusky said. "It was tough because everyone wanted to have a good season, but we didn't pick ourselves up. We may have lost touch with the coaches, but it's part our fault. We should have had a meeting or something to pull ourselves together, but we didn't."

And everything just seemed to get worse.

"The Miami game shouldn't have been a make-or-break situation, but we did a poor job as a team in handling it and the rest of the season," outside linebacker and co-captain Brett Wright said. "It was definitely a tough loss, but a good team makes things happen. We became a team of individuals and lost the team aspect. We, as captains, could have done a better job. We didn't do a good job of keeping the team's pride and tradition together.

"I feel we lost touch with the coaches. Joe's used to his system and when it appeared he would change very little, it seemed like an us-versus-them situation. We [as captains] only had three or four meetings with the coaches all year and I felt as though I was just a player and who was I to say that something was wrong? I think there was a great loss of communication, but Joe has really done his part to correct that problem and get back in touch with everyone, including the players."

Paterno began his team's turnaround by talking with his coaching staff, whom he brought together in a meeting room soon after the Blockbuster Bowl disappointment and said, "OK, let's have it. What do we do to straighten this thing out? What do you guys want me to do? Did we lose the players somewhere during the season last year, and if so, how do we get them back?"

Then it was time to discuss the matter with the players themselves. Paterno was somewhat of a changed man. He was rejuvenated and he wanted his players to see that. He chose committees — two players from each class — to air any differences between the team and himself, and he gave those committees the opportunity to meet with him once a week over breakfast to discuss any matter that was on theirs or a teammate's mind.

Tom Bradley is a man who can relate to both sides of Penn State's touchy situation at the end of 1992. As a player, Bradley was a leader. Small in stature, but big in heart, Bradley was special teams captain for the Nittany Lions' 1978 football squad that finished 11-0 during the regular season, but lost a national championship showdown, 14-7, to Alabama in the Sugar Bowl.

He was branded with the nickname "Scraps" as a player because he wasn't afraid to get involved in any play. He took on some of the giants on the field and continues to do so as Penn State's outside linebacker coach and special teams coach. Bradley is a Penn Stater in the strongest sense of the word. He grew up in Johnstown, which is two hours west of State College. He was captain of his high school football and basketball teams and earned a master's degree in sports administration from Penn State, along with an undergraduate degree in business.

Paterno admired his style as a player, and when Bradley voiced his desire to get into coaching after the 1978 season, Paterno gave him his chance. He wasn't an immediate full-time coach. Bradley had to learn the business like most young coaches do, as a graduate assistant, but it didn't take long to reach that full-time status. That opportunity came the very next season and "Scraps" has been a fixture at Penn State ever since.

Bradley falls under the category of player's coach. The kind of coach who can lead with authority, but see things from the player's perspective. He is not a go-between for the players and Paterno, but more of a guy who can put his arm around a person and say, "Look, this is the way it is . . ." His methods work well for Penn State, which is evidenced by the number of All-Americans and No. 1 draft choices he has groomed.

Bradley's influences have fallen over hundreds of players at Penn State with outside linebackers Reggie Givens and Rich McKenzie and wideout O.J. McDuffie the latest trio to join the ranks of the National Football League after the 1992 season. Givens, who was a four-year starter at Penn State, was selected by the Super Bowl champion Dallas Cowboys and McKenzie was picked by the Cleveland Browns, while McDuffie merited a first-round selection from the Miami Dolphins. Other notables who have worked with Bradley and gone on to the pros were wide receivers Michael Alexander and Ray Roundtree and Shane Conlan, who was a first-team All-American linebacker in 1986 and was the NFL's Defensive Rookie of the Year in 1987 as a first-round draft choice of the Buffalo Bills.

One of Bradley's strongest tools is his ability to land the big recruits at Penn State. Almost every player he brought in to the Nittany Lion football program has left saying it was Tom Bradley who helped him make the proper decision. Even the young recruits of the future are making career decisions based on their meetings with him.

Bradley works the Western Pennsylvania area diligently, scouting out the top high school prospects and letting them know that Penn State is very much interested in not only their football talents, but in them pesonally as well.

Ryan Fagan was a senior at North Allegheny High School near Pittsburgh in the fall of 1993. He was ranked by some scouting services as one of the top 20 offensive linemen in the country before the season started and was one of the most heavily recruited players in the state. In early December, the 6-foot-7, 270-pound offensive tackle made a scheduled visit to Penn State and upon his return, Fagan promptly canceled visits to Ohio State, Michigan, Notre Dame and Southern California after making an oral commitment to the Nittany Lions.

"I was favoring Penn State a little before I went up there," Fagan told Pittsburgh area newspapers after announcing his decision. "And after getting to know the players and staff, the place kind of grew on me when I was there. I couldn't say no."

The ultimate difference, Fagan said, was the way Penn State showed its genuine interest in him. Michigan was the front-runner when his senior year began, but Penn State pulled ahead as decision time approached.

"Michigan wasn't calling me as much on the phone and it gave me the opinion they were less interested," Fagan said. "They called maybe once every other week instead of once a week. I felt Penn State wanted me more."

Penn State worked hard in its home state after losing some top recruits during the fall of '92. It was strange how that year seemed to be a washout for many reasons for the Nittany Lions, but the coaching staff pressed on, convinced the recruiting trail would get better.

It did with the addition of Fagan and other Pennsylvania players such as tight end Doug Ostrosky, from Fox Chapel High School and Washington lineman Jamaal Edwards; Northern Bedford receiver Joe Nastasi; Harrisburg defensive back Shawn Lee; Coatesville linebacker Clint Sease, and Brad Scioli, a line-backer from Upper Merion High School in King of Prussia. The Nittany Lions received their biggest coup — both figuratively and literally—when 6-foot-7, 330-pound Upper Darby defensive lineman Floyd Wedderburn committed to Penn State in late January.

There is an annual all-star game for high school seniors from Ohio and Pennsylvania known as the Big 33 game. It features some of the best players from both states and most are headed to big-time programs all across the Division I level. When the rosters were announced for the 1994 summer classic, the Pennsylvania contingent listed one-third of its roster as Penn State signees. In all, Penn State landed eight first-team all-state selections in the 1994 college football recruiting wars and like a lot of the other players, when Ryan Fagan speaks of his decision to attend Penn State, he often points to Tom Bradley as the reason.

"He was great," Fagan said of Bradley. "He was always joking around, but he talked to you about what's important at the same time. He really made me feel like Penn State was the right place for me."

As a competitor, Tom Bradley was troubled just as much as anyone by Penn State's downer of a season in 1992. He was used to the high expectations of Penn State football, where 10-1 and 9-2 are considered the norm. A 7-5 season might be OK for some schools, but at Penn State that kind of record makes some wonder if the Lions maybe weren't interested in football and instead were just going through the motions.

Bradley faced the questions as all the coaches did at one time or another following 1992. What happened? How could a team with so much talent fall apart at the seams? Was the advanced commitment to the Blockbuster Bowl the biggest problem? Did the loss to Miami have the biggest influence on the rest of the season?

"That [Miami] was the game everyone wanted to win," Bradley said. "We set our goals around it in some form or another. When we lost, I think it was hard to refocus and get the kids to think about what their next goal was. On one hand you could say we used the loss to Miami as a crutch, but still, you always have to find the urge to win. You have a great competitor here in Coach Paterno and he doesn't care if we play Boston College the next weekend in Beaver Stadium parking lot, he still wants to win."

"The loss to Miami kind of left our team numb," Penn State quarterbacks coach Dick Anderson said. "It was like a balloon that continued to inflate in the games leading up to Miami. The balloon was at its height when we reached that game and when we lost, the balloon deflated in a big way. We should have been good enough to pick up and go on to the next game, but it didn't happen. I think that loss had an awful lot to do with the Boston College game and the rest of the season."

The entire coaching staff seemed to be aware that the players weren't collectively preparing for Boston College in the proper manner. From newspaper accounts, it appeared everyone was lamenting the loss to Miami, and doing so right up to the day before Boston College.

"Boston College had two weeks to prepare for us," Bradley said. "They were ready and we probably weren't even semi-focused until the middle of the week. I don't even think that we, as coaches, had everything tied together as well as we could have. A lot of the things BC gave us were difficult to prepare for in the particular scheme we were in. That, along with the emotional standpoint, hurt us."

Even six months later as he thinks back to the Boston College letdown and subsequent events that followed, Bradley can name every play, every situation, and every detail to a "t".

"Even in the game, we had three mental breakdowns," he recalled. "They scored 21 points on us in four minutes and 44 seconds. That's just unbelievable. It wasn't just the players, though. People can blame the players, but that's a copout for me. I did a lousy job that week, I know I did. I never wanted to see any finger pointing, nor did I think there should really be any.

"I guess the problem I have [with the way things went] is that if you're still a good football team, you should always have the competitive edge. So you lost to Miami, forget about it and move on. I don't care if there's nothing left at the end of the tunnel, you still play the games that are left on the schedule. I find it hard to believe, and accept, that anyone can just say, 'Oh well, let's just win one more game and get to the Blockbuster Bowl. It's quite possible that we didn't have enough *real* competitors.'"

Joe Paterno needed to find the competitors again so 1993 wouldn't end up like '92. That was why he went back to the drawing board in a way. It wasn't a case of teaching the basics all over again to his team, but finding the drive within himself and the willingness to listen a little more to what his players had to say. Paterno had been in the game a long time, but even he had to prove he could change just a little bit with the times.

Not only did he form his own version of the Breakfast Club, but Paterno also met with each returning player individually during the off season to talk about football and let them air their thoughts and opinions. He then carried those messages back to his coaching staff for further discussions.

"I think I let some of the kids get away from me in the latter part of the season," Paterno said of his team's '92 finish. "I overestimated some of the leadership on the squad and I wasn't as close to the situation as I should have been. It was not a solid Penn State football team, and that's what became frustrating. I blame myself for that."

"I didn't sense we lost touch with the players," Bradley said. "We just weren't on the same page with them. These guys are adults and you can't hide when you start losing confidence in them. They can sense that and we didn't really show them a lot of positives. We were probably nitpicking a lot at them without picking them back up. I look at Joe and I listen to what he says. He thinks he probably didn't do as good a job as he could have, but the players could have looked at it from his end and realized they could have done a better job for him."

At least one player shared the same feeling.

"Joe's not the one out there playing every Saturday," quarterback Kerry Collins said. "He tried week in and week out to prepare us, but our attitude was downright horrible. We weren't very fair to him at all."

"A lot of the things are not his fault, but he's willing to take the blame because he's the boss," Bradley said. "Joe's a competitor and he has a fire in his belly now just as much as he did when he first started coaching."

Enthusiasm from a coaching standpoint was another item that had to be addressed. How much did the Nittany Lion staff really want the wins in 1992? How much desire was still there? Was the majority of the coaching staff living in the past, remembering the national championship days of yesterday? And how much time would go by before everyone realized the troubles and disturbances of 1992 would not go away by themselves?

"That's why Joe took the coaches aside as well," Bradley said. "He wanted to find out where everyone stood in terms of their feelings, and what we, as a staff, had to do to get things back in the proper perspective. Our staff probably was living on some of its past glories. We had to realize that 1982 and 1986 were a long time ago, and we had to start running scared a little bit. The challenges of the Big Ten were going to be huge, and if we were going to put together another string, it had to be now."

In a sense, Paterno took a step back to his days as a starting quarterback at Brown University and handed the ball off to his coaches. It was up to them to run with it and to see if their desire to win had faded or not.

"I think everyone certainly had the desire to win," Anderson said. "While the football season's going on everyone gets wrapped up in the daily preparation and you really miss some of the things that might be right in front of you. But when the season's over and things are assessed, then you begin to find that maybe things weren't as together as they should have been."

Once the realization had settled into everyone's mind that there were problems within the framework of the team, and that maybe some of the players *had* given up after one or two losses in 1992, the coaches all seemed to agree that Paterno's extra evaluation process was the right thing to do.

"Joe did a good job with the situation in terms of assessing where we were and reviewing the players, making them understand we all have a responsibility to make our program better," Anderson said. "After that, a number of kids stepped forward and everyone seemed to be on the same page. Everyone understood and we all had a common goal."

"It was just the kick in the pants we needed," Bradley agreed. "Everyone from the coaches to the players to the equipment managers took a good, hard look and realized why we were all there. Everyone accepted their roles."

There is a specialty on every football team. Not just at certain positions, but within the very bowels of the team. If the athletic department doesn't have its plan together, how is the coaching staff supposed to prepare? And what about the equipment staff? If they are not a cohesive and competent bunch, how will the players perform with less than adequate supplies? Everything is tied together in college athletics and fortunately over the years, Penn State has been blessed with a strong and committed athletic department. The proof lies in the stability of the program and stability starts with the first name on Penn State's list, Joe Paterno.

Twenty-eight years of success can't be argued with and although he prefers to shoulder most of the blame, while giving the credit to others, Paterno is the very backbone of Penn State's strong legacy. On the field, he is a teacher and a motivator. He gets the most out of every player's ability, and then some. Off the field, he is genuine. His dedication to Penn State from an academic standpoint is second to none, and he has shown that with large annual donations to Penn State's library funds. With his help, Pattee Library, on Penn State's main campus, has increased in terms of size and access probably three times over.

"The library has to keep pace with the tremendous progress the university has made in our other academic areas," Paterno said. "It's not only a case of adding more books and other information resources, but adding needed space to better serve the students and faculty. That's how you achieve a library·system that ranks among the best at any university."

Paterno also displays a genuine interest in people, whether they are athletes or non-athletes.

A young high school senior — the star quarterback of his team — had committed to Penn State in the summer of 1993 for the '94 season. A summer diving accident left the young man totally paralyzed and survival had suddenly become his top priority. Doctors told the young man he would probably never walk again, which is a lot for a high school senior to comprehend, let alone accept.

Joe Paterno was saddened by the news of his recruit's accident and immediately voiced his concern to his family. He visited the young man as soon as time would allow after such a horrific mishap and not only calmed him, but vowed his full scholarship would be honored at Penn State, as promised, just as soon as the young man would be able to tackle the challenge.

While many consider him somewhat of a deity around this small-town setting, Paterno considers himself just your average Joe. He lives in a quaint, average-sized house just across the north end of the Penn State campus with his wife, Sue. Together, they have mulled over several head coaching positions from other places in the past. The Pittsburgh Steelers tried to lure him in 1969, but Paterno refused, and Chuck Noll landed the job. The New York Giants and New England Patriots also made great offers to him in the past.

At times, Paterno gave such notions serious thought, but his heart—along with Sue's—always told him State College was the perfect place for him. They would look at each other and ask, "Would we really be happy if we left here?" It is to Penn State's benefit that the answer has always been "No." It is the kind of foundation Paterno has built at Penn State that tells a young recruit this is the place for him. Too often, a high school senior might back off from a college if the head coach is unsure of whether his job will be safe for the next four years.

Paterno didn't want that to happen at Penn State, and that was one of the biggest reasons he has rejected so many professional offers over the years to stay in the place called Happy

Valley. The players may not always be happy, and they may not agree with Paterno. But it is rare to find a Penn State player, past or present, who would say he didn't respect the man.

Some have chastised Paterno for failing to change with the times in recent years. Change to what? To the celebratory show-boating that is too often displayed in end zones and on sidelines for a national television audience to see? To that, Paterno would kindly say no thanks.

There once was a wide receiver who ran a successful pass pattern for a touchdown during a normal practice session. The receiver held the ball in the air for all to see as he crossed the goal line, then spiked it over his shoulder a la Lynn Swann in his Super Bowl days with the Steelers. Paterno caught this action and came running over from the defensive side of the field.

"Hey!" he screamed in a voice that finds a pitch all its own when he's mad enough. "You wanna do that kinda crap, you can keep right on runnin. We don't do that stuff around here."

That scenario has probably happened more than once, and each time the point was probably well taken, just as it was by that first young wide receiver. It's an example of respect for the way Paterno's program is run, and if the player didn't know it beforehand, he surely knew it afterward.

Changing with the times . . . Paterno chuckles at the suggestion that when people can't complain about his team's poor play on the field, they complain about the way they look. "People have complained about the uniforms for about as long as I can remember," he said.

The Penn State uniform is most often referred to as generic. That, in actuality, is probably the nicest reference. Others say the uniforms are boring, bland, terrible, and downright ugly. But ask a Penn State player what it means to put on that all-white apparel and chances are good you'll get an altogether different answer.

"There's a pride that goes with wearing the uniform," tight end Kyle Brady said. "People can say what they want, but it's been successful over the years and I like wearing it."

The Penn State uniform consists of white pants, white socks and a white helmet. The school colors are actually blue and white, but you don't really know that unless you see the home jerseys, which are all navy blue with white numbers on the front and back. If Penn State were playing on the road in a blizzard, the players would not be visible if it were not for the black shoes — another change Paterno refused to make in the mid-'70s, when most teams went to wearing white shoes.

Joe Paterno has coached in four different decades now, but the clothes on the field have remained the same for his players. Heading into 1994, most teams have even come full circle, going back to wearing black shoes.

Another Paterno tradition is not to give in to the high-pressure business of commercialism when it comes to bowl games.

Case in point. Nowadays, every bowl is tied in to a major sponsor. Therefore, that sponsor feels the need to plaster its name on every billboard in town, every piece of tile in the locker rooms, even at mid-field of the very playing surface the two teams will do battle on. There is the USF&G Sugar Bowl now, the Federal Express Orange Bowl and the Mobil Cotton Bowl, just to name a few. As if those names aren't visible enough, the bowl's corporate sponsorship requests that each game jersey have the bowl logo — complete with company name — emblazoned on the shoulder pad of each jersey.

When Penn State and Stanford met in the Blockbuster Bowl, the ideal situation would have been for both teams to wear the Blockbuster Video sign that looks like a movie theatre ticket nestled squarely against a Florida palm tree. Stanford wore the patches on their visitors' white jerseys, but as is Paterno's custom, Penn State was comfortable in its blue and white attire, sans patches.

The bowl committees may frown on such actions, but there is no NCAA bylaw that says Penn State must prostitute the very players that are drawing the crowds to the bowl games and ultimately bringing in the revenue from gate receipts and concessions.

"Anyone who doesn't like the Penn State uniform doesn't know what Penn State football means to us as players," Nittany Lion linebacker Eric Ravotti said. "There's pride out there in that uniform, and I believe it takes someone special to wear it. After all, it doesn't really matter what the uniform looks like because the uniform isn't playing the game. The person inside it is. And that person wants to win just as much as anyone else."

If Joe Paterno were forced to change with the times, he might have the very thing he loves about Penn State taken away from him. That is the large campus atmosphere in a small-town setting. Students from all walks of life might be heading to one of their classes when the man with the thick-lensed glasses and dark hair walks past and offers them a friendly hello with a smile on his face.

Changing with the times would remind Paterno of a young tennis player named Monica Seles, who was attacked on the tennis court in April, 1993, by a deranged fan with a knife. It would also remind him of Nancy Kerrigan, an Olympic skater who simply walked through an arena corridor and was beaten in the legs by a man wielding what turned out to be a collapsible police club.

Almost a year later, Seles had still not returned to the tennis court. She was stabbed in the right shoulder blade and although her physical wounds had healed by the start of the new year, the scars in her memory had apparently continued. For Kerrigan, January, 1994, meant a chance to qualify for the 1994 Winter Olympics. She was a bronze medalist at the '92 games and although she was 24 years old, she knew her chances were outstanding of qualifying again.

That was until a man came out of nowhere and thrashed Kerrigan's right knee and thigh with three or four whacks from what was described by witnesses as a long, heavy object. The man got away, despite the security at Detroit's Cobo Arena, while Kerrigan lie weeping and repeatedly asking the question, "Why me?"

Monica Seles will probably play tennis again someday, and due to a special exemption given by the United States Olympic Committee, Nancy Kerrigan was allowed to compete in the '94 Olympic games in Norway. But the scars were left indelibly on these two high-profile sports figures, both physically and mentally.

It is a sad comment on our society when sports heros who have worked so hard to achieve their levels of greatness must hide from the very public for which they perform. Change would have Monica Seles or Nancy Kerrigan walk through an airport wearing wigs and sunglasses, with an army of body guards surrounding them. They would like to say hello to the public, but can the public be trusted?

Joe Paterno says hello to the public every home football weekend. Not in the way he waves to the fans during his team's pregame warmups, but in what he does after the games. Administrative aide Tommy Venturino waits for Paterno outside the stadium locker room after every game. First, there is the postgame talk with his players. Then Paterno must meet with the media. After that, he will have a chat with some of his coaches to set the times for the next day's meetings and maybe shake hands with a high school recruit or two.

Then he slips out the dressing room door and slides into the passenger seat of Venturino's small pickup truck. The fans who are buzzing around the outside fences cheer as one of the greatest coaches of all time gives a wave from the cab of the pickup as though he were in a presidential motorcade. Almost always, there is someone who is heard saying, "Did you see that? He waved at *me!*"

As the truck slowly winds through the strolling crowd and leaves Beaver Stadium far in the background, Paterno can finally sit back for a minute and take a deep, restful breath. "Another tough one," he usually says with a long sigh. It seems as though the farther away from the stadium the little truck gets, the less people seem to know or care about who is inside.

Fans are still walking, about a mile or so down Curtin Road, and most are talking about their dinner plans, or perhaps about the game they just witnessed. One can almost picture armchair quarterbacks discussing their postgame strategies. *"Boy, I wish I could tell that Paterno a thing or two about the way he called that game,"* one might say. Then the two of them might stop at the curb as the small gray pickup truck comes to a halt at the stop sign.

"See ya tomorrow, Tommy," the familiar Brooklyn accent says as the passenger door opens. "Hey fellas, how ya doin?" the coach says to whomever might be sharing the crosswalk with him. "Nice to see ya." With that, Joe Paterno is off on his leisurely stroll home. He is oblivious to the dangers that could lurk in Happy Valley just as easily as in other parts of the world. He doesn't fear it, because this is his home and the fans are his people.

You can't ask Joe Paterno to change with the times because more often than not, he has the grasp of time in the palm of his hand. Paterno had many detractors following the 1992 debacle.

It would have been easy for him to give in to the media pressure that said the game was passing him by — again. But Joe Paterno vowed to never leave his team when the chips were down and after the '92 season, the chips were about as low as they could get.

As low as things may have gotten for the Penn State football team following the 1992 season, they quickly picked up, thanks in no small part to the rejuvenated attitude of one Joseph V. Paterno as the year grew older in 1993. He kept his hand firmly on the pulse of his team through the winter workout sessions and drew excitement from practicing football while the rest of the sports world was wrapped up in events like the new baseball season, the fast-approaching NBA playoffs or the height of March Madness.

"You could see a change in the whole program," Kerry Collins said of Penn State's spring practice sessions. "That change was started by Joe because he became so focused, and so hell-bent on getting the program back to where it should be."

"It was a different atmosphere," linebacker Brian Gelzheiser said. "You had the feeling we were ready to start everything new and just forget about 1992. The thought of getting an opportunity to play in the Big Ten started to appeal to everyone, and I think we were anxious to see how we would match up with the other teams in the league."

"Oh yeah, we were looking forward to starting over," said receiver Bobby Engram, who would play a pivotal role in the '93 season. "It was our chance to just forget about everything that happened the year before and prove we were ready to play in a tough conference like the Big Ten."

In years past, players like Gelzheiser and Engram might not have had the opportunity to look forward to another season. Both players, at some point in their Penn State careers, ran afoul with the law, and that was usually a sore point with Paterno, who took a great deal of pride in the clean image that Penn State had been so highly recognized for over the years.

It was mid-September, 1991, when Brian Gelzheiser claimed to have found a woman's lost wallet on the streets of downtown State College. Years of growing up in a proper, do-the-right-thing household surged through his mind, but the allure of making just one purchase with the enclosed credit card overcame him.

Gelzheiser entered a nearby clothing store with the intent to purchase something with the card, but thought better of his actions when the store clerk eyed him suspiciously, sensing something wasn't right. Gelzheiser was recognized as a Penn State football player by the clerk, who recalled his picture in a game program.

The way his mother brought him up led Gelzheiser to realize his intentions were wrong. He even called the woman whose wallet was lost and informed her that he had found it and would like to return it to her. But police heard the story from the clothing store clerk and were led to believe differently.

The sophomore linebacker faced an uphill battle because even though no formal arrest was ever made by the authorities, the university would have its say on the issue and would ultimately render it justifiable cause for punishment. Gelzheiser was banned from football and classes for the rest of the fall semester and the entire spring semester in 1992. He could live in the area, provided it was off campus, and would need special permission from the dean of disciplinary action *anytime* he wanted to set foot on campus.

When his eligibility was restored in 1992, Gelzheiser spent most of the season backing up outside linebacker Reggie Givens. His game had always been more suited to defend against the run, but at outside linebacker, he was asked to cover a lot of wide receivers in short patterns. He didn't deny it was an uncomfortable position, but he refused to believe his assignment had anything to do with some sort of punishment that was being handed down by the coaches.

"I didn't think that was the reason," he said. "There really wasn't anyone to back up Reggie. I figured they needed someone, so I went to the position. It was hard because I'm probably slow for an outside linebacker. Covering those wide receivers usually wasn't a lot of fun."

Making tackles was, however, and when senior co-captain Brett Wright went down with an injury against Brigham Young, Gelzheiser got the call to move back inside. He started the final three games against Notre Dame, Pitt and Stanford and responded with 30 tackles, including 15 against ND and 10 against Pitt. He had 14 tackles in the previous nine games when he served the Nittany Lions as a backup.

When the '92 season ended, Gelzheiser felt secure in the knowledge that he had solidified his role as a starter in 1993 and could at long last put the great credit card escapade behind him.

"I honestly don't know what led me to it," Gelzheiser recalled long after the incident. "All I know is I suddenly thought of how my mom brought me up to do things right. And that certainly wasn't right."

In Gelzheiser's eyes, considering using the card may not have been right, but despite the allegations discussed about him over the incident, he feels he cannot show regret for something he never did. "I never used [the card]," he said. "I didn't do anything."

Joe Paterno had considered all the circumstances in the case and felt that even though Gelzheiser would lose a full season of eligibility, his player was given a fair and proper penalty.

"It hurt because I think the suspension set him and the football team back," Paterno said. "But I think it was appropriate. When somebody gets involved with what he did, even if it was a mistake, there's a price to be paid."

For Bobby Engram, it may have been a case of following a lead down the wrong path. He was destined to be a tremendous football player, this young wide receiver from Camden, South Carolina. He had the hands, the speed, the ability to find open spots and the toughness to take the hits that receivers most often do in traffic.

He was a freshman during Penn State's impressive 11-2 season in 1991. His star flickered in the shadows of teammates O.J. McDuffie and Terry Smith, but Engram still displayed a bit of Penn State's receiving future at times with four catches for 40 yards over the course of the season.

It was hoped that 1992 would be a coming-out year for Bobby Engram, an opportunity to let the entire country see what kind of talent he held inside his 5-foot-10, 180-pound structure. Instead it became the year of all lost hope for Penn State and a completely lost season for Engram.

His troubles began the year before with the death of his father, who passed away August 22, 1991. Almost one year to the day of his father's death, Bobby Engram found himself in a State College jail cell. Engram and senior teammate Ricky Sayles were arrested on burglary charges stemming from an incident in which he and Sayles were caught outside a State College apartment carrying away stolen stereo equipment.

August 24, 1992, was a warm summer night and Penn State was preparing for its season opener in just a couple of weeks against Cincinnati. Two-a-day practices were in full session and most of the players had either bedded down for the evening already or were finishing up position meetings. Engram was in his campus dorm when he got a phone call from quarterback coach Jim Caldwell.

"Coach Caldwell called me and asked if I knew where [teammate] Richie Anderson's apartment was," Engram recalled. "I told him I didn't, but I thought Rick [Sayles] did. Coach Caldwell said he had some bad news for Richie, that someone had passed away in his family. I knew what that felt like from dealing with my father's death and I thought I could be there for Richie when he found out.

"I caught up with Rick and we went to the place we thought was his [Anderson's] apartment, but it was the wrong one. We tried the door, it opened and just like that everything was going down. It all happened so fast. The next thing I knew the police were arresting us right on the spot and all I kept thinking about was, 'How am I going to tell my mom?'"

The red lights of a police car and the sound of a jail cell door slamming shut might be two of the most frightening things a person might encounter. "It was scary," Engram admitted. "I just froze. I really didn't know what was going on. Panic set in just like that."

Engram not only had to find a way to tell his mother, but he also had to talk to Paterno that evening. It was a night that went wrong from the moment Engram left his dormitory room. As he sat in a downtown police station, not only a football career, but an entire future passed before Bobby Engram's eyes. He didn't know what to say to his coach, but he knew right then he was ready to face the consequences.

"Joe called me that night and told me straight up that he was very disappointed in me," Engram said. "He said there would definitely be a suspension for the rest of that season, but he said everyone would stick by me. That really meant a lot."

The arrest brought further attention to a Penn State program that had prided itself on staying away from such incidents. Like Gelzheiser, Engram was suspended from the university for one full semester. His suspension came during the '92 season, a time when his talents would surely have been appreciated due to the loss of wideout Tisen Thomas, who suffered a season-ending knee injury. Sayles was a senior at the time of the incident with no football eligibility remaining. His suspension automatically meant the end of his collegiate career.

"I felt bad that I didn't get a chance to line up opposite O.J. [McDuffie]," Engram said. "He was such a great talent and I know I could have learned a whole lot from him. I feel I could have won a starting position and the toughest part was watching the team struggle the way it did and thinking about how I could have helped in some way."

Engram faced the same kind of punishment from the university in terms of absolutely no on-campus sightings without permission from the dean of disciplinary actions. It was perhaps the most difficult time Engram would ever face in his athletic career, because he was left with working out all alone for an entire season. No one to catch balls with. No one to push him in the weight room.

It would have been easy for a man of such a young age to pack his bags and head back to Camden, South Carolina. But Bobby Engram knew he was bigger than that. His father would surely not have approved of the stealing incident, but even more so, he probably would not condone the actions of a quitter. Not when the opportunity is still there for the taking.

So he worked alone during the 1992 season. He watched the games on television whenever he could and thought more than once, perhaps, if his contributions could have made a difference in turning around some of Penn State's losses that season. Just as importantly, he stayed in State College to take the second chance that awaited him in the spring of 1993.

"That incident was a wake-up call to me every Saturday that fall," Engram recalled. "I think when it hit me was when I drove by the stadium one Saturday from a distance and saw the huge crowd in there watching the game. Right then I told myself that outside was no place for me. I wanted to be in there, ready to play again."

His determination grew more than ever during those autumn months he had thrown away. The important thing was, however, that he didn't throw his life away. Just like Brian Gelzheiser, Bobby Engram would get a second chance to redeem himself, to show that he belonged on the football field, with the teammates that had grown to mean so much to him.

Gelzheiser made his comeback in the fall of '92, ready to put the incident behind him. He spent much of the season backing up Givens on the outside, but when Wright was lost with his injury, Gelzheiser became a starter. He led the team with 30 tackles in the Nittany Lions' last three games and served notice that he was ready to become the leader that Paterno had envisioned him to be in the first place.

Playing in those last three games meant the world to Gelzheiser, because he knew how close he really came to never stepping on the football field again, either at Penn State or anywhere else.

"It was sort of scary not knowing whether I'd ever play again," the soft-spoken Pittsburgh native said. "I just looked at everything and said to myself, 'Okay, you got a second chance. Don't blow it.'"

As the current spring practices got underway and most players dreaded the hard work that would ultimately go with it, Gelzheiser and Engram were two human beings who saw things in a different light. The football field was their comfort zone and there was nowhere on earth they would rather have been.

"What I did was stupid," Engram said with the same quiet demeanor as his teammate. "I'm fortunate to have this second chance and I plan to make the most of it. I just want to put the incident behind me and get on with my life. The best way to do that is to be myself both on and off the field."

Engram faced the consequences off the field, just like Gelzheiser, and kept a positive image throughout his suspension. He was accepted into a first-time offenders program that ultimately cleared his record upon its completion.

"Both of those guys are super individuals," linebackers and special teams coach Tom Bradley said. "If you would have come to me and said those guys would get into that kind of trouble before it happened, I would have said 'No way.' They were similar in that they immediately knew what they did was wrong, but it was really too late to do anything about it.

"You could say Bobby was just a young kid at the time and he fell into the wrong crowd when his dad died. But that's no excuse. He should still know right from wrong and he had a chance to say, 'Hey Ricky, this is wrong. We can't do this.' It's just something both Gelz and Bobby had to deal with and then it was time to move on."

Engram was the first to agree with that assessment.

"I could have said no and I didn't," he said. "I'd never put any of the blame on Rick because he didn't drag me into it. I think if he had the chance, he'd say he didn't want to be in that situation either."

And what did Joe Paterno think of his players' behavior? This is a man who has dismissed All-Americans forever from past squads for not keeping up with academics, and who never blinks an eye when it comes to sending players home from bowl trips if they so much as miss a curfew.

"I believe in kids getting a second chance," Paterno said. "I think the media really played up both incidents and I understand they have a job to do when it comes to reporting such things. Ricky Sayles was out of eligibility, so that's why his playing days were over. Bobby Engram was dismissed from the team and so was Brian Gelzheiser. Neither one got to go to a bowl game and I just felt the university's penalty was sufficient enough."

Has Paterno softened from his hard-nosed stance over the years?

"I've been in the business long enough to know it's a tough world we live in," he said. "Things like this can happen at any institution of higher learning and you have to be tough-skinned enough to not let it bother you. Those guys served their suspensions and showed they wanted to come back. They made their second opportunities, so I didn't see any reason to take such a thing away from them."

His approach to these and other considerably harrowing situations over the previous year or so were all part of Paterno's plan to get his team back on the right track. He felt the need to change, but not in the way the media wanted him to. He had to renew a strong acquaintance with his squad and find out who wanted to come along for the inaugural ride into the Big Ten Conference in just a few short months.

It was only April, 1993, but Joe Paterno had already forgotten the lost opportunities of '92. Oh, they were stored in his memory, much like the files of every other game he had ever coached. But their only future use would be to serve as a reminder of just how wrong things can go when the goals are set too high and when the morale drops to record lows. He would occasionally pull from these files over the course of 1993, but Joe Paterno was ready to face the biggest challenge of his football life.

"I have a lot of enthusiasm for this season," he said just a day before the annual Blue-White game. "We've done a lot of talking and teaching and I've found I have to be a better hands-on type of coach. I enjoy coaching. I enjoyed it last year and I thought the kids were having a good time. But when the end of the season came around, a lot of the kids opened up and said they were going through the motions at the end.

"I wanted to show the players that we could stick with this thing. I want to keep coaching as long as I'm able, and as long as I'm doing a good job. If the time comes when I'm not, I would hope there would be someone who could speak up and tell me."

The upcoming season was to be the spotlight for Penn State football. Maybe his team had to go back to the basics a little bit during those spring workouts, but in the long run the results would hopefully make up for those long, exhausting practices.

If not, Paterno could count on quite a few voices to speak up.

5

Ready for
the Big Show

The time was drawing closer for Penn State to show its worth in one of college football's classiest conferences. Incoming freshmen were the first players to report to preseason camp, each with a sense of pride in knowing he would be a part of the first freshman class to participate with Penn State in the Big Ten.

"It's a great feeling," said Brad Jones, a freshman offensive lineman from Blackhawk High School in Western Pennsylvania. "As a high school player, you dream of something like this all your life. It's hard to believe it's finally here."

Even Joe Paterno, who was beginning his 28th season in the head coaching business, was a little overwhelmed at what his team was about to embark on. "I'm excited because I've seen what the Big Ten has done for some of the other activities at Penn State," he said. "If we can get that kind of excitement at the football games, it ought to be a terrific season."

Yes, football was the final sport to get started in Big Ten play. When the announcement of Penn State's admission to the conference was officially made a little more than three years before, future schedules had already been designed for the football team. It would take a little bit of adjustment, but the conference and the university agreed that a full Big Ten schedule could be worked out by 1993.

It would seem only fitting that football would be the last official sport to participate in a Big Ten schedule at Penn State. While women's basketball has always been prominent and men's basketball has been on the rise, football is the drawing card to State College. Beaver Stadium is the resting place for recreational vehicles from all across the country every home Saturday afternoon as upwards of 96,000 fans gather to see the Nittany Lions in action.

The circumstances relate in some ways to a concert where the anticipation grows from the buildup of the opening acts until finally the headliner takes the stage. Basketball, baseball, wrestling, soccer, fencing, and many more had made their initial appearance. And now it was time for the main attraction.

September 4, 1993 was the scheduled day when football at Penn State was to change forever. No tuneups. No cupcakes. Conference play was about to begin with the opening kickoff of the new season. The Nittany Lions would host the University of Minnesota Golden Gophers in the first Big Ten game for anyone in the conference.

The big moment, however, was still a month away when the distant blare of the fog horn rolled through the dormitory hallway, bringing to life a slumbering group who could probably find better things to do on a hot summer day than spend what would amount to about seven or eight hours on a scorching football field in temperatures that were sure to rise above 80 degrees.

The fog horn is a ritual at Penn State. It is the wake-up call that sounds every morning around 6 a.m. to remind each player that it's time to start thinking about Saturday afternoons in the fall, time to start working on the fundamental things that get them to that point and help them reach for that focus.

Each student equipment manager takes his turn with the horn, walking through the hallways and hoping he doesn't get a shoe or something heavier thrown at him for triggering such a menacing sound at a dreadful hour. Every Penn State athletic team had made its first run through the Big Ten by this time and each could truly say that the football team was in for a great and unique experience.

Some teams at Penn State enjoyed great success in their inaugural campaigns in the conference. Women's volleyball finished second in the conference in 1991-92 at 15-5 and followed that with a 19-1 conference record in '92-93 and a No. 2 final ranking in the country. Women's basketball finished 22-6 overall in 1992-93 and 14-4, good for a third-place finish in its conference debut. The Lady Lions started the '93-94 season 18-0 and climbed to the top of the national polls before losing to Purdue in early February.

The Penn State wrestlers were 22-0-1 overall and 5-0-1 in their first conference schedule in '92-93, good for a second-place finish. Women's gymnastics opened conference participation in 1991-92 and finished second in the conference two seasons in a row with marks of 7-1 and 6-1. Women's swimming also had a successful Big Ten debut as the team finished 5-1 in 1992 and 7-0 in 1993 in the conference. The Penn State Lady Lion field hockey team finished 16-5-1 overall in 1992 and took second place in the Big Ten with an 8-2 mark.

Other Penn State teams struggled greatly in their Big Ten debuts. The Lady Lion softball team finished seventh at 4-24 in their first season and the baseball team was 5-23, good for a 10th-place finish. Bruce Parkhill is a coach who knows all about the struggles in his opening season. When he took over as head basketball coach for the men's team in 1983, Penn State was in a state of confusion.

Parkhill is a State College native and a 1971 graduate of nearby Lock Haven University. He earned his master's degree from the University of Virginia in 1972, and it was there that his basketball coaching career began. He started out as a graduate assistant working both with the varsity, which went 21-7 that season and made an appearance in the National Invitation Tournament, and the freshman team, which finished 11-5.

He began a two-year stint as an assistant coach at William & Mary in 1974 under Ed Ashnault and then served three seasons under George Balanis as an assistant coach and recruiting coordinator. In 1977, Parkhill's window to opportunity opened when he was named head coach at William & Mary, and his stock grew quickly when the Indians upset then-No. 2 North Carolina early in his first season.

Parkhill's first team at William & Mary finished 16-10, which was the school's best record in 25 years, and won two in-season tournaments. He compiled an 89-75 record in six seasons at William & Mary before Penn State, the school in his old home town, came calling.

The Nittany Lions needed young leadership at a time when basketball —at least on the men's side — was becoming very unpopular. Parkhill instilled a belief in his players from the very beginning. And though it would take a little time and a lot of patience, he believed his philosophies would turn into wins on the court. Coaching the Penn State basketball team was a lonely job at the time, but one man constantly fed encouragement to Parkhill, telling him the fans would see the player's efforts and they would soon come around. It gave Parkhill a tremendous boost of confidence to know he had a guy like Joe Paterno on his side.

Bruce Parkhill's first Penn State basketball team struggled through a 5-22 record and the Nittany Lions were 53-84 in his first five seasons. But then it began. The string of success that brought the fans back to Rec Hall in record numbers. The Nittany Lions finished 20-12 in 1988-89, which was only the third time in school history the men's team had won at least 20 games. The season culminated in an upset over 13th-ranked West Virginia in the Atlantic 10 Conference tournament and an appearance in the championship game against Rutgers. The Lions also defeated Murray State in a first-round NIT game, 89-73, for their first national postseason win since 1954-55.

Penn State did even better the following season as it posted a 13-5 conference record and finished 25-9 overall. It was the first time the Nittany Lions ever had back-to-back 20-win seasons. Parkhill won Atlantic 10 Coach of the Year honors and Penn State, which was 15-0 at Rec Hall that season, tied its best ever finish in a national tournament by finishing third in the NIT.

Bigger and better things continued during 1990-91 as Penn State collected its third straight 20-win season (21-11) and made its third straight appearance in a postseason tournament. The Nittany Lions won their first Atlantic 10 title and appeared in the NCAA tournament for the first time since 1965. The first round of March Madness in 1991 provided one of the biggest wins in

Penn State history as the Lions upset 16th-ranked UCLA to capture the school's first NCAA tournament win in 36 years. Penn State basketball had climbed to 35th and 41st in the final national polls.

After the NCAA tournament win over UCLA, Bruins coach Jim Harrick offered these words of praise toward Parkhill's coaching ability: "Penn State won because not only did they play better, but mostly because Bruce Parkhill did a great coaching job."

Penn State played an independent schedule in 1991-92 and finished with a 12-1 home record. The only loss, however, came in the first round of the NIT against Pitt, 67-65. At the end of the regular season, there were many believers that the Nittany Lions could go a long way in the NIT after being snubbed for an invitation to the NCAA tournament despite a 21-7 season. Pitt was a team that felt fortunate to be in any postseason tournament that year because of a late-season slump, but it showed great poise and patience in turning back the Lions in front of a hostile Penn State crowd.

"That [Rec Hall] was a tough place to play in," Pitt's senior point guard Sean Miller said afterward. "We were fortunate to get out of there with a win."

Bruce Parkhill had collected 236 Division I coaching victories through 1993 and had guided his Penn State teams to six national tournament wins — which was half of the teams' all-time total — in his 10 years at the helm. Like his football counterpart at Penn State, Parkhill is a strict disciplinarian when it comes to academics and he was once given recognition by a national sports publication for graduating all 28 of his seniors at Penn State through 1992.

He started from the ground floor at Penn State and helped turn around a struggling basketball program in just a few short years. He did this by following three simple objectives:

1:    Recruit and graduate quality students.
2:    Make sure his players maximize their college experiences, not only athletically, but academically and socially as well.
3:    Advance to postseason play.

Over time, Parkhill has seen to it that all those objectives were met, and everyone at Penn State is hoping to see him do so for a long time to come.

Just when Penn State basketball had progressed to its current level, a level that showed genuine potential for annual NCAA or NIT invitations, it was led to what many experts would consider to be the basketball gallows. While the Atlantic 10 Conference offered formidable competition year after year from schools such as Temple, West Virginia, Massachusetts, Rutgers and Rhode Island, Penn State was headed for yearly encounters with Indiana, Michigan, Ohio State, Purdue and Iowa, just to name a few.

The best greeting the Big Ten Conference might offer any new team would be, *"Welcome to the Big Ten, where there's never an easy win."*

Basketball players at Penn State heard that sarcastic greeting just like all the rest of the university's athletic teams at one time or another — and just like the football team would hear it in due time. "Welcome to the Big Ten." All any Nittany Lion fan or player could do in the early stages of this transformation was grin and bear it.

Recreation Hall, a quaint, but tiny and antiquated gymnasium on the Penn State campus, was the home for Nittany Lion basketball. It had seen many great victories for both the men's and women's programs and was home to a student contingent that was literally on top of the game. Rec Hall is a slightly scaled-up version of a junior high school bandbox. Its capacity is around 7,200, which is an off night for places like North Carolina and Duke. But every visiting coach, every player, is likely to say it was an experience he or she would never forget.

Basketball was free to the student body for many years. Until, that is, the team's first Big Ten season came along in 1992. "It was the first time we had ever charged for students," Penn State athletic ticket manager Bud Meredith said. "There was no major upheaval, however, and I think the kids understood that every school in the Big Ten charges. It was one of those necessary evils, but the students seemed very receptive and appreciative of the fact they were guaranteed a seat once their ticket was paid for."

Support for Penn State basketball never declined. On the contrary, it overflowed. Enthusiasm roared at a fever pitch through every home game as the students couldn't wait to see the likes of Michigan and its much celebrated Fab Five; Ohio State, with Indiana transfer Lawrence Funderburke; and Purdue, with freshman sensation, Glenn Robinson. And who, of course, could forget the long-awaited arrival of "The General."

Penn State fans had never forgotten the often critical remarks thrown their way by outspoken Indiana basketball coach Bobby Knight when it was first announced that Penn State would become a part of the Big Ten Conference. He took jabs at the "far-out location" of an eastern university in a midwestern conference and ridiculed the town's airport for not having a runway long enough to land a commuter plane on.

Hey, Knight has never been one to mince words and in some obscure, roundabout way, he probably did Penn State a tremendous favor by making the remarks that he did. Suddenly, Penn State was a television attraction to the likes of ESPN for some of its weekly Big Ten telecasts. The Lions hosted Ohio State and Michigan on national TV and the entire country was suddenly witnessing the closed-in atmosphere that was Rec Hall. The Penn State Lady Lions were also featured on a couple of CBS' weekend telecasts of women's college basketball, and rightfully so as their top-ten ranking through much of the season would attest.

The biggest, and probably most exciting ESPN telecast all season came on a cold Tuesday evening in early February, 1993. That was when Bobby Knight led his Hoosiers into State College (yes, Indiana's commuter plane somehow found its way through the mountains of Pennsylvania) for their inaugural appearance at venerable Rec Hall.

Earlier in the conference season, Indiana toasted the Nittany Lions by 48 points at the Hoosiers' Assembly Hall in Bloomington. Coming into the second meeting, Indiana was ranked No. 1 and Penn State was struggling in its new surroundings. Week in and week out, the Nittany Lions were repeatedly forced to discover just how deeply committed its new conference really was to basketball.

Penn State was destined for a 7-20 overall record in 1992-93 and would snap its string of four consecutive 20-win seasons by winning only two of its 18 conference games. But on this night, when blue and white smothered the surroundings, Penn State would send a message to the rest of the Big Ten Conference. The Nittany Lions matched Indiana point-for-point through much of the first half and refused to wilt under the Hoosiers' disciplined pressure defense in the second.

Rec Hall was deafening as Penn State tried desperately to maintain a two-point lead in the closing minutes of the game. Indiana hit the offensive glass with every missed shot, but couldn't put the ball in the basket. Finally, a Penn State rebound resulted in a fast break with about 20 seconds remaining.

The crowd roared as Indiana's Chris Reynolds grabbed the jersey of Penn State's Greg Bartram around half-court in an attempt to stop the sure two points. Referee Sam Lickliter's whistle blew from under the Penn State basket and the Lions apparently would have a chance to put a wrap on the biggest upset in school history from the foul line. What Lickliter saw and what everyone else in the building saw — including Bobby Knight and the national television audience — were two different things.

As Penn State's players congregated around the foul line, Lickliter approached the scorer's table and waved his right arm several times in a backward motion. A confused Bruce Parkhill, a distraught Bobby Knight, and a raucous crowd all watched in disbelief as Lickliter signaled an offensive foul against Bartram. The arm motion was a signal that Bartram had pushed off on Reynolds from behind to gain better position for the ball and the breakaway layup.

With under 15 seconds left in regulation, Indiana had the ball and a chance to either tie the game or win it with a three-pointer. Parkhill was enraged at Lickliter's hugely erroneous call, but kept his poise enough to talk to his team about defense during Indiana's ensuing timeout.

Ever since the inception of the three-point basket in college basketball, the Indiana Hoosiers had learned to make it one of their team strengths. The Hoosiers were characteristic for having some of the best three-point shooters around and this season was no different as the Nittany Lions were facing two of the best in Damon Bailey and Calbert Cheaney. Parkhill did not want his team to concentrate so much on the inside in the closing seconds that it would forget about those two or anyone else from beyond the arc.

When Indiana inbounded to a heavy chorus of boos, Bailey went to work setting up the offense. The ball was whipped around the perimeter as the seconds wound down and the Penn State players stuck to their men like glue. Suddenly out of nowhere, however, Bailey spotted teammate Greg Graham alone in the left corner for a three-pointer. The shot got off cleanly as the Penn State defender tried desperately to disrupt Graham's rhythm. The shot missed, but Graham was fouled with no time left on the clock.

The new rule in college basketball for the 1992-93 season said any player fouled in the act of shooting from beyond the three-point line would be awarded three shots from the foul line. So, the game's outcome suddenly hinged on Graham's foul-shooting ability, much to the unhappy disapproval of the 7,300 or so who were packed inside a smoldering Rec Hall.

Three shots from the foul line were all that was left in one of the most hard-fought contests in Penn State basketball history. "Win or lose, Penn State has shown the country a gutsy performance tonight," one of the ESPN commentators surmised above the tremendous crowd noise. Meanwhile, Dick Vitale, who was the color analyst for ESPN, criticized Lickliter's call profusely and pronounced over and over that Indiana did not deserve the "W" should they go on and win it.

As Graham toed the line for Indiana, the Penn State crowd — most of which were positioned literally a few feet away — waved their arms all around him, begging for a miss. Graham dribbled once, then twice, and eyed the basket. The cheer from the crowd told the story as Graham's first shot left his hands and clanged lazily off the front of the rim. The knot in Graham's stomach suddenly pulled just a little bit tighter as Knight watched from the sideline and showed no sign of emotion.

Graham needed to make both of his remaining shots or Indiana would return to Bloomington with one of its most shocking defeats ever. One dribble, then two, this time three. A deep breath and the shot was on its way. The rippling of the nylon cord was music to Graham's ears, not to mention the silence that fell just as quickly inside this 65-year-old gymnasium. Indiana's deficit was down to one as Graham readied for his third shot.

The crowd picked up the noise again, but Graham showed a confidence that every good foul shooter must have. He blocked out the crowd and tuned his concentration in on one thing only

— the basket. Again, he dribbled once, then twice, then thrice. His deep breath then changed to a sigh of relief as the shot nestled in the hoop to send the game into overtime.

Parkhill had few words for his team during the timeout and instead spent most of the time glaring at Lickliter, the official whose call eventually set up the overtime session. Indiana had been let off the hook and would surely show the underdog Nittany Lions why the Hoosiers were one of the best teams in the country.

There was pride and determination on both sides, and Penn State refused to believe it should give in to a team that rightfully had the better talent. There is a quality called heart that sometimes wins games also, and Penn State displayed the greatest abundance of it on this occasion. Indiana jumped out to a quick six-point lead in the extra session and seemed like it was on its way to victory.

Penn State fought back, however, and tied it halfway through the overtime with a three-point basket. Incredibly, the Lions forced a second overtime with their refusal to melt under the tremendous amount of pressure they were facing.

Eventually, however, the fight wore out of the Nittany Lions. Indiana was deep in talent and when Penn State center John Amaechi fouled out early in the first overtime, the Hoosiers put the game away both in the paint and from the foul line.

Not many heard the words, but Bobby Knight admitted to Bruce Parkhill during the coaches postgame handshake that his Lions deserved to win. It was small consolation for Parkhill, but he knew the General's words were spoken in sincerity. Every Penn State basketball player made a stand for the university that night. They stared down the advances of a Big Ten juggernaut and proved to one of the sport's greatest legendary coaches that Penn State had arrived in the Big Ten.

"The Indiana game generated excitement like I had never seen before in Rec Hall," Bud Meredith said. "It was an easy sellout and we could have added a few thousand more fans if it weren't for the fire safety restrictions."

Indiana's 88-84 double-overtime victory was easily the most exciting game Penn State basketball had ever been involved in. The crowd cheered right through the national anthem, the first half, the second half and both overtimes. And afterward, all anyone could talk about, whether they were in attendance at Rec Hall or watching on national TV, was "The Call."

"He [Reynolds] had a hold of my jersey with one hand and his other hand was on my waist," said Bartram, the Penn State player who was involved in the play. "I didn't know what the call was until I saw them giving the ball to Indiana. I couldn't believe it."

Parkhill's words were spoken carefully after maybe the toughest loss of his coaching career, but clearly he was seething inside.

"It's a league policy that coaches aren't allowed to discuss officiating," he said at the time. "I've had to bite my tongue to the point that it's almost cut off."

Richard Falk, supervisor of Big Ten officials, spoke to all three members of the officiating crew for the Penn State-Indiana game, including Lickliter, the day after the incident and said that Lickliter "was very down and distraught about the call because he knew, only later, that he had missed it. He didn't get any sleep that night because of it."

According to Falk, Lickliter was in his proper position and the other two officials were handling their responsibilities on the floor. When Reynolds' hand grabbed Bartram's jersey, none of the officials had a clear view of what was happening. All Lickliter saw was Bartram gesture with his arm to try to free himself from Reynolds' hold. That was when the whistle blew.

It was only later that evening, when all three officials were at their respective bedding places for the evening, that any of them saw the true accounts of the final seconds.

"Clearly, it would have been an intentional foul call," Falk said. "Two shots for Penn State and they also would have gotten the ball out of bounds. It was missed clearly, but if you don't see it, how can you call it?"

Maybe it was destiny, some sort of proof that Nittany Lion athletics belonged in the Big Ten Conference. It may have been a horrible call, but Penn State basketball was suddenly magnified not only in Pennsylvania, but all over the country. True, it was playing the best team in the land at the time, but every college basketball fan in North America knew on the night of Feb. 9, 1993, that No. 1 should have been knocked off. Bobby Knight knew it and he said so to Parkhill immediately after the game. Knight also told the country through the media that Penn State had an outstanding program and proved it belonged in the Big Ten.

"If you know anything about basketball, then you would understand that these people have done a great job with basketball [at Penn State]," Knight said. "I really like Bruce [Parkhill]. I like what he stands for and what he does. I would hope the kids here tonight know they can play with anybody. I really tip my hat to Penn State."

Parkhill became a true believer that night, as well. He was always positive that his team could do well, but was particularly pleased with the way it played against the best team in the country. The way his players carried themselves with pride and determination all night long. And the way each one showed class afterward, even though emotions could have taken over very easily.

On the night when David almost knocked off Goliath, Penn State basketball showed every quality that Big Ten officials had looked for when they went searching for an 11th member just a couple of years before. That evening only heightened Parkhill's enthusiasm for his team's future in the Big Ten.

"I really enjoy coaching in the Big Ten," Parkhill would say not long after that near upset of Indiana. "Every game is a war. It doesn't matter whether you're in the second division or the first division. All the kids play hard and every team is well-coached. I enjoy the atmosphere, and I've enjoyed getting to know the coaches around the league.

"The competition is tremendous, and every arena is fun to play in. There is a lot of outstanding talent on all the teams and I believe we can be very competitive in this league. To me, it's what big-time college basketball is all about."

Joe Paterno is a regular at Penn State basketball games in the winter. One of the reasons he was so enamored with the university's decision to join the Big Ten was because of his friendship with Knight and the similarities both men share when it comes to the importance of academics and athletics. Paterno admitted he had some concern as to how the fans would react to Penn State's departure from independence, but after attending a few basketball games during conference play, all concerns and fears were alleviated.

"That Indiana game was tremendous," Paterno said as his football team prepared for the start of its Big Ten wars. "All the way through it I kept thinking of how great it will be if the football crowds get into the games like the basketball crowds were. There was so much excitement around there, I couldn't wait till we got started."

Penn State was 15-0 at home during the 1991-92 basketball season when it played a "lame duck" independent schedule because the Atlantic 10 basically said it didn't want the Nittany Lions as part of its conference if it intended on jumping ship.

While the team struggled for much of the '92-93 season, it played to roaring crowds game after game and learned what it was like to belong to one of the most prestigious conferences in the country. As the aging rafters of Rec Hall shook from the fan's enthusiasm against the likes of Indiana, Michigan and Ohio State, a massive hole was being dug almost two miles away. It was the beginning of a long-awaited project that would sadden some Penn State basketball faithful, but could ultimately put the program on a more even level with its new-found peers.

The Bryce Jordan Center, named after a former Penn State president, is due for completion in 1995. It is a 15,000-seat academic/athletic facility that will ultimately replace Rec Hall as the home for many of Penn State's indoor athletic teams, most notably men's and women's basketball. It will be located at the eastern end of the university, right down the road from Beaver Stadium. The Jordan Center was funded by both the university and the state of Pennsylvania. It was a much-talked about project in Happy Valley, perhaps 10 to 15 years before its completion and to many, that day will be most welcome.

Bud Meredith is one of those people. He has been the ticket manager for athletic events at Penn State for over two decades. It is his job to fill the seats at Penn State sporting events, whether that be basketball, football, wrestling or any other athletic contest. Everyone should have a job that easy. For Meredith, selling the tickets is never the problem at Penn State. Having enough to go around, now, that's another matter.

Meredith has seen four additions to Beaver Stadium during his tenure. The football site — where it stands today — has grown from a horseshoe-type stadium that held around 60,000, to a full enclosure that currently fits over 96,000 Nittany Lion faithful inside its steel structure. It is currently the third largest on-campus stadium in the country behind those at Michigan and Tennessee, and Meredith estimates if Beaver Stadium were expanded to around 120,000 capacity, it would still sell out.

The list of season ticket holders is a half-mile long and the list of those wanting to get on that list is even longer. Penn State officials believe the university's basketball programs will fall under the same kind of burden for ticket requests because of the addition of a Big Ten schedule. With the addition of the new arena, that is certainly the hope.

There are several reasons why the university went ahead with its plans to build a new arena. First and foremost was for recruiting purposes. In a day and age when young high school stars ponder higher education, they dream of playing in the spotlight of the national audiences; the fancy new arenas with 15,000 to 20,000 fans — sometimes more — packed inside. Some of the best programs in the country have the best facilities as well.

With Penn State's entrance to the Big Ten, university administrators didn't need to add two plus two to figure out that Rec Hall was more of an eyesore than an attraction to most recruits. As antique and charming as it may be, the old place was just not going to cut it when it came time to compete with the likes of others in the Big Ten. A young kid with confidence almost has to figure, *"Hey, if I'm gonna play in the Big Ten, give me Michigan; Indiana; Iowa. Let me play in a place where the people can see me."* With a maximum capacity of 7,200, probably more than the fire marshal would allow in the place, Rec Hall would no longer be a prime recruiting device.

Economics is also a contributing factor. It may have cost into the thirty millions to build the Jordan Center, but the prospect of selling out the new arena on a near-regular basis will help pay that off in no time. Bruce Parkhill knows that the only way his basketball team has a chance to become a true challenger in the Big Ten is to play a better non-conference schedule. Every team has a few of the cupcakes on its schedule every season, but Penn State sometimes finds itself with too many.

Penn State found it difficult to get more powerhouse teams to visit Rec Hall in the past, because those teams had everything to lose and nothing to gain. Suppose that Duke, North Carolina, Kentucky or any top-ten team committed to a Rec Hall appearance. It would be a non-conference game for both teams on the court, and Penn State would be the clear underdog. But everyone knows what can happen to the favorite when it is playing away from home against a team whose fans are literally on the floor with it.

In Rec Hall, the fans in the lower level seats are the students, and they are right on top of the action. When a visiting player brings the ball in after a timeout, he can be sure to get an earful from the stands. True, the better teams — the truly disciplined teams — will block such a thing out, but any given team can be intimidated on any given night, and those better teams sometimes look at such a visit as though it could be their night. It happened one season to a talented Illinois team that ventured into Rec Hall before Penn State gained official acceptance into the Big Ten.

The better teams are also used to playing in front of the larger crowds. This in turn means more gate for the schools involved, and when there are only 7,000-plus in attendance, it just doesn't make sense financially for Duke, North Carolina, or Kentucky to risk such a venture into hostile territory.

As long as Penn State continued to call Rec Hall its home, one thing was certain. If Parkhill wanted his team to face the upper echelon of competition on a more regular basis, he would have to take his team to Chapel Hill or Lexington. With the construction of a new arena, the Penn State athletic office would suddenly have more clout in asking teams of such stature to maybe schedule a home-and-home type series over a two- or four-year period.

"We can definitely sell the tickets," said Meredith, who reported seven sellout crowds during the Lions' first Big Ten season. "I haven't seen the seating configuration for the new arena yet, and although I think 15,000 will be a great environment for basketball, I'm not so sure we'll have the closeness that we did in Rec Hall. I don't think the people will be as close to the floor as they were in Rec Hall."

For at least one Big Ten coach, that will be a blessing.

"I don't know why they want to build a new field house," Purdue coach Gene Keady said after an already improved Penn State team upset his Boilermakers 71-68 during the 1993-94 season. "They ought to stick with this one. There are at least 15 high school gyms in Indiana bigger than this place."

The home court advantage matters a great deal to Parkhill, but he isn't so much concerned about how close the fans are to the action as he is to how many fans are there to witness it. He looks forward to Penn State's next big step and thinks the move will have a tremendous impact on the future success of his basketball teams.

"It's wonderful to know that the Jordan Center is on the horizon," he said. "It'll provide many benefits to our entire campus community and will certainly mark a new era in Penn State basketball. The impact will be felt in several ways, but first and foremost, the Jordan Center will have a very positive effect on our recruiting. The new place will be a necessary complement to our move into the Big Ten."

Slowly but surely, Parkhill hopes to build Penn State basketball to a level where it can compete with the best the Big Ten has to offer some day. That was his hope when he took over in 1983 and the Nittany Lions belonged in the Atlantic 10 Conference. The results — after a few years of maturing — were four straight 20-win seasons, a conference championship, an NIT final-four appearance and an NCAA first-round tournament victory.

The rafters may be aging in old Rec Hall and soon its halls will be silent. But Penn State had to look toward its Big Ten future in all areas, not just football. With the addition of its new athletic/academic facility, the Nittany Lion athletic program had clearly taken a step in the right direction.

The last piece of the Big Ten puzzle was about to be put into place. All the other Penn State sports had taken their turn in the spotlight and the curtain was about to be raised on Joe Paterno's football team. Many would wonder if Penn State's disastrous 1992 would have any ill effects on its first season without independence, but Bud Meredith was quick to dispel any such notions.

"Everyone seems to be looking forward to the new rivalries," he said. "The request for season tickets has been about the same as any other year, but I think the push will be a little bit greater as the season goes on. Especially if we start out with a couple of wins."

There were at least two things Penn State fans could be sure of in 1993. First, that the Lions would play 11 regular season games and second, there was no predetermined bowl game to either look forward to or anguish over as was the case in 1992.

Penn State was set to open its first Big Ten football schedule September 4 against Minnesota at Beaver Stadium. Following that would be the first of three non-conference games on the Nittany Lions' schedule. This one would be at home against the University of Southern California, a team the Lions lost twice to in 1990 and '91. Both of those games were played in Los Angeles and after not playing the Trojans in 1992, Penn State would host USC in '93 and '94.

The following week would take the Nittany Lions on the road for the first time in '93. They would have to face the Iowa Hawkeyes, a team they had faced quite a bit as an independent in the early 1980s and were 6-3 against overall. Now, however, Penn State would be looking at Iowa as one of the many tough conference foes that would lie ahead.

The next two games would be against non-conference opponents and both were teams that Penn State was not only well acquainted with, but also held some sort of hex over. The Nittany Lions were 19-2 against Rutgers, but had packed 15 of those wins inside the first loss to the Scarlet Knights in 1918 and the second one in 1988. Penn State had fared even better over the years against Maryland having won 34 of the 36 meetings between the two teams. The Terrapins' only victory in the series — a 21-17 decision — came in 1961, while Penn State teams under Joe Paterno have gone 22-0-1 against Maryland since 1966.

The first of two bye weeks during the season would follow the Maryland game, and Penn State was about to start the first of many great new rivalries. The Michigan Wolverines were the preseason favorites to win the conference championship and their trip to State College was expected to go a long way in determining whether that prediction would come true.

After that, it would be another week off for the Nittany Lions before they traveled to Columbus to face another conference favorite, Ohio State. Penn State had a short history with the Buckeyes also, having won six of the eight meetings. The last time the Nittany Lions faced Ohio State was in the 1981 Fiesta Bowl, a 31-19 victory, and before that was in 1978, when the Lions won 19-0 at Ohio Stadium.

The last four regular season games would come against conference foes as Indiana and Illinois were scheduled to visit Beaver Stadium in Weeks 8 and 9, and Penn State would travel to Northwestern and Michigan State to close out the regular season. It would be a formidable schedule, but nothing the Nittany Lions weren't used to. The only question mark would be in how the team would face the new season knowing it was no longer working on an independent schedule.

There would be very few automatic wins on the Penn State schedule in 1993, the Big Ten would see to that. Paterno doesn't like to think of any team as an "automatic" win, but he certainly knows what teams his players must absolutely be prepared for. There were probably eight teams like that on the Lions' '93 schedule, and that was about the same number of teams Paterno and his squad would be facing for the first time.

"That's probably the toughest thing about joining the conference," Paterno said. "There are eight or nine new teams on our schedule that we're seeing for the first time. That means we have to learn eight or nine different game plans and study dozens of tapes of each team. At this point, I think it's a little bit easier for the other teams in the conference to get used to Penn State than for us to get used to them."

The best way to handle that was to assign each assistant coach an opposing team on the 1993 schedule and let them break down film, dissect, and then construct a formidable game plan. Where does such a task begin?

"Literally, from scratch," Penn State assistant Tom Bradley said with a shrug. "Sometimes you sit back and think about a certain team and you just don't know where to begin. You have to see how much they've changed their system over the last few years and try to get used to the personnel that was on the team last year, and who you figure to be on it this year. It's a big job."

And a tough one. But Paterno was ready to run with his team through the Beaver Stadium tunnel just as he had done every season for the last 27 years.

"Going into the Big Ten is very exciting," he said. "Any time you take a program into what is the greatest all-sports conference in the country, there is a tremendous level of excitement and anticipation. I am obviously nervous as to just how well we can compete in the conference."

Penn State has had little opportunity to see just how well it could stack up against Big Ten opposition. Through all the years of independence, the Nittany Lions had played only 35 games against foes from their new conference. The last time Penn State had faced a Big Ten team was in September of 1984 when it defeated Iowa, 20-17, at Kinnick Stadium in Iowa City.

"I realize I'm going from one era to another," Paterno said. "I've obviously never been in a conference, so it's a whole new thing to get used to. But it's kind of exciting. I've had to do a lot of homework to get a feel for the different coaches in the conference."

While Paterno and his coaching staff did a lot of studying in the off season, they also had to think of ways to prepare their own players. The rigors of preseason two-a-days were about to come to a close, and the first game was just a few days away. The goals Paterno had set for his team were about to be tested. He could only hope those goals would be fulfilled.

Intensity was a key word around the Penn State football offices as the 1993 season approached. Over and over again, Paterno and his staff would remind anyone who cared to listen that the Big Ten was loaded with intensity. "The players are gonna learn that kids in the Big Ten come at you on every play," Paterno said. "They never take a break and when the game's over, you're gonna feel like you ran into a brick wall a few times for no apparent reason."

That word was something he preached to his players during winter workouts and the intensified spring practices. And he continued preaching right through preseason drills. There were 40 returning lettermen at Penn State in 1993, but only about 12 that could be considered regulars from the season before, and 15 who had at least one start on offense or defense. They heard their coach, and they learned that the rigors of the Big Ten would be demanding, both physically and mentally.

"Oh yes," returning defensive tackle Tyoka Jackson said. "Coach said to us over and over that the players in the Big Ten, especially the linemen, were big and strong. They had the ability to knock you around, so you better be prepared to give it right back."

One of the reasons Paterno preached intensity so strongly was probably to serve as a reminder that his squad may have lost some of that quality when things got ugly in 1992. Another setback like that, and the Nittany Lions had great potential to be blown out of the new waters they were about to set sail on before their feet even got damp.

"One of the things we established as a goal going into spring practice was to get back to where we could be a really tough football team again," Paterno said just before the season began. "We wanted to enjoy being physically tough, to look forward to a difficult practice and to come off the field feeling good about the fact that we had a tough workout and achieved something in doing it.

"Secondly, I wanted to come out of the spring practices with a bunch of guys and a bunch of coaches all on the same page. That's what it's going to take to be a good football team. You're never quite sure, but I think we're pretty close to that."

Despite losing 22 lettermen from 1992, including All-American wideout O.J. McDuffie, Paterno was encouraged by the attitudes he saw in spring practices and felt his team was taking its first season in the Big Ten quite seriously.

"I think the kids wanted to put [1992] behind them," he said. "We had a lot of enthusiasm in the spring and things were very intense. Although we tried to stay loose and have a little fun, when we went after things, we went after them tough."

Penn State's strength going into 1993 was nothing new. The defense would feature seven returning starters, including the senior defensive tackle tandem of Tyoka Jackson and Lou Benfatti. Both made the 1992 Associated Press All-East team (Benfatti first team, Jackson second) and were rated as two of the best in the country going into '93.

Benfatti, who was also a second-team All-American selection by *The Sporting News* in 1992, led all defensive linemen at Penn State with 43 tackles the season before, including eight behind the line of scrimmage. He was one of three defensive players to start every game for the Nittany Lions. Jackson's playing time was somewhat limited during the second half of the '92 season because of an ankle injury he suffered against Boston College, but he still managed 25 tackles and three quarterback sacks despite missing three games and being hobbled against Notre Dame and Pitt. Jackson's 16.5 career sacks led all Nittany Lion defenders going into the 1993 season.

Linebacker Phil Yeboah-Kodie was listed as the "surprise" of the 1992 defense for his outstanding work on the inside position. His 63 tackles led the team, and he added six tackles behind the line of scrimmage for losses of 30 yards and three sacks for 32 yards lost. His position was to be challenged heavily by senior Brian Monaghan, who came on strongly in spring drills while Yeboah-Kodie's availability was limited due to a back ailment.

"Monaghan was one of our most improved players," Paterno said in his preseason synopsis. "He's one of those guys that sees this as his opportunity to have a good year before he gets out of here. He showed consistent effort and good leadership in spring ball."

The return of Brian Gelzheiser would be a welcome bonus for Paterno's squad. With his legal troubles far behind him, Gelzheiser was ready to continue in the role that got him a lot of playing time at the end of '92 and a total of 30 tackles in the Nittany Lions' last three games. His 44 tackles were the third highest number on the defense, even though he played as a backup through the first nine games.

Senior Eric Ravotti missed all of 1992 with an injury, but he was back as a redshirt senior. His presence would be felt a great deal because Ravotti has the capability to play up as a linebacker and down as a defensive lineman. A three-time letterman with 8.5 career sacks, Ravotti displayed the kind of versatility Paterno would need heading into 1993.

Penn State was also expected to be strong in the secondary where three starters were expected to return. Cornerback Shelly Hammonds, hero back Derek Bochna and free safety Lee Rubin all manned starting positions in 1992, and although two of the three missed spring practices, the Nittany Lion defense wasn't expected to miss a beat upon their return.

Bochna is probably the most versatile of the three. He entered the '93 season with 147 career tackles, eight interceptions, six quarterback sacks, and 18 tackles behind the line of scrimmage. Bochna, who plays baseball for Penn State in the spring, had three interceptions in '92 and played more minutes than any member of the team.

When one thinks of versatility at Penn State, Hammonds should also come to mind. He is one of those rare college football players who defiantly insists he'd rather play defense than jump into the spotlight of the more glamorous tailback position on offense.

As a freshman in 1990, Hammonds was asked to carry the ball at Boston College because the Nittany Lion tailback situation was severely depleted. He responded with 208 yards — including 191 in the second half — on 24 carries and had touchdown runs of 65 and 48 yards. Hammonds also had a 58-yard touchdown run called back by a clipping penalty. It was the best performance ever by a Penn State freshman and his second-half total was second best.

Joe Paterno thought seriously about keeping Hammonds on the offensive side of the ball on a more permanent basis, but Hammonds said he preferred to play defense. "I don't mind helping out when we're short [on offense]," he said. "But I like the hitting on defense and I think that's where I can help us the most."

Hammonds was pretty good at hitting also, and he proved so when Paterno left him on defense through all of 1992. His 39 tackles tied Bochna for seventh place on the team, and his 19 pass deflections would have made him the 1992 Big Ten leader. Hammonds still reached the end zone in '92 thanks to his 32-yard interception return for a touchdown against Eastern Michigan.

Hammonds missed the heavy work in spring practices because of an off-season shoulder surgery, but junior Tony Pittman, the son of former Penn State All-America tailback Charlie Pittman, stepped up big in spring ball to earn a substantial amount of playing time in 1993. Pittman was the recipient of the Jim O'Hora Award, named for a former assistant who served 31 years on the Penn State coaching staff until his retirement in 1977. The award recognizes the most improved defensive player after each spring practice period is concluded.

Lee Rubin missed five starts in 1992 due to an ankle sprain in the first game and the problem lingered all season. Despite his periods of inactivity, Rubin led the Penn State secondary with 41 tackles and ranked fifth overall in the cumulative defensive statistics. He too, was limited in spring drills, but his overall intelligence and awareness allowed him to act as another coach in a way for the rest of the up-and-coming safeties.

As much as a Penn State defense is always expected to be strong, a Penn State offense often goes into the new season with a lot of question marks. This season would prove to be no different as the Nittany Lions were hit hard by graduation and injuries.

Quarterback Kerry Collins, the starter at the end of '92, missed spring drills because of a broken finger he suffered in the Blockbuster Bowl, which eventually led to off-season surgery. Fullback Brian O'Neal was sidelined in the spring by an off-season back operation and kicker Craig Fayak was still rehabilitating his painful back in the spring. Paterno was cautious, but confident when asked about the absences of his players.

"Everything indicates that Brian O'Neal is going to be fine," the coach said. "But not knowing the kind of physical things a fullback has to do in our system, we're keeping our fingers crossed. Everybody was encouraged by Fayak's progress, but we're still not home free. He was just starting to kick the football at the end of spring drills.

"Kerry did not do a lot of throwing [in the spring] and was rusty when he did. If he's healthy, he will be a big factor at quarterback."

Quarterback is a large factor in the success of any good football team and as 1993 approached, Collins, a junior, was locked in a three-way duel with junior John Sacca and sophomore Wally Richardson, both of whom saw considerable playing time in 1992.

Sacca and Richardson took all the snaps in spring practices and it appeared that both would be just a little bit ahead of Collins on the depth chart, even though Paterno left the door open for any of the three to get the starting assignment against Minnesota.

Sacca connected on 81 of 155 passes in 1992 for 1,118 yards and nine touchdowns in six starting assignments. He had only three interceptions and if Penn State's statistics were included in the Big Ten in '92, Sacca's 128.1 passer rating would have put him at No. 3 in the conference.

For Richardson, the first game of 1992 was a freshman's dream — or maybe nightmare. Imagine dressing for your first college football game ever, taking a few snaps in pregame warmups and then settling in by the offensive coordinator on the sideline to get the feel for things and examine the system slowly. Suddenly, it's the first quarter and the starting quarterback is lying on the stadium turf, writhing in pain from a shoulder injury.

That was the plight Richardson faced in his very first game. Collins was out and so was another backup with little experience, Matt Nardolillo. Sacca was through for the afternoon, and the Cincinnati Bearcats were hungry to avenge a humiliating 81-0 defeat at the hands of Penn State the season before.

The game was called conservatively from Penn State's offensive point of view as Richardson only passed in obvious situations. He completed five of 10 for 35 yards, but the Penn State running game accounted for 243 yards, and the Nittany Lions prevailed, 24-20. Richardson made his first career start the following weekend against Temple and responded admirably with a 10-for-19, 164-yard performance that included no sacks or turnovers.

Richardson went on to appear in five regular season games for the Nittany Lions and the Blockbuster Bowl. His completion percentage of 53.3 was the best of any Penn State quarterback in 1992.

His star appeared destined to shine in the future and many people at Penn State felt Paterno would do everything possible to redshirt Richardson in 1993 so he'd have three years of eligibility left and the opportunity to collect a lot more playing time in the future. That probably would have happened in Richardson's freshman year were it not for the urgent need to be pressed into service.

"Never having had a spring practice, I think Richardson's improvement may have been a little bit more dramatic," Paterno said. "Sacca was a good quarterback for us last fall and he and Wally have both done well in the spring. We tried to play them in a way that both kids had the chance to work with both teams."

In the spring of 1992, it was actually Kerry Collins who appeared to have a handle on the starting quarterback situation for the '92 regular season. Collins served as the backup to John Sacca's older brother, Tony, in 1991 and appeared to have a lock on the position upon Tony's graduation.

A broken finger suffered in a family volleyball game prior to fall camp in 1992 set Collins back, however, and he wouldn't be ready until around mid-season. He came back to play the second half against Boston College in Week 7 and started the final five games of the season. That included the Blockbuster Bowl, where Collins broke the same finger again, which necessitated the January surgery.

With Brian O'Neal's back ailment raising a big question mark, Penn State was looking at a severe depletion from the fullback position. Two redshirt seniors, Brian Moser and Brian Kurlej, elected to pass up their final year of eligibility and that left Paterno with an interesting dilemma.

O'Neal was the only returning fullback with any relative experience, so once again, Paterno went to the defensive side of the field to find a running back. This time he plucked a linebacker, sophomore Jon Witman, to help fill the void. The move wasn't a total shot in the dark, considering Witman had gained almost 4,000 yards during his career at Eastern York High School in Pennsylvania and had scored more than 40 touchdowns.

"He had a great spring," Paterno said of Witman. "He's a tough runner with speed. He has to catch the ball a little bit better, but other than that he was fine. We always thought Jon was a good fullback and, based on what we saw in the spring, this move has really helped us."

Another addition that would figure to help the Nittany Lions in 1993 was the return of senior Brian Milne. His story is another example of a coach such as Paterno sticking by a commitment to one of his players.

Milne was an outstanding high school prospect in football. He gained 2,430 yards and scored 31 touchdowns during his junior season at Fort LeBoeuf High School in Waterford, Pennsylvania, to earn All-American honors. He also set state records in the discus and shot put for his high school track team and had his sights set on both football and track and field in college.

Expectations were pretty high for his senior year, but as happens for many potentially great athletes, adversity stepped into Brian Milne's life and challenged him to the very fullest.

"Hodgkin's Disease" was the diagnosis. Suddenly, there would be no football in Milne's senior year of high school. No discus. No shot put. No chance to better any of the records he had set the season before.

Life was the most important thing now to this young man, and those around him knew he could beat the disease if he just attacked it in the same manner that he approached the sports he loved so much.

Most schools would turn their backs on such a situation. His courage and determination were to be admired, but the fact remained that he was missing out on the all-important senior season, the one that should have answered the question of whether he could follow up on all the records from the year before. Athletic scholarships didn't grow on trees and there was very little room for charity.

Brian Milne preferred not to seek charity, however. He knew and believed in his abilities as an athlete. Whether the venue would be the gridiron or the infield of an Olympic track stadium, he was confident he would make it there some day.

He spent the 1991 football season at Penn State moving from tailback to fullback to tight end. It was mostly an experimental type of situation as he was more suited in this, his first season, to play on the foreign team, which meant he would run the other team's plays week after week to help the starters prepare for another Saturday afternoon.

In 1992, Milne turned his attention solely toward track and field. He missed all of the spring football workouts due to track and an emergency appendectomy. His purpose was to become a world-class competitor in both the discus and shot put. He became a two-year letterman in track and his perseverance would be rewarded with an NCAA discus championship during the 1993 season with a toss of 200 feet, 5 inches. Milne also won the discus gold medal at the World Junior Track Championships in Seoul, Korea in September, 1992, and he won the championship in the 1993 Penn Relays. His personal best discus throw of 207-5 is a Penn State record.

In events such as discus and shot put it takes dedication, concentration, commitment, and a lot of heart to be successful. Brian Milne displayed all of these qualities coming into Penn State's 1993 football season, and Joe Paterno was one happy coach to see a young man with so much versatility return to the team.

"Brian is going to be a big addition to our football team," Paterno offered in his preseason assessment. "He's a big man who can run and we consider him a big league prospect. I think he is much more comfortable with his physical status now than when he was out the last time for football. He wasn't quite sure he could handle it all at that time, but now I feel he's a story in himself. I'm excited about him coming back and I think his addition will give us a really good fullback situation."

With the fullback position looking better every day, Paterno should have felt even more comfortable at the tailback spot. Richie Anderson gave the Lions outstanding production from the position in 1992 with 900 yards rushing and 19 touchdowns, which placed him second nationally in scoring. Anderson opted for an early departure to the professional ranks and that left an opportunity for three budding stars to take center stage.

Mike Archie, Stephen Pitts and Ki-Jana Carter were redshirt sophomores when they played sparingly in 1992. At one time or another during the season, however, each one had his chance to impress the coaches. And none of them disappointed. The trio combined for 525 yards and eight touchdowns in their limited amount of action, but Paterno could see their promise.

All three tailbacks were given nicknames by the coaching staff soon after their various talents were showcased in early practices. They called Carter "Flash," because of his explosive speed. Pitts' ability to dodge tacklers along the line of scrimmage earned him the nickname "Slash." Archie was given the name "Cutback," because of his unique ability to make the right moves in the open field.

Each displayed a special talent and offensive coordinator Fran Ganter soon realized they would be a trio like he has never worked with before.

"I can remember having Curt Warner and Jonathan Williams in the early '80s," said Ganter, who had seen a number of great tailbacks in his 22 previous seasons as a member of the Penn State coaching staff. "We thought we could win with either one of those guys, but we've never had three of the same caliber at the same time.

"All three players have ability," he said. "They're not great yet and they're going to have to work awfully hard for everything. Each one has his own specialties and I believe that's what is going to make them so important to our team this season."

Carter displayed the best rushing numbers of the three in 1992 with 264 yards — a per-carry average of 6.3 — and four touchdowns. He also totaled 76 yards on four kickoff returns. Pitts had a 6.4-yard per-carry average with 148 yards and two touchdowns and also averaged 23.8 yards on four kickoff returns. Archie had an all-purpose total of 269 yards with 113 rushing, 67 receiving and 89 in returns. His resume from 1992 included an impressive 62-yard punt return for a touchdown against Pittsburgh in the last game of the regular season.

When Paterno and Ganter put together the offensive depth chart for 1993, they knew it would be impossible to list the tailbacks from 1 to 3. Instead, they were figured to be listed as 1, 1A and 1B. There was no sure starter for the upcoming opener against Minnesota, and the coaches figured none of the three backs would average 20 carries per game.

"There wasn't really a set plan," Ganter said. "Those things tend to take care of themselves. We plan to use them each week in the best way we can. All I know is I don't want to see any of them standing on the sideline in the fourth quarter with a clean uniform."

One very impressive factor about the three young players vying for Anderson's vacated position was the lack of animosity. Each player knew there would be room for the other to do his thing and each was determined not to create a controversy over who would carry the ball the most.

"No, we believe in each other and we're gonna support each other," Carter said. "What better situation could you ask for? When one back gets tired or a little bit sore, you have another one ready to step in and take his place. That can only help our offense.

"[The competition] is hard, but it makes you a better person. You don't want anything handed to you. You don't want to get lazy. We're really pushing each other, but we want to see each other do well, too."

"I'd describe it as a friendly rivalry," Pitts added. "We're all going for the same position, but the competition stops once we get off the field."

That is the kind of competition Ganter can appreciate.

"None of them sulk," he said. "After coaching for so long, you tend to see that a lot, and that's what creates problems. It's fun to be around these guys. It's fun to walk into my meeting room. Sometimes when I'd walk in there in the past, people would be sitting there with their heads down and their hoods up. That would make the job more difficult because it seemed like I'd have to worry about how many carries this guy or that guy is going to get. Something like that can be a cancer and it can spread through the team."

Even though Richie Anderson was set at the tailback position, the three young high school stars felt good about their future careers at Penn State. When Anderson turned pro early, their feelings got even better.

"I went with my heart," Pitts said about his decision to attend Penn State. "Penn State is very similar to my high school program, doing the little things right and not taking the short cuts. Life goes at a slower pace here in State College and I like that. If I were closer to home, I don't think I'd be able to study as much."

Pitts grew up in Atlantic Highlands, New Jersey, about 30 minutes from Asbury Park along the Jersey Shore. He rushed for 1,923 yards in his senior season at Middletown South High and scored 23 touchdowns. He had also considered Notre Dame and North Carolina before settling on the Nittany Lion program.

Mike Archie is Pitts' roommate at Penn State. When the 5-8, 206-pound Pennsylvania All-State selection made his decision to attend Penn State, he already knew that Pitts had done the same. He was also aware that the Lions were in hot pursuit of another tailback named Carter. Michigan State, Pittsburgh and Tennessee were all attractive opportunities for Archie, but the challenge awaited him at Penn State.

"I knew I'd face competition wherever I went," said Archie, who ran for 5,136 yards in his career at Sharon High School in Western Pennsylvania, including 2,334 yards and 32 touchdowns his senior season. "I love the competition. It's a stiff challenge, and I love to be given challenges."

Carter was the last of the three to announce his plans for college. He hedged just a bit on his verbal commitment to Penn State, but the Nittany Lions won the final recruiting battle over Colorado, Notre Dame, Michigan and Carter's hometown school, Ohio State.

"I went to a lot of Ohio State games," said Carter, who rushed for 1,723 yards and 23 touchdowns as a junior at Westerville South High in suburban Columbus, Ohio before a knee injury set back his senior season. "That's a big tradition in Columbus. I ran on the track [at Ohio Stadium], but I wanted to get away from home. I really wanted to grow up and mature. I wanted to start something new and meet new people."

Carter is the fastest of the three young tailbacks, with 4.3 speed in the 40. He is well built at 5-10, 205 pounds, but his production was somewhat limited in the spring due to annoying back spasms and an ankle sprain.

"Everyone knows he can run like the wind," Ganter said. "We've been watching him and making sure he stays healthy. He just needs to play and get the repetitions."

Archie used the winter and spring of 1993 to work on his blocking during pass protection, and also worked in the weight room to build some extra bulk and strength to his stocky frame.

"Mike Archie has worked hard and he's turned into one of the best [backs] coming out of the backfield that I've ever been around," Ganter said.

While the other two worked on their specialties, Pitts was no different. He needed to work on his receiving skills and that's what the coaches drilled him in during spring football.

"He's not a natural catching the ball, but he really has made great strides," Ganter said after spring ball. "He can scare a lot of teams because he's really a good inside runner."

"All three of those kids have ability," Paterno said immediately following the conclusion of spring practices. "None of them are great players yet. I think they'll all get plenty of work. They'll just have to stay healthy and work it all out.

"[The tailback situation] is a little like the quarterback situation. Nobody has really established himself as *the* tailback. I'd like to have someone come to the front and say beat me out."

They may not have spoken out just yet in terms of a leadership role, but Carter, Archie and Pitts were heading into the '93 season with thoughts of being No.1 in both the country as a team and No. 1 on the team in terms of field position. They know about all the past names at this position and they wanted to use the fun in the competition to make some names for themselves.

"They appreciate the competition," Ganter said. "They want to work harder and it makes me appreciate even more the fact that they're team guys and not 'I' guys. They just want to win."

Penn State would have another all-star position to fill at wide receiver due to the graduation of All-American O.J.

McDuffie. His presence was felt on all sides of the field in '92 as he and tight end Troy Drayton caught a combined 99 passes, accounting for 57.5 percent of the Penn State pass receptions in 1992. The two also totaled 61.3 percent of the Nittany Lions' receiving yardage.

As camp opened, Penn State had high hopes for a successful return from senior Tisen Thomas, who was slowed in '92 from a severe knee injury suffered the season before. Thomas caught eight passes in 1992 and had a 20.1-yard average per reception. He had also proven before his injury that he could return punts, which happened to be another area in which the Lions would miss McDuffie.

The high hopes for Thomas' successful return were quickly dashed, however, when he suffered the same injury to his opposite knee early in Penn State's preseason drills. He worked hard in the off-season and had seemingly established his presence once again during spring ball, but just as quickly as the optimism had been rebuilt, his career was over.

Redshirt sophomore Justin Williams was a pleasant surprise in 1992 as his 25.6-yard average per reception was the best on the team among those with more than just a few catches. His presence in '93 was to figure heavily in the Penn State offense along with steady senior Chip LaBarca and redshirt freshman Freddie Scott.

"I feel O.J. [McDuffie] was one of the greatest players I've ever seen," Scott said before the season. "But with him gone, I feel we have a more balanced group of receivers. Instead of one standout, we have a good mix and we should be able to complement each other. I think people will have to concentrate on us as a group."

That group would also be enhanced by the return of another redshirt sophomore in Bobby Engram. He contributed immediately as a freshman in 1991, but was forced to sit out the entire '92 season because of his run in with the law. With that all behind him, Engram was ready and willing to finally make his mark at Penn State.

With the loss of Drayton at tight end, Penn State would count heavily on two players who were seemingly followed at every turn by injuries or illness throughout their careers. Redshirt junior Kyle Brady checked into preseason camp at 6-6, 256 pounds and was prepared to take more of a responsibility in the

Penn State offense. There was no doubt he presented a big target for any of the Nittany Lions' three quarterbacks, but his stamina would be questioned early due to a severe bout with a flu virus that hit him early in the team's '92 camp and set him back for much of the season.

"I feel fine this season," said Brady, who played in all 11 regular-season games for Penn State in 1992, but was limited to just nine catches. "Last year it just seemed like my whole season was wasted because I couldn't shake what was bothering me. I expect to come back strong this season and do everything I can to stay healthy.

"Sometimes when you have a bad season, your confidence goes down and you start to have self-doubts. I was here [in State College] all summer doing lots of things, like lifting and running, and I'd sometimes look at myself and say I could do a lot more things than all of these guys up here of similar size. I just had to regain that confidence and that focus."

"As long as people don't expect him to be Superman, Kyle will be fine," Paterno surmised. "He's a lot more relaxed and confident and we just told him to go out there and do it."

Brady won the 1993 Red Worrell Award, which goes to the most-improved offensive player during Penn State's annual spring practice sessions.

"I wasn't expecting the award at all, but it's a great honor," he said. "I felt more a part of everything in the spring drills, like I contributed more. This is the best I've felt about myself since I came here."

Brady wasn't alone at the top of the depth chart heading into the 1993 season. Senior Ryan Grube ran neck and neck with Brady through the entire spring session and Paterno was bold enough to say on several occasions during the '92 season that Grube had a better grasp at the position in terms of blocking, reading and all-around play than any of the Nittany Lions' tight ends.

The wealth at tight end was to be spread between the two players, but misfortune struck the position early in 1993 when Grube suffered a severe knee injury in camp. He was expected to miss at least the first half of the season and suddenly the weight had shifted all on Brady.

The area where Penn State perhaps needed the most re-building after the 1992 season was in its offensive line, where three starters and another regular would have to be replaced. Center E.J. Sandusky, guard John Gerak and tackle Greg Huntington were gone, and that left guard Mike Malinoski as the only returning lineman who started all of Penn State's games the season before.

Malinoski was among the leaders on the line in minutes played in '92 and would be counted on to provide experience to the newcomers. Bucky Greeley had shared time with Sandusky at center during the previous season and was ready to step in full time. Derick Pickett also shared time at long tackle with part-time regular Todd Rucci in 1992 and was ready to step to the front.

"Being able to identify things on the field really helps a lot," Malinoski said of his role as Penn State's most experienced offensive lineman for 1993. "If you don't know what you're up against, you're going to have a real hard time. Playing a lot last year helps me to see what's going on and what I have to do to get the job done."

"Malinoski and Pickett really set a tone during spring drills," Paterno said. "They were both absolutely great. They are a couple of guys who could have gone through the motions but they hustled over to practice from late classes when they could have missed 20 minutes here or a half hour there."

With Malinoski, Pickett and Greeley set to man three-fifths of the offensive line, Paterno was looking to fill the other two spots left open from graduation. Jeff Hartings and Marco Rivera saw limited playing time in 1992 but showed a lot of promise in spring drills to take over the long guard and short tackle positions, respectively.

Redshirt sophomore Keith Conlin was also expected to get a good look on the offensive line going into preseason camp, while another redshirt sophomore, 6-5, 284-pound Andre Johnson, was switched from defense to offense in the spring to add depth to the line. Johnson gave Rivera stiff competition before settling into the No. 2 spot on the depth chart.

The 1992 foreign team provided Penn State with much promise but little experience on the offensive line as guards Bill Anderson, Paul Ingrassia, Pete Marczyk and Boris Oden; tackles Dale Harvey and Ken Lupold and center Barry Tielsch all figured to get important minutes in 1993.

Paterno was optimistic about his young offensive line going into the 1993 preseason camp, but only to a certain extent:

"If you'd ask me where our offensive line stands right now, I'd say we are OK one deep, but after that we have some problems."

One of the compelling problems during the 1992 season was the weekly status of the Penn State kicking game. At times the punter was doing the place-kicking, while the regular place-kicker spent much of the latter part of the season in the trainer's room.

Craig Fayak headed into the 1993 season just four points shy of the Penn State career scoring record for place-kickers, but would have broken the mark midway through 1992 were it not for a mysterious back ailment that caused him to shank two short kicks in the Nittany Lions' gut-wrenching loss to Miami. The injury was later diagnosed as a stress fracture in a vertebra and it forced Fayak to miss the rest of the season.

Punter V.J. Muscillo handled both duties during Penn State's final five games and connected on three of four field goal tries and 12 of 16 extra points. He also averaged 35.8 yards on his punts through the season and didn't allow one to be blocked.

"I would prefer V.J. concentrate on the punting and be really good in that department," Paterno said. "He's been a solid punter, but he had some trouble in the spring being as consistent as you'd like him to be. We didn't have a quality long snapper in practices, and V.J. didn't have the chance to do some things that would help determine if he's going to get better."

Fayak worked on his kicking in a different way during spring drills. While others worked with the hard leather footballs, the senior from Belle Vernon, Pennsylvania, practiced kicking the spongy nerf footballs that are so popular with children. It wasn't until the end of the spring drills that he was allowed to kick the real thing.

"We really don't know whether he'll have more back problems when he gets back to kicking seriously," Paterno said. "Everybody is encouraged by his progress, but we're still not home free."

Besides the scoring record for place-kickers, Fayak faced the opportunity in his last season of breaking Lydell Mitchell's all-time school scoring record of 246 points. Fayak, who also established himself in the classroom as a two-time CoSIDA-GTE Division II Academic All-American, is a tough nut to crack in terms of trying to break his concentration, but even he displayed a great amount of concern and caution about the possibilities of a healthy return.

"Records are nice and I certainly would like to have them, but they're not first and foremost on my mind right now," he said after spring workouts. "The injury was probably the toughest thing I've ever had to go through, and there still aren't any guarantees. The doctors feel it will heal and be stronger than it should be normally. I want to be better for the season, but it's scary to think it could fracture again just as easily."

Paterno came into the preseason with the idea that the majority of his team's success for 1993 could depend on the kicking game.

"There was a lot of concern in spring ball," he said. "When your kicker is up in the air, it affects everything you're doing. If your kicking game is good, it makes things easier for the defense and when the defense shines, that helps the offense. Until we're comfortable with our kicking, I'll be a little uneasy about the 1993 team."

Because of the misfortunes and maybe even dissension of the season before, Penn State was facing a lot of concerns and question marks as it headed into the 1993 season. When the entire roster had arrived in State College for the long and grueling camp that was laid out for them, Paterno seized the moment to further instill that belief he took hold of just a day after the Blockbuster Bowl loss to Stanford almost nine months before.

"You're gonna have a lot of doubters," the 67-year-old teacher told his students in the theatre-like team meeting room. "Every school in this conference, every one of 'em wants to see you fall flat on your face. They don't want Penn State in their league. They've said a lot of things about you, and not one of 'em thinks you guys can do anything in this league."

His voice had risen just a bit.

"Last season's over with and I'll tell you right now, I'm forgetting about it," Paterno continued. "Let all the non-believers say what they wanna say or think what they wanna think. But I know, and I believe that we're gonna have a great season. It's gonna take more heart and more guts than you've ever had to give in your whole lives. But you can get it done.

"We need a commitment from every single person in this room starting right now. We had good winter workouts and we had a great spring. Now's the time to put it all together. The last thing the Big Ten wants to see is Penn State coming in and winning the conference championship in its first year. Who cares what they want? It's what you want, and what you feel right here (pointing to his heart). We start right here, today. And we're gonna have a fun season."

Paterno then went over the list of rules and regulations that every player was to adhere to through his entire stay at Penn State. These included promptness for meetings and appointments; the proper dress code for trips as well as appearance in general. There would be no association with drug usage and gambling, and the acts of taunting or hot-dogging would be strictly forbidden.

All of Paterno's rules fall into the discipline category and each player would be constantly reminded of Penn State's glorious past and how the public truly does look up to them because they are Penn State football players. The coach reminds them that little kids will want to act like them, dress like them and look like them. All he asks is for each player to set a good example.

The next few weeks would be strenuous for everyone. Players had to pass their physicals and then they had to pass the dreaded 40-yard dash test.

"[The 40] is one of the most difficult parts about camp," assistant strength coach Kevin O'Dea said.

"It's a big challenge, but it goes a long way toward helping you get through the season," defensive tackle Tyoka Jackson said.

The 40-yard dash test actually begins in the spring. Each player runs the 40 at the beginning of spring drills to establish an individual time and is then grouped into a certain bracket for the following preseason based on that time.

Using Jackson as an example, the 6-2, 265-pound senior ran a 4.76 40 at the beginning of the 1993 spring football session. His time was then rounded off to 4.8 and .6 was added to that time to make his required running time in the fall, 5.4. Jackson was considered a Group C runner because of his position, as that group consists of all linemen. Group B is made up of quarterbacks, fullbacks and linebackers and Group A consists of all defensive backs, tailbacks and receivers.

When preseason camp begins, all players are grouped into their required time slots. Because Jackson's time was faster than most of the linemen, he was actually grouped with the linebackers when it was time to run because his time compared more so with theirs. All players who are in the 5.4 time slot are lined up on the goal line of the team's indoor practice facility. A clock with a buzzer is set at 5.4 and when the whistle blows, the clock is started and the players take off.

The players must cross the 40-yard line (the finish line) before the buzzer sounds to have their run considered successful. The grueling part is the players don't get by with running just one timed 40-yard dash. They are required to run 14. And they must pass at least 12.

The key, according to Jackson, is how you use the staggered rest time in between each run. For example, the Group C runners are allowed 40 seconds rest before their next run; Group B, 35 seconds and Group A, 30.

"You have to pace yourself, set a good rhythm after the first three," Jackson said. "That's why a lot of the younger guys don't pass their first time through. They want to run so hard to impress the coaches that after the first five or so, they're running out of gas, and they still have eight or nine to go."

Some players, like tailback Ki-Jana Carter, are in a group by themselves. Carter's qualifying time in the 40 was 4.4. As a tailback, he had only .4 added to his time and thus was forced to run at least 12 of 14 timed 40s in 4.8 or less.

"Concentration is one of the biggest reasons the coaches have something like that," Jackson said. "If you can really set your mind into how you're running, how you're pacing yourself for the whole picture, it really helps your concentration when you're in a game. It makes you see and realize a whole lot more of what's going on out on the field."

For a lot of people, running even one 40-yard dash would cause pain and discomfort. When their timed efforts are concluded, most of the players wouldn't be blamed for heading to the locker room for a long hot shower or an ice bag to the knees. Instead of doing that, however, the players that are finished usually stick around to encourage those that find the going not as simple.

As a hefty lineman struggles to meet his goal, Carter, Jackson, Shelley Hammonds, Bobby Engram and a host of others are taking turns running beside him, urging him with their voices, pacing him with their own tired legs. It is a sign that no one affiliated with Penn State football wants to let the same disparaging circumstances from 1992 follow this year's team around. Their efforts on this first day seemed, at least for a while, to prove the ugly albatross of the previous season had disappeared.

While most of the players were able to pass their 40-yard times, some could not. It would be easy for the coaching staff to say, "Oh well, better luck next year." But that's not the way it goes. Sadly enough, the players that don't pass the first time must rise at 5 a.m. the next day and go through the paces again. The runs are followed by the normal two-a-day practice sessions and if they don't pass a second time, they do it again the next day. Repeated failures also mean a drop in practice jersey color (from light blue to green, or first team to second team on offense, for example) and that could go a long way toward determining how much playing time a player will receive during the season.

While the players were doing their part to prepare during preseason camp, the coaching staff was also hard at work. Between practices, the players eat and rest. Coaches, on the other hand, may take time for a quick lunch, but then it's back to the meeting room to discuss the previous practice session and plot the next one.

Paterno is not always present at these meetings, but he knows his staff will be well prepared thanks to offensive coordinator Fran Ganter and defensive coordinator Jerry Sandusky. All the Penn State coaches prepared for this unusual season in a special way because it marked the first — and maybe only — time the Nittany Lions would have to prepare from scratch for *eight* new teams.

"It was kind of unusual because of the new situation," linebackers and special teams coach Tom Bradley said. "We were basically assigned one [opposing] team each and told to literally dissect film from every aspect and every angle. That made preparing for the season a little easier, but it was still a real challenge."

Another part of the coaching staff's assignment was to study every coach's tendencies in the films they observed. What would John Cooper (Ohio State) do in a fourth-and-one situation at mid-field? How would Gary Moeller (Michigan) handle a fake punt? Every question had to be plotted. Every question needed an answer. The Penn State coaching staff was bound to face situations during the season where their homework would be tested.

It was a test the Lions couldn't afford to fail.

6

MINNESOTA:
The Road Begins

Part of the fun of college football is following the polls. Coaches and players will say the only ranking that counts is the last one, but most catch themselves looking through the local newspapers come every Monday morning in the fall, searching for their team's name in some publication's Top 25. It is true the final polls handed in by the writers and coaches after all the New Year's Day bowl games are completed carry the most clout. That is when a champion is crowned, and there is no more looking over your shoulder, at least for the next few months.

At the end of the season, those two polls are the only ones that count. A panel of Associated Press writers — some on the regular college football beat, some not — and the nation's Division I-A coaches decide the best college football team in the country. No one else has a say, not even the players who toiled for the last five months or so with hopes of reaching that lofty goal.

To date, college football's national champion is not decided on the field at the end of the season, nor is it decided at the beginning. But at the beginning of every season, there are a host of prognosticators who chomp at the bit to sell their publications and release their preseason predictions. Everyone has a say in the beginning. Whether it's the professional analysts who get paid big money to make their predictions on television, or the average fan who stands around the office water cooler and goes on forever about why Florida State is better than Notre Dame, or vice versa.

At Penn State, there was a curiosity about where the Nittany Lions would be ranked in most of the preseason polls. Tradition would perhaps be on their side in terms of success and consistency over the years, but how much respect would the Penn State football program receive in the wake of 1992's disastrous conclusion? Many fans had to wonder if tradition would be enough.

Another factor was the move to the Big Ten. Penn State would be facing eight new opponents beginning with Minnesota. The new teams all came from the conference that seemingly wished for very little success from the Nittany Lions in their first full venture into conference play. It was an interesting dilemma, one that Joe Paterno could hardly wait to dive into.

"It's time to get going," he said. "We've been waiting around and preparing for this the last few months. It's our chance to see how we're going to do and I'm really anxious for it."

Paterno, at least publicly, really wasn't one of those people who spent too much time looking at predictions. He had his mind solely focused on preparing his team, so it didn't matter what ESPN analysts Lee Corso and Beano Cook, or any others for that matter, had to say about the fortunes of Penn State football for 1993. All he hoped for was a little respect and a chance to get his team back in the national spotlight for all the right reasons.

Corso, for the record, had the Lions finishing 16th in his preseason poll, citing the tough new schedule that Paterno and his coaching staff had very little advanced knowledge of. Other national magazines and newsletters had Penn State finishing anywhere from 14th or 15th to 20th.

Michigan was the team most experts picked to win it all in the Big Ten Conference. The Wolverines were coming off a 9-0-3 record in 1992 and were out to defend their Rose Bowl victory from the season before. Ohio State got at least one nod to win the conference title, while Penn State was picked by most to be the conference's bridesmaid. Obviously, tradition meant a lot to the preseason prognosticators, because most teams are placed somewhere in the middle of the pack when starting out in a new conference.

All Paterno cared about heading into the season was getting his team focused. Everyone asked him about the Nittany

Lions getting "back on track," which was a question he wasn't quite sure how to answer. All he could look at and pass on to his players were the realities that faced them in this new challenge.

"I don't know what getting back on track means anymore," Paterno said. "All I want to do is make sure we play with some enthusiasm and make sure we hit people and play with pride. I sense we lost that in a couple games last year. Where that takes us, who knows?

"This is not a great squad. It has a chance to be a pretty good squad, but it needs to stay healthy. It's got a chance to be competitive, but it's just not a great squad. People hate to hear that, but right now those are the realities of the situation."

Almost every preseason article about Penn State mentioned the idea that the team lost interest following the game it gave away to Miami in the middle of 1992. Each analysis then followed with these words of caution: "That won't be the case in 1993." To a man, the Penn State players definitely believed there would be no fold in '93. They said so all winter, spring and summer. Now was the time to start delivering on those promises.

SEPTEMBER 4, UNIVERSITY PARK, PA — The weather in Happy Valley wouldn't exactly remind fans of Pasadena. The skies were mostly cloudy and gray; sprinkles of rain tried their best to wash out the season's first giant tailgate party. Inside the Penn State locker room, players dressed quietly, getting mentally prepared. They pondered last-minute assignments; sat down to some final coaches meetings; tried to quell the excitement of this history-making day.

For the past few months, Paterno had been facing a tough decision. It was getting to be an annual event, this quarterback situation. One player appears to have the inside track to the position, another comes along and stakes his own claim. In this preseason, no less than three players were out to convince the head coach that he should be the starting quarterback.

John Sacca, Kerry Collins, and Wally Richardson had all taken their turns in the spotlight during the 1992 season and each succeeded in making an impression on Paterno and offensive coordinator Fran Ganter. Richardson was a true freshman in '92 and, as is the freshman quarterback custom under Paterno, appeared headed for a redshirt, which would have made him inactive, but would have given him an extra year of eligibility.

Fortunes changed, however, for Richardson when Collins couldn't start the season due to a broken index finger, and Sacca went down with a shoulder injury in the first quarter of the Nittany Lions' first game. Richardson handed over the clip board, snapped on his chin strap and led Penn State to a season-opening win. He followed that with a start against Temple the following week and another win.

Suddenly, Penn State fans everywhere showed a little less concern for Sacca's or Collins' return. Instead, they wondered if Penn State had found the second four-year starting quarterback in school history. Paterno had cautioned all along that Richardson's appearance was more due to emergency than anything and that Sacca was still the team's No. 1 quarterback.

True to Paterno's word, Sacca was back in the starting lineup by the third week of the '92 season, and Richardson was back on the sideline to learn the position he had just filled so admirably. Patience is a virtue at Penn State, especially if you're a quarterback, as Richardson was quickly finding out. The chances for a medical redshirt were gone for '92, but Richardson felt relief that he had played the game on a big-time level and did so with a fair amount of success.

Coming into 1993, Paterno faced the same situation as usual. The quarterback derby was on, but now there was a proven third person bucking for the position. Sacca, Collins and Richardson were all healthy, although Collins was probably behind just a little due to his absence in spring practices because of surgery on his broken finger.

Paterno knew what *he* wanted to do with the situation. The question was, how would he convey his message to the three young men who expected to lead his offense? During the summer months, Paterno said he wouldn't wait a long time to name a starter. Confidence was everything in this move to the Big Ten and Paterno wanted to give his quarterback all the reassurance he could. His idea was to name a starter early and let him take charge of the offense almost from the beginning of camp.

It was only five days before the season-opener when Paterno made up his mind. His intentions of naming a starter well in advance were good, but sometimes pulling the trigger on such a decision is the most difficult and critical dilemma a coach can face. Only one person is going to approve and the coach can only hope the others will stay in tune with the program. When he informed the three leading candidates for the position, there was no pouting from the runner-ups. As things so often go, however, circumstances would change throughout the season and feelings would eventually be hurt. It's just that the hurt feelings were to come from the most unlikeliest source in this trio of quarterbacks.

John Sacca was Paterno's choice to lead the Penn State offense in its Big Ten debut. It was widely felt that Sacca had earned his shot because of his consistent performances through-out an otherwise inconsistent season in 1992. He had displayed leadership qualities while completing 52.3 percent of his passes (81-155) in '92. Sacca threw for 1,118 yards and nine touchdowns and had just three passes intercepted in his first full season of quality playing time. According to Paterno, the position was Sacca's to lose all along.

"Yeah, I went into the preseason with the idea that some-body had to beat John out," Paterno said. "I felt John had played well in '92, maybe a bit better than Kerry. Nobody came in and beat him out. If I had started the other way, I'm not sure anybody would have beaten Kerry out. They're that close. All three kids are good, but you have to start with some guidelines."

While discussing his decision to make Sacca the opening day starter, Paterno made frequent mentions of Kerry Collins' ability as a backup, and his confidence in Collins' stepping in at any time. Little was said of Wally Richardson and his abilities as a starter, backup or otherwise. That left reporters again with the question of a possible redshirt for the talented sophomore.

The 6-foot-4, 208-pound sophomore from Sumter, S.C., had the body of a wide receiver, but his position was to be quarter-back from day one at Penn State. The Nittany Lion football program had never been blessed with a quarterback who was termed a *great* one. Even during the national championship seasons of 1982 and '86, and several other years when the Lions were contenders, the starting quarterback was not someone who could be labeled the prototype quarterback.

Chuck Fusina and Todd Blackledge went on to play in the NFL, but never became the stars that college had made them out to be, although Fusina was a star in the United States Football League, where he led the Philadelphia Stars to two consecutive USFL championships. But Penn State has never really had a Dan Marino or John Elway or Jim Kelly. Not even a Charlie Ward, the Heisman Trophy winner from Florida State, or Heath Shuler, another Heisman hopeful in 1993, from Tennessee.

The label that has been most often placed on the quarterback position at Penn State is "winner." There's nothing wrong with that, however, and after all, those "winners" were the players who led the Nittany Lions to their two national championships in the 1980s.

Blackledge turned the corner at Penn State when he won the starting quarterback position at the beginning of the 1981 season. He beat out current NFL quarterback Jeff Hostetler, who ultimately transferred to West Virginia, and settled into the position with relative ease. It was his leadership quality that Paterno trusted so much on the field and Blackledge probably solidified that trust when he led the Nittany Lions to a come-from-behind 48-14 win at Pittsburgh in the last game of the regular season when the Penn State-Pitt game was still a heated rivalry.

It was a sweet win for Penn State despite the lopsided score because the Panthers were 10-0 at the time and seemingly headed to the Sugar Bowl with thoughts of a national championship on their minds. In those days if there was one thing Penn State fans liked to spoil, it was a Pitt march to a national championship, and vice versa. Marino was the All-American candidate and he showed it by passing the Panthers to a 14-0 first-quarter lead.

Blackledge responded with a cool head and the Penn State defense never buckled again that afternoon. In fact, it bottled up the Pitt receivers and chased Marino all over the field for the next three quarters while the Penn State offense opened the flood gates.

The following season was Blackledge's chance to shine as a leader, and that he did. Penn State lost just one game in 1982, but that loss was early enough in the season to a very talented Alabama team. At a time when a lot of teams might pack it in and play out the string, Blackledge showed his leadership as the quarterback and quietly vowed the Lions would lose no more. He had the players around him on offense: tailback Curt Warner; fullback Jonathan Williams; wide receivers Kenny Jackson, Kevin Baugh and Gregg Garrity; and offensive linemen like Pete Speros, Mike Munchak, Sean Farrell. But they listened to Blackledge and believed they could win it all, which they did with a 27-23 Sugar Bowl win over the No. 1 Georgia Bulldogs on Jan. 1, 1983.

Todd Blackledge will go down in school history as the first quarterback to ever win a national championship at Penn State, but John Schaffer has the best chance of being remembered as the winningest quarterback in school history. Schaffer was the Nittany Lions' starting quarterback in 1985 and '86. Like Blackledge, he waited patiently for his chance and won the position when the opportunity was there.

Joe Paterno was best remembered at Brown University as the quarterback who couldn't run or pass; all he could do was win. Schaffer could only be compared to his coach in probably one of those categories because although he wasn't the best passer or runner Penn State had ever seen, he did both well enough to succeed. One thing Schaffer *could* do was win. He did it in high school for three years as Schaffer's team was 33-0 with him as the signal caller.

When he took over as Penn State's starter in 1985, the Nittany Lions rolled through the regular season with 11 straight wins, a No. 1 ranking and a national title shot in the Orange Bowl against No. 2 Oklahoma. The Sooners' offense was too much for Penn State that evening as Schaffer lost his first game ever as a starter, 25-10. The loss was even more devastating to Schaffer because it was in a national championship game.

The loss could have affected a lot of people because of the implications surrounding it, but Schaffer only seemed more determined. His 44-game winning streak as a starter went by the wayside in Miami that night, but 1986 brought the opportunity to start another streak, which was exactly what Schaffer did.

Penn State finished 11-0 during the '86 regular season and matched up with undefeated and No. 1-ranked Miami in a specially arranged January 2, nationally televised showdown for the national championship in the Fiesta Bowl. The Hurricanes seemed to thrive on the bad guy image they had achieved with their green fatigues and utter lack of respect for Penn State.

Meanwhile, legions of Penn State fans around the country either tuned in to their televisions or flocked to Tempe, Arizona, to cheer for their heroes in the white hats. It was John Schaffer's last game in a Penn State uniform and his last chance to achieve the national championship for which he had worked so hard these last few years to pursue.

Miami had Heisman Trophy winner Vinnie Testaverde. Penn State had its usual outstanding defense. Miami had a defense about as talented as it was arrogant, while Penn State had an offense that methodically worked its way to the end zone.

Schaffer had tasted losing just once in his last five years or so of football and for him, once was more than enough. The Miami defense chased him, hit him, harassed him and taunted him. But there was one important thing the Hurricane defenders could not do to John Schaffer. They never once got to him. The Miami players sacked Schaffer a few times, but they never once got inside his head. If he was hit, he got back up. If it hurt, he didn't let them see it. If they talked to him, he turned the other way.

Schaffer did just enough that evening and Penn State came away with its second national championship, a 14-10 winner. It was a classic case of good reigning over evil if you were a Penn State fan, and Schaffer was proud to be a hero representing the good guys. His high school and college career wasn't perfect, but 56 wins out of 57 games as a starter wasn't exactly a setback.

Penn State always seems to be the model when football experts speak of consistency at the quarterback position. Most have the capabilities to throw on third down when they have to, but they usually spend most of their time handing off to one of the many great tailbacks that seem to grow on trees in State College. That was the case even before the Sacca-Collins-Richardson saga began in '92. John Sacca's older brother, Tony, was another one that fit the Penn State mold to a tee. He wasn't one to put up the great numbers week after week, but he did the little things well enough to win with consistency.

Wally Richardson appeared to at least have the chance to break that seemingly long-standing Penn State mold. Many fans grew excited at his signing because they had heard of, or read about his size and exceptional quickness, not to mention his strong and accurate arm. For the first time in a long while there actually seemed to be at least a two-dimensional quarterback that might see action in a Joe Paterno offense.

Once Sacca had been named as the Nittany Lions' opening game starter, however, Richardson began to face the definite possibility of seeing no playing time in 1993. It can be hard on a player to face a long, hard season of practice without the reward of a game to participate in. It is a dilemma Paterno has faced many times before, but never seems easy to discuss with the player.

"You want to see a guy get his chance," Paterno said. "I mean he works hard for his opportunity to play. But at the same time, if he can see the reasoning behind the decision, he'll realize we want to redshirt him because we value his talents so highly. The best thing for a young quarterback with potential such as Wally is to take the extra year and work without the pressure. It should ultimately put him in a lot better position for the future."

Richardson's position for 1993 was pretty much decided at the end of Penn State's preseason camp. To his credit, he never moped or complained once informed of the coaching staff's direction. Barring any unforeseen emergency such as Sacca's injury in the '92 opener, Wally Richardson would be a candidate for a redshirt and would be held out of all games in 1993.

"Wally did very, very well in the preseason," Paterno said after naming Sacca his starter. "We certainly realize he has tremendous potential. He may have the most potential of all three of our quarterbacks, but our offensive football team has been decimated by injuries, and we have to have some people in there who have experience. Wally and I have talked and it seems likely that we'll redshirt him. But I really don't want to make that decision for a couple of games."

With Richardson's case being somewhat decided, Paterno also had to make sure he would still have the cooperation and commitment of his other quarterback in the feature battle for a starting position. Kerry Collins came into camp just a few paces behind Sacca because of the off-season surgery on his broken finger, but he hoped to impress enough in camp to win the job back. When Collins didn't quite do it, Paterno made sure he discussed the situation with him openly and frankly.

"I talked to Kerry about playing a series of downs here and there," Paterno said. "I discussed a couple of scenarios with him and to his credit, Kerry said, 'Hey look coach, if I was the QB, I wouldn't want to be looking over my shoulder.' I appreciated his attitude about it. He and Wally Richardson are mature young people and understand what football is all about. You give it your best shot and if a decision is made that's not in your favor, you live with it and you continue to be an asset to the football team."

No matter which quarterback Paterno selected as his starter, the rest of the Penn State players were glad to see just one guy in the light blue practice jersey instead of three.

"It's tough [in practice] when you go into the huddle every day and you're seeing a different face," tight end Kyle Brady said. "You're not really sure who your leader is going to be. Sometimes you'd just like to know."

Penn State was set to open its 1993 season at home, which was always a good sign when considered that the Nittany Lions were 67-7-2 overall in season openers at home. This was a special one, regardless of the rolling mist over Mount Nittany and the gray, threatening skies. The Penn State logo was painted in blue and white in each end zone, as had been the case for the past several years. But those in attendance saw something else painted inside those end zones, something that signified the end of a 106-year tradition, and the beginning of a new one.

It was the rectangular logo of the Big Ten Conference that caught many eyes as they strolled into Beaver Stadium. The letters were blocked and powerfully displayed in white paint with blue background. The B and T stood in capital letters just a bit taller than the rest and the logo seemed complete when one noticed the numerals 1 and 1 intertwined between the G, T, and E. It seemed to take a moment for the meaning to sink in, but once it did it became very clear.

The new logo stood for the tradition of a longstanding conference that wasn't afraid to take the first steps in expansion. Conference officials didn't know whether to change the name of the conference or leave it as it was, so they did a little of both. The big block letters seemed to stand for the solidity of the conference, while the numbers in the middle highlighted the addition of a new member in its ranks. At least for now, the conference remained the Big Ten, but there would now always be that little reminder in the new logo of the 11th member.

As a new member of the conference, Penn State expected to start several new rivalries. Fans and politicians would get in the act by putting their state's pride in the athletes' hands.

Lt. Governor Mark Singel of Pennsylvania, and Governor Arne Carlson of Minnesota were on hand to participate in a pre-game ceremony to announce the institution of the "Governor's Victory Bell," a trophy that would go annually to the winner of the Penn State-Minnesota game. At halftime, Penn State president Dr. Joab Thomas and athletic director Jim Tarman would receive a framed certificate of Big Ten membership from Conference Commissioner Jim Delaney, Minnesota president Dr. Nils Hasselmo and Minnesota athletic director McKinley Boston. Even the fans received commemorative coins that had the Nittany Lion logo on one side and an inscription on the other side that said, "Penn State vs. Minnesota, Nittany Lions' 1st Big Ten Conference game."

The stadium had received a facelift as well, in the form of new electronic scoreboards in the end zones, and the game was the first in a new attempt to draw even more Penn State fans to State College by the experimental pay-per-view system over much of Pennsylvania and the surrounding states.

The numbers and records set by both teams over the years seemed to be staggering. The University of Minnesota came into Penn State's first Big Ten game as a charter member of the conference when it began in 1896. Since that time, the Golden Gophers had played 605 games — more than any other school in the conference. Joe Paterno had been Penn State's coach for the last 27 years and had amassed 247 career victories. But coming into this one, the numbers meant nothing.

"We want to play well against them, that's for sure," Paterno said. "It's our first Big Ten football game and we certainly want to be a good team when we play Minnesota. I'm nervous enough just going into the conference, but I'm probably going to be awfully nervous when it gets close to game time."

Despite all the numbers, Paterno needed only remember that Penn State was 0-0-0 in conference games and had never met Minnesota on the football field. The Golden Gophers were coming off a dismal 2-9 season in 1992 and both teams were looking to erase the bad memories of a season before. In Minnesota's case, a win over Penn State to kick off the historic season would do wonders for an otherwise struggling program.

"Minnesota gives you a lot of problems," Paterno said in the days leading up to the first game. "I know that sounds like an old coaching cliche, but [Minnesota coach] Jim Wacker is a very ingenious coach who does a lot of things defensively and offensively. I expect it to be a wide open football game, because Minnesota will have us spread all over the place.

"Defensively, they are very, very aggressive. They play the kind of defense that has traditionally given trouble, with a lot of blitzing and eight-man fronts and things like that. Jim Wacker is a very enthusiastic guy and his players should come out and play the same way."

When Penn State made the move to the Big Ten Conference, it was met with some harsh words of criticism from several of the conference's coaches in sports other than just football. Wacker, however, was one who gave the Nittany Lion program a vote of support.

"It's great for the Big Ten," he said. "It's great for Penn State; great for the Rose Bowl and great for big television audiences. The addition of Penn State can do nothing but enhance an already great conference, both academically and athletically."

Eight months of pain and struggle had come down to this moment. So many lost souls that needed to be corralled. So many questions that needed to be answered. It was a whole rebuilding job in an incredibly short time. Success would be difficult in this new conference; failure would be a major step backward. As the Penn State football team prepared to take the field for the first time in 1993 — and for the first time in a new era —everyone looked back on the past year's preparation and remembered what they were out to accomplish.

"We learned a lot about putting off-the-field distractions behind us," defensive tackle Tyoka Jackson told one newspaper reporter. "We learned about not going out and doing things that could hurt this football team. We learned that practicing with intensity every single practice pays off. You just can't show up against teams and think you can play hard on Saturday. We learned about what it takes to win in tough situations.

All those are things we can take with us out on that field. Everything else can go in the garbage."

The Nittany Lions won the coin toss, which in itself became an eerie habit for the team throughout the '93 season. Another strange story unfolded a day earlier in State College when a gunman armed with an assault rifle fired several shots randomly while at a construction site less than two miles from Beaver Stadium. Locals were urged to stay in their homes and fans coming into town for the game were asked to either stay in their hotel rooms or their motor homes. Traffic was closed on one of the main access highways to the stadium through much of Friday as police and special weapons officers conducted an eight-hour manhunt. It was early evening before the man's lifeless body was discovered in a trailer at the site of the construction from an apparent self-inflicted gunshot wound.

University of Minnesota officials were kept abreast of the situation throughout the day and the team was housed in a hotel about four miles away from the incident. Minnesota coach Jim Wacker said it would be something to remember for his team's first visit to Happy Valley. "Next time I come here I'll have to bring a six-gun," Wacker said.

Although Wacker did not carry actual firearms in his possession, Joe Paterno knew well enough that Minnesota certainly had the firepower. Quarterback Tim Schade was about to start his first game for the Golden Gophers after transferring from Texas Christian University the season before. He brought a powerful arm with him and he wasn't afraid to use it.

Schade did his part to welcome the Nittany Lions to the Big Ten by setting a non-bowl record for most passes completed and attempted, and most yards gained by a Penn State opponent. The 6-6, 230-pound junior set a Minnesota school record with 478 yards, completing 34 of 66 passes.

"How many passes?" Paterno asked the media afterward. He was once again told 66. "You mean combined?" The answer was no. "Geez, no wonder the game took so long."

The game lasted three-and-a-half hours as the Golden Gophers seemingly passed on almost every down. The teams combined for 1,095 yards and 178 offensive plays. While Schade and Minnesota accounted for most of those numbers, Penn State surprised many in the sold out crowd with some offensive firepower of its own. Minnesota outgained Penn State 591-504 and totaled 90 plays to the Nittany Lions' 88.

For the sixth straight year, a Sacca would start the first game of the season for Penn State. Tony started the openers from 1988-91, while younger brother John kept it going in '92, and now '93. John Sacca lent credence to Paterno's decision to start him against Minnesota by completing his first six passes for 114 yards. For the game, Sacca completed 18 of 32 for 274 yards, but it was his four touchdown passes that got the Nittany Lions' first Big Ten experience off to a positive start as Penn State rolled to a 38-20 victory in its first game under the Big Ten spotlight.

While the offensive display was a surprise, the Penn State defense simply delivered its usual steady performance. The Lions elected to kick off to Minnesota and the game was barely two minutes old when the defense made its first contribution.

Schade completed his first pass for 11 yards on a second down play, but the next time he dropped back to pass he was faced with a heavy Penn State rush. Schade wasn't sacked all day, but when Nittany Lion defensive tackle Tyoka Jackson got in his face on a second-and-seven situation, it appeared a sack would have been the most fortunate thing to happen for Minnesota. In his haste to get rid of the ball, Schade's pass floated like a wounded duck into the hands of Penn State hero backer Derek Bochna.

"That was a big play for our defense," Bochna said. "That was our goal coming in, to make some big plays. To have it happen right away like that, I was happy."

Suddenly, Penn State had a first down at the Minnesota 29. "I just wanted to call a simple out pattern to get our passing game going and to give John [Sacca] some confidence," Paterno said of Penn State's first scoring play.

On first down, Sacca dropped back and looked to his left. He spotted wideout Bobby Engram, who was making his first start in a Nittany Lion uniform, with a pass toward the sideline. Engram juked one defender and picked up a key block from guard Mike Malinoski. Twenty-nine yards and a lot of zig-zag moves later, he was in the end zone and the Lions had a 7-0 lead on their first possession — and first play — of Big Ten football.

Stephen Pitts was Paterno's choice as the starting tailback for Penn State, but the plan also called for rotating perhaps four, sometimes five different running backs throughout the game. The rotation system was put to good use on Penn State's next possession as the Nittany Lions took over following a Minnesota punt at their own 11-yard line.

Pitts, Ki-Jana Carter and Mike Archie, along with fullbacks John Witman and Brian Milne supplied the ground force that carried Penn State to the Minnesota 31. From there, Sacca looked again to Engram, this time down the right sideline on more of a timing pattern. The 5-10, 180-pound receiver used every inch of his body in making a diving, sprawling catch in the corner of the end zone.

The first quarter was barely half over, and Penn State was out to a 14-0 lead. Fans were cheering Sacca and discovering what the Nittany Lion offense missed in '92 when Engram sat out the season during his disciplinary suspension. A lesson Penn State players and fans alike would soon learn, however, was that no Big Ten team should ever be counted out of a game, regardless of the deficit.

While many in State College envisioned a blowout, Minnesota quarterback Tim Schade would hear nothing of the kind. Embarrassed by the Golden Gophers' first two offensive series, Schade quickly completed four consecutive passes, including a 42-yarder to slot back Omar Douglas, and Minnesota was at the Penn State 13-yard line. Before the Nittany Lion defense could adjust, Schade cruised into the right side of the end zone on the next play on a quarterback draw. The extra point made it 14-7 and Penn State would have to quickly take an attitude adjustment toward the Minnesota offense.

The momentum seemed to have shifted toward Minnesota thanks to its strong drive, but Penn State quickly rebounded. On the ensuing kickoff, returner Shelly Hammonds broke free up the middle and returned the ball 67 yards before Minnesota's Tony Levine wrestled him down at the Golden Gophers' 26-yard line. Hammonds was the defensive back who filled in at tailback on several occasions during his first two seasons at Penn State. He showed he could still run with the ball as he returned four kickoffs during the game for 148 yards.

"Our kickoff coverage was the most disappointing aspect of the game," Minnesota coach Jim Wacker said. "I thought that would be one of our strengths."

Over the long part of the season, Penn State would rely heavily on its running game, but today it looked like Air Paterno.

It took three plays for Sacca to roll right and find his new favorite target. Three minutes and 40 seconds still remained in this breathtaking first quarter when Engram hauled in his third touchdown pass of the day — this one for 20 yards. The redshirt sophomore broke a school record that 30 other players shared in just one quarter.

"I think it was just a mix-up in the defensive backfield," Engram said of his third touchdown, which saw no Minnesota player even near him. "Their coverage probably got a little confused."

A little?

"I made one terrible mistake, asking a true freshman to play cornerback," Wacker said. "Blame Wacker for that one."

The first quarter finally ended, but Minnesota's mistakes continued. Running back Chris Darkins fumbled on the Golden Gophers' next drive and Penn State's Tyoka Jackson recovered at the Minnesota 17. Penn State's drive stalled at the 9, but Minnesota jumped offside on a Nittany Lion field goal attempt and Paterno elected to take the first down at the 4.

Carter, who would finish as the day's leading rusher with 120 yards on 15 carries, turned wide to his left two plays later and lunged for the pylon to give the Nittany Lions a 28-7 lead early in the second quarter.

Finally, Minnesota's mistake-prone offense calmed down and Schade was able to lead his team 57 yards in eight plays — the final one a five-yard TD pass to Douglas. Kicker Omar Salas missed the extra point and Penn State held a 28-13 lead.

Penn State kicker Craig Fayak would see his struggles throughout the afternoon as well, but he connected on a 32-yarder to give the Nittany Lions a 31-13 halftime lead. Despite missing three other field goal attempts in the game, Fayak hit all five of his extra points and his eight-point total was good enough to set the Penn State career scoring record for kickers.

Penn State had an early chance to build on its lead in the second half, but Mike Archie's fumble at the Minnesota 2-yard line thwarted the effort. The Gophers once again failed to capitalize on what little good fortune they could find as Schade moved his team 40 yards in seven plays before throwing his second interception. Linebacker Rob Holmberg returned the interception for Penn State to the Minnesota 6, but the score remained the same when the offense stalled after four plays and Fayak was wide left on a 24-yard field goal attempt.

This time Schade found the end zone as he moved Minnesota 80 yards in five plays to cut the gap to 31-20. The big play in the drive was a 36-yard pass to Aaron Osterman. Safety Lee Rubin's late hit cost the Nittany Lions another 15 yards and Schade spotted running back Chuck Rios with a 17-yard scoring pass.

Depth turned out to be the key factor as the game wore on and Paterno could sense his team was wearing Minnesota down. Penn State shuffled several players in and out all afternoon and by the end of the third quarter, Schade's passes weren't nearly as crisp and the offensive line was dragging. Still, the Nittany Lions' pass rush did not register a sack during the entire game, which was not a pleasant experience for several defensive players.

"You'd think I'd like going up against an offense like that," Penn State defensive tackle Tyoka Jackson said. "It got frustrating after a while. We got close a lot of times, but we weren't able to sack him. You've got to give Schade a lot of credit. He got rid of the football fast and found his receivers, but we did a lousy job of shedding our blocks and putting pressure on him. I hate it when I don't get any sacks."

Penn State allowed Schade too much time to stand in the pocket through much of the first half as he sometimes had four or five seconds to look around for receivers. He completed seven of his first nine passes and was 17 of 25 in the first half for 257 yards.

"We wanted to play seven guys back in coverage most of the time," defensive tackle Lou Benfatti said. "It wasn't in our game plan to do a lot of blitzing. I think the coaches felt that [blitzing] would create a lot of opportunities for their pass offense. It was our job to create the pass rush and we just didn't get the job done. We're really going to have to work on our pass rush in practice. We won't be a good defense if we have to do a lot of blitzing."

Penn State's defense forced Minnesota to go three-downs-and-out on two straight possessions late in the third quarter and it added the speed of sophomore outside linebacker Terry Killens to help contain the Gophers' five-receiver set.

Still, however, the Penn State defense believed it could do a whole lot better than it showed in its Big Ten debut. While

Schade was throwing for nearly 500 yards, Minnesota gained 113 rushing yards on just 24 attempts for a 4.7 yards per carry average. Schade also ran the quarterback draw seven times and racked up 58 yards rushing. Most of those yards came in the first half, before Penn State could make the necessary adjustments to shut it down.

"I know I'm not pleased [with the defensive effort]," hero linebacker Derek Bochna said after the game. "We have a lot of athletes on defense and we can be good. But that won't happen if we continue to play like we did today. We've got to become more aggressive and not be afraid of making mistakes. It's time for this defense to start playing up to its potential. One game isn't a season, but this wasn't a good start. We could have done a lot better."

No, it wasn't as top notch a defensive effort as Penn State is so often associated with, but it was enough to keep Minnesota fairly silent through much of the second half. After their third quarter touchdown, the Gophers made it past the Penn State 40-yard line only once more, but on fourth and goal at the Penn State 10, cornerback Tony Pittman intercepted Schade in the end zone with just under five minutes remaining.

Minnesota even tried a fake punt midway through the final quarter on a fourth-and-10 situation at its own 31-yard line. Penn State sniffed it out nicely, however, and took over on downs. Three plays later Sacca hit Engram from 31 yards out for a fourth touchdown and the final outcome was no longer in doubt.

The game was a highlight film for John Sacca, who seemingly proved himself to be the correct choice by Paterno as Penn State's starting signal caller. He completed 56 percent of his passes for 274 yards and more importantly did not throw an interception. A performance like that should have given the redshirt junior a tremendous dose of confidence in his leadership abilities, but the coming weeks would somehow only bring Sacca confusion.

While Penn State fans could feel satisfied — at least for a while — in their quarterback, they were surely elated to see the return, and full-time debut, of Bobby Engram. He hadn't seen action since the 1992 Fiesta Bowl, but his eight receptions against Minnesota for 165 yards and four touchdowns earned Engram the season's first Big Ten Offensive Player of the Week Award and made it look as though he had never missed a beat.

"It just so happened that you looked down the field, and there's Bobby celebrating every time I threw a touchdown pass," Sacca said.

Minnesota coach Jim Wacker chastised himself on several occasions after the game for concentrating so much on Penn State's running game that he overlooked the possibility of the Nittany Lions actually being able to produce a decent passing offense.

Even better for Engram, the Golden Gopher defense spent much of the afternoon in single coverage against him. Needless to say, he found a few ways to exploit that strategy.

"I love man coverage," Engram shyly told reporters after the game. The hot lights and swirling cameras of the press room all seemed so new to him. "It's one-on-one and the way they play it, they brought the safety up and the whole middle of the field was wide open."

As the weeks would wear on, it would seem doubtful that Engram would see much more of that coverage. Especially once the other Big Ten teams got their first look at Penn State in its first conference game.

"In the future, people are going to have to do some different things with Bobby," Sacca said. "They may have to double him or force him off his route a little bit. You can't use single coverage on Bobby Engram. That's what I think the bottom line is."

Since his run-in with the law that forced his suspension for 1992, Engram had displayed himself as a model citizen. He became the good guy and it wasn't just an act. He simply wanted to move on, play football and forget the past that haunted him through a season of inactivity in '92. He wanted his teammates to believe in him the minute he stepped back out on that football field and mostly, he wanted to believe in himself.

"I was a bit nervous, this being my first game back," Engram said of his return. "There was a lot of excitement around the team and in the locker room before the game. We just turned that into positive energy and tried to do positive things on the field."

When senior Tisen Thomas went down in preseason with a career-ending knee injury, Engram's importance to the team became even more crucial. His four career catches wouldn't seem like much on any statistical chart, but with as little experience that Penn State was faced with at receiver, Engram's career numbers could have been on the Nittany Lions' leader board. He was suddenly a veteran in this group of young, inexperienced receivers.

"Tisen going down was obviously a huge blow to our receiving corps," Engram said. "Chip LaBarca was the only senior left, and after that it was redshirt sophomores and redshirt freshmen. We had a meeting before the [Minnesota] game. We all knew we had to step up for this game because we knew what kind of defense they were going to play."

Engram and the others did step it up, which was a good sign for Penn State considering a lot of the heavyweights on the schedule were still to come. Paterno was just glad to get the first one over with. He had said all along that Minnesota was a team on the rise and should not be taken lightly.

"I went into the game with a lot of anxiety about how it would go," Paterno said. "I feel pretty good about it now. I don't mean that in a gloating sense, I just feel good about it."

The question of whether Penn State belonged in the Big Ten would linger throughout the season. The Nittany Lions were preparing to defend themselves week after week against those who felt success away from an independent schedule was just not possible. For now, the Nittany Lions were in first place in the conference at 1-0. And they found at least one person who believed they belonged.

"Penn State played unbelievable," said Wacker, who had words of praise for both the football team and the institution it represents. "We weren't just flopping around out there, they were good. This is the greatest atmosphere I've ever seen for college football. Classy fans, they clap for both teams, and they even talked to our players. This is great for the Big Ten."

With the first conference win in school history tucked safely under their belts, the Nittany Lions could only hope to convince the rest of the Big Ten that what Minnesota witnessed was very real and something to believe in. There was a lot more proving to be done as the welcoming committee had only begun to take shape.

7

USC:
A Time for Payback

This was a special date on Penn State's schedule. It had nothing to do with the Big Ten. All the talk about conference play could have been put on hold for at least this one week and not a soul in State College would seem to have minded. In a season that would be filled with tests, this was to be the first for the Nittany Lions to tackle. The Trojans of Southern California were invading Beaver Stadium for the first time ever. USC, believe it or not, came into Penn State's first season in the Big Ten as the Lions' only connection to the Rose Bowl in team history. The two teams met in the first ever Rose Bowl, before it was ever decided that the Big Ten champ would meet the winner of the Pac-10 Conference.

The date was January 1, 1923, and USC defeated Penn State 14-3, in the bowl that was to become the "grandaddy of 'em all." The two teams would not face each other again until the 1982 Fiesta Bowl. Joe Paterno wasn't around in 1923, but he was the coach of the Nittany Lions for the second meeting and this time Penn State came out a winner.

On that day, tailback Curt Warner ran for 145 yards and two touchdowns, bettering the 85 rushing yards by Heisman Trophy winner Marcus Allen, to lead the Nittany Lions to a 26-10 victory. Penn State used that victory as a springboard to its national championship in 1982, while Trojans' coach John Robinson would leave USC one year later to coach the Los Angeles Rams.

Ten years later, Robinson was back. From 1976-82, USC had won 82 percent of its games, captured the 1978 national championship and was ranked No. 2 in '76 and '79 under Robinson's leadership. USC fans had grown tired of Larry Smith as coach because he couldn't seem to win the games that counted — those within the conference.

Robinson achieved very little success with the Rams and felt rejuvenated upon his return to the Southern California campus. "I can't wait to see the horse and hear 'Conquest' again," said Robinson, who was 67-14-2 at USC. "We feel this is a program that should be in the Top 5 every year. We can never be an underdog here."

During his coaching days at USC, Robinson was famous for running the tailback-oriented offense with the even more famous Student Body Right, Student Body Left concept. "I can promise you that Student Body Right will be run the same number of times as Student Body Left," he told the fans. "We'll go back to that kind of approach, to a tailback offense."

To back that commitment even further, Robinson hired one of his former pupils to coach the USC running backs. Charles White was a two-time All-American and won the Heisman Trophy in 1979. One of White's new students would be sophomore Dwight McFadden, who led the Trojans in rushing six times in 1992 and figured to be a rising star in the Pac-10.

"Somehow, I always feel better with Charlie White standing next to me," Robinson said. "He was the toughest, most intense running back I've ever coached."

If USC proved anything in its opening game against North Carolina in the Disneyland Pigskin Classic, it proved just how far the Trojans have to go before they can relive the glory days of Robinson's first time around. North Carolina ran up 291 yards on the ground and rolled to a 31-9 victory. Meanwhile, the Southern Cal offense totaled a meager 101 rushing yards and lost McFadden indefinitely to a broken ankle in the first quarter.

USC rebounded with a win over Houston the following week and hoped to get its running game going against Penn State behind an offensive line that averaged 6-foot-6, 248 pounds and returned five starters, including junior All-America candidate Tony Boselli, who had been a starter at left tackle since his freshman year.

McFadden was being touted as one of the top running backs in the Pac-10 before his injury and it appeared the Trojans' offense might suffer without him. Robinson wasn't short on bodies. He had probably six or seven tailbacks on his roster that seemed to have credentials, but lacked the experience needed to help right away.

USC had an experienced quarterback returning in junior Rob Johnson, who came into the season ranked ninth on the Trojans' career passing chart. He completed an impressive 163 of 285 passes in 1992 for 2,118 yards, but threw 14 interceptions compared to 12 touchdowns. Robinson's ball-control type of offense was hopefully going to improve that ratio somewhat.

The Trojans returned nine starters on defense, including All-America defensive end Willie McGinest. The 6-6, 250-pound senior led the Pac-10 with 16 sacks in '92, and totaled 63 tackles, including 23 for losses. McGinest was starting as a sophomore in 1991 when USC last played Penn State, and it was his blitzing defense that led the way to a 21-10 Trojan upset over the Nittany Lions. The year before that, Southern Cal hosted Penn State in the Los Angeles Coliseum and pulled out a close win, 19-14, in front of 70,594 fans.

Those were two frustrating games for Penn State because it had several chances to win both, but whether it was offensively, defensively, or on special teams, the Lions made some kind of blunder in each game to seal their doom.

That's why payback was so important in 1993. Penn State believed it had a better team than what national television audiences saw in both 1990 and '91 against USC. There was no game between the two schools in 1992, but this season the Nittany Lions would have their shot at hosting the next two games in the series.

"I don't think Penn State was prepared for what we did on defense [in 1991]," McGinest said in the week leading up to the game. "but I'm sure they'll be ready this time. We have a lot of work to do before we're ready to play those guys. We know Penn State's a good football team, and they'll have the advantage playing at home. But I know we'll be ready to play them."

"This is one we've been looking forward to," Penn State tight end Kyle Brady said. "We'll have to be sharp, but we certainly have a lot of incentive. We owe them one, or two."

SEPTEMBER 11, UNIVERSITY PARK, PA — Over the last few years, Penn State had been labeled a team that couldn't win the close games. Something was always going wrong when the game was on the line. It happened in the two previous losses to USC. There were the losses to Miami in 1991 and '92, and the two-point conversion pass that Notre Dame successfully completed in the final seconds at South Bend in '92. If it seemed frustrating as a fan, think of how the players who lived those agonizing final seconds felt time after time.

When those things happen, however, the best thing to do is just keep trying until you finally get it right. For three-and-a-half quarters, it appeared Penn State would need no miracle finish to pull out a win. Its defense was back on course after a rough ride against Minnesota the week before. The famed USC running attack was being gang-tackled at every turn. Student Body right? Student Body left? Student Body nowhere!

Coach John Robinson's running game was held to just 34 yards on 31 carries as Penn State's defensive line of Lou Benfatti, Eric Ravotti and Tyoka Jackson combined for 17 tackles. The Nittany Lions delivered a dose of USC's own medicine as tailback Mike Archie weaved his way to a career-best 107 yards rushing on just 10 attempts. Ki-Jana Carter added 104 yards on 21 carries for his second straight 100-yard effort (120 against Minnesota).

"Today, our offensive line had a great game," Carter said. "They had the holes there for us to run through all day. I have to thank our fullbacks, also."

Penn State's offense wasn't quite as flashy as it was against Minnesota the week before, probably *because* it stayed on the ground more, instead of going to the air. Out of its 347 yards of total offense, Penn State chewed up 282 of them on the ground.

"I think Joe [Paterno] wanted us to establish the running game right off the bat," Archie said. "He knew that when you looked at the films of their first game, their defense got tired when North Carolina wore them down running the football. So I'm sure that's why he wanted to establish the running game right away. After our offensive line figured out their line was slanting their rush, we just rolled in the second quarter."

That was when the Nittany Lions controlled the ball for 12 minutes and 31 seconds, totaled 103 yards on the ground, and sustained scoring drives of 41, 80 and 70 yards.

"After we realized what they were doing with their defensive line, we controlled the line of scrimmage," offensive tackle Marco Rivera said. "They ran so many fronts against us in the first quarter, they had us a bit confused. They were slanting inside with their rush and we tried to run the ball inside.

"In the second quarter we found that since they slanted the line inside, we could have a lot of success running the ball outside. We went to our pitch game and we ran a lot of counter plays where I and the guard next to me pulled and led the sweep to the opposite side."

And the rather simple adjustment helped the Lions through the rest of the game.

"Absolutely," Rivera said. "We were able to get the proper angles on our blocks, and that really helped us to take control up front. Once we got it rolling, it seemed that everything we did in the second quarter worked. I know Joe told us at halftime that we were really firing off the ball."

"The offensive line has really surprised me the most this early in the season," Paterno said. "They've been very poised, very steady. They've not made foolish mistakes and have been good with penalties. I felt comfortable with them going into the season, but they've been a nice surprise."

The Penn State offense used some of that fire to build a 7-0 lead early in the second quarter when Archie carried three long gainers to the USC 4-yard line. Sacca then rolled right, dodged blitzing safety Mike Salmon and hit Archie alone in the end zone for the game's first score. It was about the only highlight for Sacca during an otherwise dismal performance (6-for-17 passing for 65 yards and two interceptions).

One of those interceptions came on the Lions' next drive. Sacca looked to senior wideout Chip LaBarca downfield, but Salmon stepped in front of the pass and returned it to the PSU 1-yard line. Three plays later, USC's Rob Johnson scored on a quarterback sneak to pull the Trojans even.

Mistakes like Sacca's interception were what cost Penn State in their last two encounters against Southern Cal and it seemed paramount at the moment not to fold to such pressures again. The Nittany Lions responded to the challenge in a positive way by putting together a pair of long scoring drives of their own. The first covered 80 yards in 11 plays, while the second was a 13-play, 70-yard march. Both ended with two-yard touchdown runs by senior fullback Brian O'Neal, who was still bothered by a preseason foot injury but managed to walk in for both of his scores.

It was 21-7 at halftime and except for the interception return that led to USC's only touchdown, Penn State was playing an outstanding ball game. The Nittany Lions were shutting down the opposition's running game and pouncing on every Trojan miscue. Johnson would complete 25 of 43 passes for 291 yards, but most of that would come in the game's final harried moments. Johnson spent most of the game running for his life under a heavy rush of dark blue jerseys. The Penn State defense registered four sacks — four more than against Minnesota — and pressured USC's junior quarterback into numerous hurries.

"We were manhandled a little bit," John Robinson said.

"They had good pressure in the first half," Johnson said. "I was getting hit a lot."

Penn State's defense continued its pressure in the third quarter when it recovered USC running back Deon Strother's fumble at the PSU 24-yard line. Although there was still plenty of time left, that turnover would appear to be Southern California's last chance at a serious challenge. Everything it tried wasn't working. Every opportunity seemed to end in either a hurried incompletion or a costly turnover. Then came the most unlikeliest of turnarounds.

USC was being dominated and could do nothing for three-and-a-half quarters to stop the Nittany Lions, either statistically or physically. Somewhere along the way, however, the Penn State defensive pressure waned, and the game turned into one that made many resurrect the demons of 1992.

"I thought about last year," Penn State defensive tackle Tyoka Jackson said. "I thought, oh no, not again."

It started simply enough. Southern California had possession with a little under six minutes remaining in the game. It was running sideline pass patterns in a harried effort to move down field when receiver Ken Grace took a pass from Johnson, slipped a pair of tackles and found a hole to the end zone from 30 yards out with 5:11 left in the game. All of a sudden Penn State's lead was cut to 21-14.

The next Nittany Lion possession moved nowhere and the 95,992 fans in Beaver Stadium were less than amused when Paterno called for a pass on second down — especially when the pass fell incomplete forcing the game clock to stop. A third down pass also fell to the ground and the Trojans would get the ball back with still plenty of time remaining.

Rob Johnson, USC's quarterback who had been harassed through much of the game, had suddenly found a Heisman-like touch on the Trojans' last-chance drive. It started at their own 30-yard line as Johnson moved his team methodically down the field. He completed nine of 10 passes during the drive, including a 19-yarder to receiver Edward Hervey on third-and-17.

With the drive still moving, Johnson spotted wideout Johnny Morton along the left sideline at the Penn State 2-yard line. Morton made a great diving catch, while keeping one foot in bounds at the same time. It was first-and-goal now, and the Lions were the team that appeared frazzled. Johnson wasted little time in heightening the suspense as he dropped back and threw a quick toss to sure-handed tight end Johnny McWilliams, who made a sliding catch about five yards deep in the end zone.

The crowd was as stunned as the Penn State sideline. There were 37 seconds remaining and a two-point conversion was all that separated USC from a spectacular come-from-behind win, and Penn State from another gut-wrenching loss. Right then, however, in the second game of a still young season, the Penn State defenders gathered together and vowed to do everything possible not to let the Trojans in their end zone any more, even though some thoughts admittedly went back to South Bend almost one year ago.

"I thought, oh no, another Notre Dame," Tyoka Jackson said.

"I know what was going through everyone's head — no Notre Dame, no Notre Dame," said linebacker Brian Gelzheiser, who had a team-high eight tackles, including six in the second half. "We didn't want a repeat of last year."

That was when the Nittany Lions held a 16-9 lead late in the game against Notre Dame, only to watch Irish quarterback Rick Mirer complete a miraculous comeback with a late touchdown pass and subsequent two-point conversion.

Knowing his players may be harboring such thoughts in their minds, Paterno made what may have been one of the smartest decisions of the game in the moments following USC's touchdown. That was when he called his team's third and last timeout to discuss the defensive strategy for the deciding two-point conversion.

"Poise was the main thing I was looking for," Paterno said of the timeout. "We just wanted to make sure the kids were playing the defense that was called and kept the containment on the quarterback and their poise."

The Nittany Lions seemed calmed by the extra time as they held hands in the huddle and banded together to face the consequences — win or lose. "We wanted to have good coverage," safety Lee Rubin said. "We put four defensive backs on four potential receivers, and I think it was a good call at the time."

"I was thinking it was going to be the same play as the touchdown, and I almost intercepted the touchdown," Gelzheiser said. "[Linebacker Rob] Holmberg was lined up on the wrong side at the beginning of the play. He ran over and I told him to watch the tight end running in and back out, and he was right there."

With the backs covering the receivers and linebackers covering the middle, it was up to Penn State's defensive line to put a rush on Johnson like he had never seen before. As he had done throughout the game, Jackson collapsed the pocket and forced Johnson out of his drop-back and set position. Moving hurriedly to his right, Johnson short-armed a throw to McWilliams in the middle of the end zone and everyone held their breath when they saw the ball cradled in the sliding tight end's arms.

All heads turned to the nearest official, who came running in from the side. His ruling was quick, confident and precise. The ball had skipped the surface of the end zone and was therefore ruled a trapped ball and an incompletion.

"The ball just got by my hand again," Gelzheiser said of the final play. "Thankfully, I looked back and saw it skip on the ground."

This Penn State squad came into the 1993 season with new life and believed it could have an undefeated season. Sometimes, that means believing when no one else does — not even your truest supporters. This was a game Penn State needed. A lot of thoughts did turn to the last-second loss to Notre Dame, and the other close losses to Miami, Boston College and even USC over the last couple of years. This was a time when everyone on the Penn State sideline felt destiny was about due to deliver them a kinder finish.

"I felt inside we were going to stop them," hero backer Derek Bochna said. "We all did. I don't know if you could say we willed it to happen, but we've been in this situation before and we weren't going to let it happen again."

"I think the will was strong enough that the guys went out and got it done," senior defensive lineman Eric Ravotti said. "We knew our backs were against the wall. We just had to stop them, and we did."

Jackson looked at the finish and remembered several things about previous losses such as this, and how important hanging on for the win really was. He called it playing to win, instead of playing not to lose.

"Last year, [against Notre Dame] we did a lot of looking at the clock," Jackson said. "We were looking at the clock, thinking, 'When is this thing going to be over?' This year, it was, 'Who's gonna make the play?'"

"We needed this one," Bochna said. "A lot of us have been on the field the last three years when stuff like this was happening to us. It was good for us to have it happen this early in the season because if it happens again, I think we know we can stop it."

Paterno agreed that the experience — despite the anxiety — would probably do wonders for his team's confidence.

"In a lot of ways, this kind of game was good for this football team," he said. "They've got to learn to get in there. We haven't won those kinds of games in the past couple of years, where a couple of things could have gone their way. In a lot of ways, it was an ideal game for this club.

"I think it was a good, tough football game. A game where kids learn how to play under pressure. I was pleased about that part of it."

"We lost two years in a row [to USC]," defensive tackle Lou Benfatti said. "We came out determined and we ended it the same way. I think to come into this game and play like we did for three-and-a-half quarters was excellent."

With the win, Penn State remained undefeated and kept alive its still lofty goal of a Big Ten championship and a national championship in the same season. Next up was the Lions' first road trip of the season and first away Big Ten game, against Iowa. The USC game was history and no one wanted to think of the consequences had Johnson's pass to McWilliams been completed.

"Who cares?" Jackson said. "All I know is we have to go to Iowa in the cornfields next week and we'll be undefeated."

Not only were the Nittany Lions undefeated, they were also unshaken. They faced the first of their many big tests in the 1993 season and came away unscathed. The best was yet to come.

8

IOWA:
A Trip to
the Cornfields

Life on the road for the Penn State football team is somewhat unique. At home, the players see the fans come rolling into State College a couple of days or so before the game. Tens of thousands of people decked out in blue and white line the path to the stadium, hoping for a glimpse of their favorite players. When the Nittany Lions go on the road, it would figure they would get away from the adoration that is so steadily present at home. But it isn't that way at all.

Joe Paterno has some steadfast rules for his team when it plays in someone else's back yard. Coats and ties at all times. On the buses, on the airplanes, and in the team's hotel. No exceptions. To Paterno, when you're traveling with Penn State, you're representing the university, and the way you carry yourself in public will leave a lasting impression on those that see you for the first time.

Penn State was about to get a number of first looks in 1993. Players, coaches and staff boarded two charter planes in State College for the team's longest road trip of the season. Iowa City, Iowa was the destination for the first conference away game in Penn State football history. Ironically, Iowa was the one Big Ten team that Penn State had developed a familiarity with over the years. The Nittany Lions and Hawkeyes had met nine times previously with Penn State winning six. Furthermore, the Nittany Lions had won in their last four trips to Iowa City, including a come-from-behind 20-17 win in 1984. That was the last time the two teams had met and the last game against a Big Ten opponent for Penn State until its meeting with Minnesota two weeks before.

As the first of the two planes touched down at Cedar Rapids Airport, a view out the window displayed the beauty of the vast midwestern scenery. The stereotype of the midwest is miles and miles of flat land, wheat fields, silos and dirt roads. The Penn State players soon discovered at least one of those perceptions to be false as the buses pulled away from the airport and rolled down a smoothly paved two-lane highway. The land was incredibly flat, however, and the number of wheat fields and silos in sight were very abundant.

But it was a relaxing picture that kept everyone's eyes searching from one side of the spacious land to the other. Not far away, evidence of the cruel summer rains that seemingly never stopped torturing the midwest in 1993 left everyone in awed silence.

"Sand bags are lined up everywhere," the bus driver pointed out to no one in particular. "At one time, the road we're driving on was closed in some places because it was completely under-water."

"It really makes you think of how much people suffered through such a thing," Penn State wide receiver Bobby Engram said. "You heard about this place all summer long and now we're right in the middle of it."

When the buses reached the Sheraton Hotel in Cedar Rapids, there was a banner inside the lobby that read:

PENN STATE NITTANY LIONS
"Welcome to the Big Ten"

The sign was a gesture of greeting and courtesy from the hotel's management and employees, but Penn State would get used to hearing that familiar refrain no matter where it visited in '93.

The road is not always the place to get away from the fan adulation, as some of the players might have thought early in their careers. The hotel lobby had its share of blue and white clad well-wishers, who seemed giddy at the thought of standing so close to some of the players they watch on television or read about in the papers. Penn State alumni are everywhere in the United States and it seems the Lions will have a following wherever they travel. But no one really seems to mind.

"It's great to look up in the stands when you're away from home and see people cheering you on," punter V.J. Muscillo said. "I think we'll take the fan support anywhere we can get it."

For the regulars in the Penn State traveling party, the routine is quite simple. Pick up your room key, find your room and follow the itinerary to a tee. Paterno has always been precise about timing and schedules. The player's itinerary states when the team will meet for dinner, when position coaches will have individual meetings, when offense and defense meets separately with the respective coordinators and when a full squad meeting will take place.

There is a snack in one of the hotel ballrooms the night before the game, and that is usually when Paterno has an informal meeting with his players to discuss any final preparations or to go over last-minute concerns that might mean the difference in a win or loss the next day. It is a science, right down to the final bed check, when the coaches must knock on doors of their position players to make sure they have met the curfew.

Jerry Sandusky, Penn State's defensive coordinator, is often a perfectionist, himself. He isn't the demanding kind of teacher who makes ultimatums to his players. He is a motivator who expects, and counts on, his players to follow the lessons instructed to them. Football at Penn State is a classroom activity almost as much as a field activity. Scouting reports are drawn up almost every week, with new designs for the current play book.

Coaches teach the system with a blackboard and video projector almost endlessly, until the knowledge is absorbed by the players and can be executed on the field. It is often in these last-minute bed checks that Sandusky will ask his defensive players if they have any questions about tomorrow's strategy, or if they are the least bit unclear about their assignments. When the last room is checked, he still clenches the rolled-up room list in his hands and silently hopes his players have it all ready in their minds and in their hearts.

"You never know what you're gonna get out of them until you see it on the field," he said. "Most of the time though, they don't let me down."

SEPTEMBER 18, IOWA CITY, IA — Game day was cloudy and somewhat rainy as the Penn State buses rolled down Interstate 80 for the 25-mile trip to the University of Iowa campus. Police escorts weaved their way through the brisk traffic, making way for the huge transporters to travel as smoothly as possible. Further evidence of sand bags piled high along the banks of what were normally small streams brought images of locals cringing at even the slightest sprinkle of rain.

The campus entrance was just around the bend when the first signs of a town came into view. Restaurants and hotels in the area plastered their marquees with encouraging words to the Iowa Hawkeyes. Fans dressed in black and gold looked twice to see if these were the buses that carried their Hawkeye players or the bad guys. Once they knew, they either gave the thumbs down signal or said, "Go back home to eastern football!"

The Penn State players noticed literally thousands of people strolling the sidewalks of the Iowa campus, either making their way toward the stadium or looking for a tailgate party to crash. One good sign was the blue and white mobile home parked alone off a small side street, with the words "PENN STATE" and "NITTANY LIONS" covering its surface. The occupants were right there to wave to Joe Paterno and company as the team buses rolled by.

The rain had stopped by the time the buses pulled up to the visitors' entrance at Kinnick Stadium. Even the Iowa fans nearby cheered when Paterno stepped off the first bus. One by one the players filed into the visitors' dressing room and snickered somewhat at the bright pink walls.

It is an attempt at intimidation toward the visiting team, this idea of pink walls. The thinking at Iowa is pink is soft, and that is how the visiting team should feel when it travels into Hawkeye territory. The tactic even drew a smile from Paterno's normally game-ready face.

"If somebody hadn't told me, I wouldn't have even known [the walls] were pink," Paterno said of the locker room decor.

The stadium wasn't even half full when the first of Penn State's warm-up unit took the field. There seemed to be a jitter or two in the step of a couple of young special teams players who were getting their first taste of life on the road in major college football. The fact that it was Big Ten play made the situation even more intense.

Brett Conway came to Penn State all the way from Lilburn, Georgia, just outside of Atlanta. Kicking was his specialty in high school and he was one of the most sought after place-kickers in the country. Craig Fayak was entering his last season at Penn State in '93, and Conway liked the situation in Penn State's northern setting. A one-year apprenticeship would probably do him wonders, and Paterno had him pegged as the Nittany Lions' regular kicker by 1994.

When preseason drills got underway, Conway worked a lot with Fayak and developed a kicker's kind of relationship with him. He knew that in this, his first season, much of his activity would involve holding the practice kicks for Fayak on the sideline into a net. What he didn't know, however, was Paterno's intention to use him in a much more productive manner during games.

With Fayak's back problems the season before and subsequent rehabilitation during the off-season, Paterno wanted to keep the senior kicker in the best shape possible through the '93 season. Conway came to Penn State with a powerful leg and Paterno told the 6-foot-2, 180-pound freshman he'd like him to handle all the kickoff duties.

"I was glad for the opportunity, especially so soon," Conway said. "I figured I'd spend a lot of time watching Craig and learning from him this season. I just wanted to be ready to go in case his back bothered him again."

Conway did well in Penn State's opener against Minnesota as his kicks either made it to the end zone or provided little return opportunity for the Golden Gophers. He kicked off against Southern California the following week, but definitely seemed to have a case of the jitters. The opening kickoff sailed out of bounds and so did three others through the course of the game. Each occurrence started the Trojans' possession at their own 35-yard line and made the fans a little more restless in their seats.

"I don't like to think it's because the game was on national TV," Conway said. "I thought about everyone at home having the chance to see it, but I tried not to let it cross my mind [during the game]. I really just think it was a bad day and for whatever reason, my concentration wasn't there. I sure don't want it to happen like that all the time."

Brad Pantall's path to Iowa was even more unusual. In the spring of 1993, Pantall was a normal student at Penn State who had aspirations of playing football on the major college level. He was paying his own way through school and working out on his own. Small in stature (5-9, 225 pounds), but big in heart. That's how he would come to be known.

He approached the Nittany Lion coaching staff about his talents, told them he was a pretty decent snapper. They gave him a look in early summer and told him to stick with the workouts. He was invited to participate in preseason drills, but much like the non-roster player in baseball camps, there was no guarantee for a promising future.

Pantall was too small to play center on a regular basis, but he knew he could fill the long snapper opening that was vacated with the graduation of Bob Ceh, the former student equipment manager who put on the pads for Penn State and turned the position into a near art form. Pantall continued the weight workouts on his own — even during preseason camp — and was not permitted to eat any meals at the team's training table. All he could do with the team was practice.

But that was all he really asked for and all he wanted to do. There were a couple of candidates in Paterno's mind to fill the long snapper position, including regular starting center Bucky Greeley. Brad Pantall kept hanging around, however, and the coaches soon realized the young man had worked hard enough to win himself the position. So here he was, No. 62 in the generic white uniform that signifies Penn State, taking in the scenery of Kinnick Stadium from field level, almost gasping at the thought of whether it was all true or not.

"He's as steady as they come," said punter V.J. Muscillo, who is the one player among all others on the squad that must have a good rapport with the long snapper. "He puts the ball right in my hands every time and that helps my concentration because it gives me one less thing to have to worry about. If there is a problem, I know I can talk to him about it and he just nods his head and works it out with himself. I'm very comfortable with him snapping the ball to me."

Iowa hoped to see a lot of Pantall if it meant Penn State's offense could be kept under control. The Hawkeyes were 2-0 after non-conference wins over Tulsa and Iowa State and were anxious for their first Big Ten encounter against Penn State. Coach Hayden Fry was optimistic about his team's chances, but also took a cautious approach because the Hawkeyes had finished 5-7 the season before.

"We're still a young team with several guys learning their roles," Fry said. "We're looking forward to playing in front of a sellout at home and having the crowd on our side. I won't kid anybody, though. Our offensive line is very inexperienced and Penn State has some of the best pass rushers in the conference."

Actually, Iowa's fortunes in 1992 were severely depleted in the first half of the season. The Hawkeyes finished 4-3 in their last seven games, but couldn't overcome a dismal 1-4 start.

"Last season was one of the most frustrating experiences in my coaching career," Fry said. "We had a brutal schedule that had us playing North Carolina State, Miami, Colorado and Michigan in four of our first five games. We were banged up, and we found ourselves entering October with a 1-4 record. My team hung together for the rest of the season, but we weren't able to overcome that start."

Sounds a bit like Penn State's 1992 problems, only the Nittany Lions failed to find a way to stick together when adversity seemed to bite them during the middle part of the season. The Lions finished 7-5, but lost five out of their last seven after a 5-0 start. Those kinds of setbacks were what made Paterno and his coaching staff just a little bit edgy about how this afternoon's game would play out.

Brett Conway, the freshman kicker, would get the chance to start the game as Penn State won its third straight coin toss and deferred its choice to the second half. That put Conway on the field with the kickoff team, more than likely thinking about last week's game against USC and how to avoid such similar results.

The first kick brought a sigh of relief to Conway and many others on the Penn State sideline as it rode high and true — and deep — into the Iowa end zone. There was no Hawkeye return and for now at least, Conway seemed to feel a lot better about his presence in a Penn State uniform.

"That one felt really good," he said moments later on the sideline. The skies were still gray around the stadium, but the dark cloud that lingered over Brett Conway for the past week or so had finally lifted itself and floated away.

Iowa went nowhere in its first possession and after an exchange or two of punts by both teams, the Penn State defense made the first of its several big plays of the afternoon. Iowa quarterback Paul Burmeister had only begun to feel the pressure of Penn State's heavy pass rush when he hung a long pass to wideout Harold Jasper along the right sideline late in the first quarter.

Safety Lee Rubin and cornerback Shelly Hammonds stayed with Jasper step for step and Hammonds picked off the hanging pass and returned it 19 yards to the Penn State 30-yard line. Quarterback John Sacca, who had trouble moving the Lions during their first couple of possessions, led his team on its first scoring drive.

Most of Penn State's yardage came on the ground, but Sacca completed a key 22-yard pass to tight end Kyle Brady to put the Nittany Lions deep in Hawkeye territory. The drive stalled three plays later, however, and Fayak gave the Lions a 3-0 lead with a 22-yard field goal. The successful kick was Fayak's second in six attempts on the young season.

Little did any of the 70,397 observers know it at the time, but Sacca's pass to keep the drive alive would be his only completion in seven attempts through the whole afternoon. Joe Paterno appeared annoyed right before the field goal when Sacca failed to spot a wide-open Brady crossing the goal line over the middle of the field on third down, as well as wideout Bobby Engram, who was standing alone in the left corner of the end zone. Sacca, a redshirt junior, seemed to look in just one direction and when that option was covered, he tucked the ball under his arm and tried to run it into the end zone.

Sacca threw another incompletion on the next series and was benched in favor of Kerry Collins, another redshirt junior. Sacca appeared shocked at the quick hook displayed by his coach and pointed out after the game that it was "time [for him] to sit down and think about my future."

"It's just really hard to sit on the bench," said Collins, who was only slightly better as he completed 6 of 16 passes in his three quarters or so against Iowa for 57 yards. "It was tough watching during those first two games, but I knew the best thing to do was keep my mouth shut and wait for my opportunity. I was glad to get it in the Iowa game, although I was a little surprised at how soon."

Penn State relied on its defense to keep Iowa at bay, while its offense searched for an answer to getting the ball in the end zone. Midway through the second quarter that answer came in the form of an opportunistic interception by defensive end Eric Clair. Six plays later, fullback Brian O'Neal scored from a yard out and the Lions were up 10-0.

The Penn State defense had given up more than 450 yards per game in the first two weeks of the season, but were out to drop those numbers significantly at the Hawkeyes' expense.

Clair and teammate Todd Atkins registered four of the Nittany Lions' nine sacks, as Burmeister received little support from his offensive line during the game. The Hawkeyes rushed 41 times but netted only 32 yards on the ground thanks to the Penn State sack total, which resulted in 89 lost yards.

Penn State scored just one touchdown as the result of a long, sustained drive, but pounced on Iowa's mistakes at almost every turn. The opportunistic effort continued at the start of the second half when Hammonds took the opening kickoff and raced 54 yards to the Iowa 36-yard line. Collins completed a big fourth-and-four pass to Engram for a 15-yard gain during the drive and tailback Stephen Pitts skirted around right end for a nine-yard touchdown run two plays later to up the Nittany Lions' lead to 17-0.

With just over three minutes left in the third quarter, linebacker Brian Gelzheiser picked off a pass intended for Jasper at the Iowa 40-yard line and tailback Ki-Jana Carter ran for 23 of his game-high 144 yards and a touchdown five plays later to make it 24-0, Penn State.

With the fourth quarter still to be played, the Penn State defense took it as a mission to hang on to the shutout.

"That was important to us," defensive end Eric Ravotti said. "We even told the second- and third-teamers to preserve the shutout. Our attitude is if they can't score, they can't win."

That "attitude" was an element that most Penn State players felt was severely lacking in 1992.

"We were missing emotion last year," Ravotti said. "[This year] we're thriving on team unity and camaraderie. Our attitude is completely different from last year."

Penn State added its final score with 10 minutes remaining in the game when Pitts completed a 52-yard drive — the longest scoring effort of the afternoon for the Nittany Lions — with a three-yard touchdown run. Penn State's offense may have struggled at times, but Iowa had nothing but kind words toward the Nittany Lions' defense in their 31-0 blowout.

"I feel sorry for our quarterbacks," Hayden Fry said afterward. "Our offensive line had been coming along, but today, collectively, it was just terrible.

"The way we played in the first half, I couldn't believe we were so close at halftime. I still felt good about our chances at coming back, but then the roof fell in."

Paul Burmeister, Iowa's quarterback who took most of the punishment, played despite not being able to practice all week due to a bruised back. After the further beating he took from Penn State, he may have wished he had sat this one out.

"It said more about Penn State's defense than our offense," Burmeister said. "They just have a great front seven and always have. I'm not going to get down on our guys. Penn State just blew us away with their great pass rush."

"We were taking some criticism [in the first two games]," Shelly Hammonds said. "But there were some plays in the first two games where we were just missing. We came through on some of those plays today and hopefully we can carry it through the rest of the season."

The win was the 250th of Paterno's coaching career and his players presented him afterward with a game ball. But the coach, as always, was just happy to get the win, no matter what number it happened to be in his career.

"I'm just glad the kids won and played a solid game," he said. "That's what it's all about."

The Penn State players also hoped to serve notice with the win that the team was carefully treading that road to respectability after the disastrous finish to 1992.

"I think [the win] will give us a little confidence and maybe put some fear back in some of the other teams we play," defensive end Eric Clair said.

"It was something big for us," defensive tackle Tyoka Jackson said. "It was the first Big Ten road game in the history of Penn State football. There are a lot of firsts this year. We have a lot of pressure on us as far as our history is concerned and we wanted to show well."

The Nittany Lions did carry themselves well defensively and although much of the postgame talk was about the impressive shutout, the media and even the players, wanted to find out more about Paterno's quick decision to bench quarterback John Sacca in mid-stream. In his weekly press conference a few days before the Iowa game, Paterno spoke of stability in the quarterback position and stressed how important that was.

"I think at times you bring kids in," Paterno said when approached with the subject of bringing Kerry Collins in off the bench, "It's not a question of a lack of confidence in Collins, but I don't want to get to the stage where you stick a kid in when things aren't going well and then you stick the other guy back in. That's when you get in trouble.

"There's a tendency to think the quarterback's the answer to the problems you have. You have to be careful. You don't want to wash a kid down the drain if he throws a couple of interceptions."

Judging from Sacca's postgame mood, he appeared to have the feeling he was not only washed down the drain but on his way to the deepest part of the river.

"I really have to take a good, long look at things," Sacca said. "I don't see myself as a backup quarterback this late in my career. I've done the things to earn the starting job, I was handed the starting job. I deserved it. If I'm going to exit the football game in the first quarter, then I don't see myself as quarterback here much longer. That's what it comes down to."

Sacca entered the game having completed 24 of 49 passes for 339 yards, five touchdowns and two interceptions. In 1992, he completed 52 percent of his passes, threw for nine TDs and three interceptions and was 4-2 as a starter. He was 1-for-6 for 22 yards when Paterno opted for Collins midway through the second quarter against Iowa.

"I was a little shocked," Sacca said. "It seemed like we just started to get things going."

Paterno, who had already met the media by the time Sacca had voiced his disapproval, said he was going to play Collins even if Sacca "was as hot as a firecracker." He also stated he was not pleased with the Penn State passing game over all and he would still be reevaluating the situation.

"This may go on all year," Paterno said. "I'm going to play it by ear if I sense something. [In this case] I felt it was time to change. I'm not sure John would have done as well. I was going to play Kerry no matter what because I felt he might be getting away from things."

Collins concurred with that statement, saying Paterno had mentioned to him the day before the game he would be getting him some playing time, but Sacca said there was no indication the coach was going to pull him. When it happened, Sacca claimed he was told by Paterno that Collins was going in "for a series."

Collins played all but the last nine minutes of the game. That was when Paterno put Sacca back in the game. He had one incompletion and was sacked once to finish out the game.

"At that point, going back in was sort of pointless," Sacca said.

Sacca said his immediate thoughts were of discussing his situation with his family and deciding what to do with his future. He was pretty much out of options with Division I football because he was a senior academically, but had eligibility through 1994 because he had redshirted in 1990. Since NCAA rules require a transfer to sit out one year, Sacca knew his options were very few.

"My back's to the wall," he said. "It's a tough situation and I don't want to make a judgment too quickly."

Sacca was awarded the starting job during preseason after Paterno said Collins or sophomore Wally Richardson would have to beat him out, but did not. Paterno made that decision based on Sacca's strength of performance during Penn State's spring practice.

"You look at what I've done," Sacca said. "I don't think I get the proper respect. If you look over my career, I've done the job, and to get lifted, frankly, I'm a little burned up."

Things had rolled along fairly smoothly for the Nittany Lions through their first three games. They were 2-0 in their new conference, 3-0 overall, and about to take a four-week hiatus from conference play. A pair of non-conference games against Rutgers and Maryland were on the horizon, then the first of two frustrating mid-season bye weeks before the long-awaited first ever meeting with Michigan.

Paterno had a lot to think about during the next week or so, including an unwanted and unnecessary controversy at the

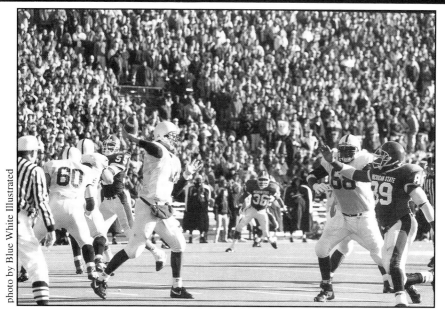

Kerry Collins (#12) stepped into the starter's role at quarterback in the fourth game of the season. The 6-foot-5, 235-pound quarterback completed 142 of 274 passes for 1,767 yards in guiding the Nittany Lions to a 10-2 finish and a Citrus Bowl victory over Tennessee.

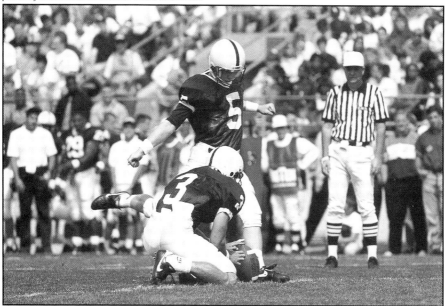

Kicker Craig Fayak (#5) overcame a back injury that sidelined him halfway through the 1992 season to become Penn State's all-time leading scorer with 289 career points, including 86 in the Nittany Lions' inaugural Big Ten season. Fayak earned an honorable mention selection in the conference's All-Star voting.

Junior tight end Kyle Brady (#8) came back from an illness that hampered much of his 1992 season to catch 27 passes for 289 yards and three touchdowns in '93 to earn second-team All-Big Ten honors.

photo by Blue White Illustrated

Senior defensive tackle Eric Ravotti (#94) cased this Iowa fumble with his steady, relentless pressure. Ravotti registered eight sacks for the Nittany Lions in 1993 despite missing two games from a seizure he suffered in a Big Ten game against Indiana.

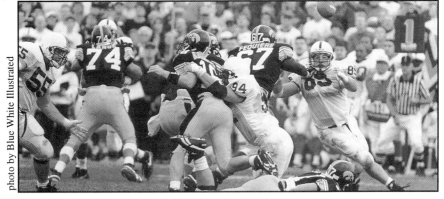

photo by Blue White Illustrated

Quarterback John Sacca (#9) gained some yardage against the University of Miami in 1992, but quit the Nittany Lion football team halfway through the '93 season when coach Joe Paterno benched him in favor of Kerry Collins.

photo by Mark Selders of Blue White Illustrated

Penn State trailed Michigan State, 23-10, but this touchdown pass from quarterback Kerry Collins (#12) to wide receiver Freddie Scott (#31) just before halftime helped the Nittany Lions rally to a 38-37 victory.

Junior tailback Ki-Jana Carter (#32) led the Nittany Lions' ground game with 1,119 yards, despite missing the last two regular season games against Northwestern and Michigan State to a calf injury. Carter was selected second-team Big Ten All-Star by the coaches and media.

Senior Derek Bochna (#35) registered 48 tackles at a secondary position Penn State refers to as the "hero" back. Bochna's consistency and leadership made him a hero in the eyes of Nittany Lion football fans for four years and his career was culminated by an All-Big Ten second-team selection.

Brian Gelzheiser shows his intensity against Iowa as he did all season. The junior linebacker led Penn State with 118 tackles, which earned him a second-team All-Big Ten selection.

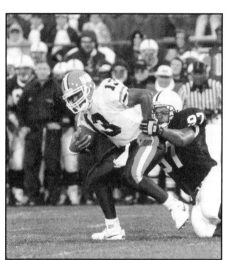

Senior End Tyoka Jackson (#97) registers one of his eight sacks in 1993, which was a team-high for Penn State along with his 13 tackles for losses that totaled 82 yards. Jackson was selected to the first-team All-Big Ten by the conference's coaches.

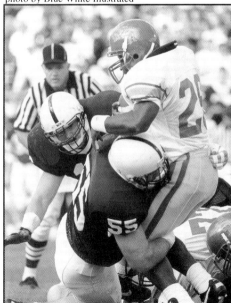

Senior defensive tackle Lou Benfatti (#55) stood up opposing running backs all season long for Penn State as he led the defensive line with 69 tackles, which earned him second-team All-Big Ten honors.

Head coach Joe Paterno discusses offensive strategy with quarterback Kerry Collins (#12) and fullback Brian O'Neal (#29)

photo by Blue White Illustrated

Senior fullback Brian O'Neal (#29) totaled 272 offensive yards in 1993 and cleared pathways for Penn State's outstanding tailback trio of Ki-Jana Carter, Mike Archie, and Stephen Pitts.

Nose guard Eric Clair (#89) set up Penn State's first touchdown against Iowa with this interception. The 31-0 victory started the Nittany Lions off to 3-0 in their first Big Ten season.

photo by Blue White Illustrated

photo by Blue White Illustrated

Sophomore tailback Mike Archie (32) gained 835 yards on 145 carries as part of Penn State's high-powered backfield.

photo by Mark Selder of Blue White Illustrated

photo by Blue White Illustrated

Junior linebacker Brian Gelzheiser ponders a rain-soaked 28-14 victory over Illinois in Penn State's first season of Big Ten football.

photo by Blue White Illustrated

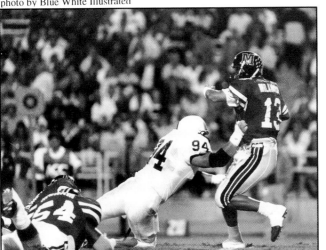

Defensive tackle Eric Ravotti (#94) pressured the Maryland offense all evening as the Nittany Lions closed (at least temporarily) an annual rivalry with the Terrapins in 1993. Penn State rolled to a 70-7 win over the run-and-shoot Terps.

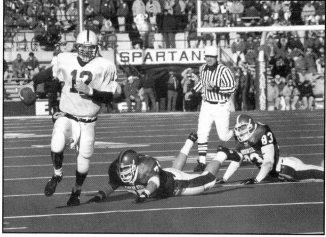

Quarterback Kerry Collins gains some much-needed yardage in Penn State's come from behind 38-37 win over Michigan State. The Nittany Lions trailed 37-17 midway through the third quarter before Collins threw for three quick touchdowns to cap the impressive rally.

photo by Blue White Illustrated

Defensive end Tyoka Jackson (#97) sacks USC quarterback Rob Johnson in the Nittany Lions' 21-20 win over the Trojans.

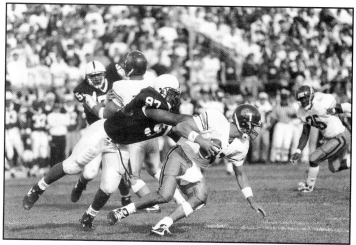

photo by Mark Selders of Blue White Illustrated

photo by Blue White Illustrated

Defensive tackle Lou Benfatti (#55) forces Tennessee quarterback Heath Shuler (#21), the Heisman trophy runner-up, into an early incompletion in Penn State's Citrus Bowl victory over the Volunteers.

photo by Blue White Illustrated

Sophomore wide receiver Bobby Engram (#10) gave the Big Ten an eyeful in Penn State's first season of conference play. His 48 catches for 873 yards and 13 TDs earned him a unanimous first-team All Big-Ten selection and he capped his season with 184 all-purpose yards in the Nittany Lions' 31-13 Citrus Bowl win over Tennessee to earn MVP honors.

photo by Blue White Illustrated

Sophomore tailback Ki-Jana Carter (#32) celebrates Penn State's 31-13 pounding of Tennessee in the Citrus Bowl. Carter's 93 yards rushing helped the Nittany Lions rally from a 10-0 deficit, including a sparkling 14-yard touchdown run with three seconds left in the first half.

team's most fragile position. He said he had lost touch with some of the players in 1992 and vowed that would not happen this year.

Now was the time to see if he could follow up on that vow.

9

A Break From the Big Ten

It was widely hoped the John Sacca story would simply fade away without much further interruption to Penn State's preparation for its last two non-conference games against Rutgers and Maryland. The Nittany Lions were 3-0 and ranked No. 9 in the latest polls. They were heavy favorites against their next two opponents, but did not need a distraction such as this quarterback change that could easily cause a drop in team spirit and allow a team such as Rutgers or Maryland to pull off an unlikely upset.

Sacca was still upset upon the football team's return to State College and had not rescinded anything he said earlier. He spent all day Sunday stewing over Paterno's decision to bench him against Iowa and once again threatened to quit the Nittany Lions and leave the university. After discussing the situation with his father and other family members, Sacca seemed to back off just a bit on his strong remarks.

"By late Sunday night, John had settled down and he agreed to stay and continue playing football at Penn State," John Sacca Sr. told the Associated Press. "Everyone in the family talked to him and, afterward, I think he finally realized that it would be a big mistake if he did anything else."

Sacca talked with everyone from his mother to his former high school coach. His brother Tony was a record-setting quarterback himself at Penn State, and who better than him would know about run-ins with Paterno. It seemed they disagreed on everything, but Tony, who was currently in his second season with the Phoenix Cardinals of the National Football League, was able to put aside the grievances with his coach and enjoy a standout four-year career as the Nittany Lions' full-time signal caller.

"I think it helped a lot that Tony talked to [John]," John Sacca Sr. said.

Sacca reported to practice the Monday of the Rutgers week and found the green practice jersey in his locker that signified second-team offense. Paterno, however, said very little about who would be the starting quarterback that Saturday against the Scarlet Knights. In his weekly Tuesday press conference, Paterno remained vague on the subject, saying only that he wasn't sure who his starter would be. It was clear from his words, however, that Paterno was tiring of the whole situation.

"John is a fine young man who probably said a couple of things he wishes he wouldn't have said," Paterno told the media gathering. "He's a good quarterback and he's got a bright future. As to which kid is going to start, we'll work that out. Enough has been said about that situation and, I'd rather talk about what I felt was a good job by our football team against a fine Iowa team."

Although neither Sacca nor Kerry Collins was brought to the media room, a couple of other Penn State players were present and they felt there was more being made of the situation than needed to be.

"I think John just overreacted and said some things in the heat of the moment," guard Mike Malinoski said. "I really think everything's going to be okay."

Defensive tackle Lou Benfatti said a talk by Paterno in a team meeting on Monday helped everyone understand all the distractions that could surface because of the situation.

"Joe was very concerned that it would affect us," Benfatti said. "He wanted to make sure we put it behind us. I don't think it'll be a distraction."

Paterno had said immediately after the game he was not pleased with the Nittany Lions' passing game against Iowa and that was part of the reason for taking a look at someone else.

"Our quarterbacks have not been as alert as I'd like them to be," he said. "Also, we have not caught the ball well. There were a couple of easy catches [against Iowa] we didn't make in key situations and a couple of others we didn't make. We have not come up with a great catch. Bobby Engram is the closest thing to it. Our wideouts, tight ends . . . we cannot drop two, three passes a ball game. Part of our problem is that as well as the quarterback reads. They're going to have to get rid of the ball quicker."

Kerry Collins' numbers (6 of 16, 57 yards) were equally unimpressive against Iowa, but logic would have had him starting in Penn State's nationally televised (ESPN) Saturday night home game against Rutgers simply because of Sacca's initial postgame tantrum and incessant pouting throughout the week.

It took Paterno much of the week, but by Thursday, he made it clear that Collins would be his starter. The question was raised once more about the status of Wally Richardson as a possibility at quarterback, but Paterno said he was still evaluating the now very strong probability that the sophomore would be redshirted to save an extra year of eligibility.

"I'm still considering that possibility," Paterno said. "I know I said I'd have a better feel for it after the first three games, but there's no reason to rush him into anything unnecessarily."

It had become a soap opera.

The setting: A quiet little town in central Pennsylvania that would be a ghost town were it not for the large university that engulfs it.

The subject: A nationally-ranked Division I football team that tries to seek acceptance in a conference that was none too keen on the idea of welcoming the school in the first place.

The main characters: A group of young men who are trying to convince their loyal fans that 1992 was all a bad dream and that they really do care about playing football in 1993. This group centers around a troubled young quarterback, wrought with confusion and jealousy because he had his starting assignment pulled out from under him; the second-team quarterback, who kept his mouth shut, bided his time, and took back the position he silently felt should have been his all along; and the embattled head coach, who sorted through the wreckage of a lost season the year before and now must pull all the right strings to prevent his ship from sinking again.

Stay tuned.

SEPTEMBER 25, UNIVERSITY PARK, PA—Rain seemed to be the ongoing forecast for football Saturdays for Penn State, only this time it was a deluge. The Nittany Lions agreed to move their game against Rutgers from an afternoon start to prime time to accommodate ESPN's cameras for their weekly Saturday night broadcast. The Scarlet Knights were 2-0 coming into Beaver Stadium and although they had never fared well against Penn State, they always looked for that one possible upset.

As expected, Kerry Collins got the start at quarterback for the Nittany Lions and John Sacca was relegated to backup duty. Once he knew of his starting assignment, Collins wanted only one thing, to get into a good rhythm. He did that by completing six of his first seven passes for 105 yards in the first quarter.

That feat was even more appreciated considering the game began in a driving rainstorm, which not only made for bad footing, but also made it difficult to just stand up. The defense was affected by the weather on both sides as Rutgers used its impressive running game to reach the Penn State 11-yard line on its second possession.

Hero back Derek Bochna saved face for the Nittany Lions when he intercepted quarterback Ray Lucas' pass in the end zone. Penn State then drove 80 yards to score the first points of the game. Tailback Ki-Jana Carter accounted for 40 of those yards on six carries. Collins gathered his first touchdown pass of the season when he spotted tailback Mike Archie from four yards out on a screen pass.

"Rutgers started to get a little momentum going, but that drive seemed to take a lot out of them," Bochna said. "For us to come right down and score was really big."

Penn State wasn't finished as Collins found wideout Chip LaBarca in single coverage and hit him with a 46-yard bomb that set up a 28-yard Craig Fayak field goal and a 10-0 lead early in the second quarter.

Fans, coaches and players all wanted to see tight end Kyle Brady get more involved in the Nittany Lions' passing game and although he caught just two passes for 16 yards against Rutgers, his contributions were of paramount importance. Brady's first reception came late in the first half when he took a pass from Collins along the right sideline and bulled his way past linebacker Jamil Jackson for a 15-yard touchdown.

"We've been doing that play for years," Brady said. "It's the old misdirection play. I just delay at the line for a couple of seconds and wait for everyone to go to the opposite side of the field. Then, I race over to the other side. Usually, there's no one there. This time there was, but it still worked out pretty well."

"We've been trying to get the ball to Brady," Joe Paterno said. "We finally got that chance once we got the ball to some of the other receivers."

Collins completed 18 of 25 passes against the Scarlet Knights, but more importantly, was able to spread them around to six different receivers.

"I think we've got to get the ball more to Kyle," Collins said. "He's a great tight end and a real important player for us. I think he's a great part of our offense and we need to get him the ball more."

"The coaches have been talking to me, and so have the players," said Brady, who had three catches for 49 yards in the Lions' first three games. "Everybody says we have to get me the ball more to take some pressure off the wideouts and the running game. It worked out well [against Rutgers]. Hopefully, I can just keep helping in the future."

Brady's touchdown helped Penn State to a 17-0 halftime lead and the defense also came up big by stopping Rutgers twice inside the Nittany Lions' 10-yard line in the first half.

Penn State's defense allowed 184 yards on the ground, with most of those coming in the first half. The Nittany Lions put the clamps on Rutgers' backfield duo of Bruce Presley and Terrell Willis in the second half and held the two to 59 and 39 yards, respectively, for the game.

Collins, who would finish with 222 yards and a career-high four touchdown passes, continued to move the Lions effectively in the third quarter as the offense took advantage of some solid special teams play to put the game out of reach.

Terry Killens, who is a promising linebacker in Penn State's future, blocked a Rutgers punt and set up shop for the Nittany Lions at the Knights' 18. PSU drove to the 1-yard line in five plays and set up with their three-fullback alignment on third down. Collins crossed up the defense, however, by rolling to his right and throwing to his right to a wide-open Brady in the back of the end zone. Fayak's extra point made it 24-0, Penn State.

Rutgers tried both Lucas and senior Brian Fortay at quarterback, but the Penn State defense was pounding. The two QBs combined for 14 of 29 passing for just 95 yards against another stingy defensive performance by the Nittany Lions.

"We're not playing error-free," Derek Bochna said. "We're making mistakes, and we're still holding teams down. That's because we're flying to the ball. If we make a mistake, we make it going full speed. When you do that, you're going to hold teams down."

Penn State added a score with less than five minutes remaining in the third quarter when Bobby Engram took a screen pass along the center of the field, slipped a couple of tackles and darted 20 yards for his fifth touchdown of the season.

The Nittany Lions' bid for a second straight shutout collapsed when Fortay broke loose for a 22-yard touchdown run against Penn State's third-team defense with just 49 seconds left in the game.

"We're close," defensive end Tyoka Jackson said of the Lions' 31-7 victory. "But we're not there yet because teams are still moving the ball on us effectively at times. The great defenses that I can remember [at Penn State], like in 1986 and 1991, and like Alabama last year, they dominated for four quarters. We haven't quite done that yet, but we're leading to it. The ball is definitely rolling that way.

"We still have some improving to do, and that is our goal. It's right there in front of us and I know we can get to it."

Jackson went on to stress the fact of how much fun it is to play Penn State football again this season.

"We have a lot of leaders on this team," he said. "We've got guys who are enthusiastic and we feed off that enthusiasm. That's just a great feeling to play with a bunch of guys who enjoy playing the game as much as I do. They like to play it the right way. They love getting after it and really being aggressive. I'm glad to be a part of that and it's why I believe this defense will do something special before the season is over."

Coming into the game, Paterno hoped to see his offense do something special. Like throw the ball better, and also catch it better. Against Rutgers, he seemed to have gotten both.

"I tried to go out and get into a rhythm right away, and I was able to do that," Collins said. "Once I got into a rhythm, everything started clicking."

"Kerry came out and was hitting us right on the money," said Engram, who caught eight of Collins' passes for 107 yards. "We had no choice but to catch the ball. He was really sharp, considering the [weather] conditions and considering it was only his second week of playing."

Collins kept his cool through the week's turmoil, wondering whether he would see more action against Rutgers or if his stint against Iowa was just a cosmetic appearance.

"I was a little nervous," he said. "But I think it was nervous excitement. The story was there all week and I can't say it wasn't tough, because I was involved in everything that happened. I think we tried to put it behind us and look ahead to Rutgers. I think it says a lot about the team that we were able to do that."

Collins, whose only interception came late in the game, also felt pretty good about his first start of 1993.

"I was ecstatic," he said. "It was probably my best effort to date. And because of all the stuff that happened, it was a great win for the team."

Paterno refused to immediately discuss the quarterback situation for the Lions' next game at Maryland, and at one point of his postgame press conference, he politely asked the reporters to talk about the game that was just finished when the question of Collins or Sacca arose. "I thought he [Collins] did a pretty good job in there," were Paterno's only comments relating to the subject.

Although the rest of the team had been fairly quiet on the subject from the beginning, most would have preferred to see it resolved before the season went much further.

"It's tough to say who should play," said Brady, who shares an off-campus apartment during the school year with Collins. "Kerry and John are both so good, and I'm not just saying that. But I think everyone would like to see just one guy stay in there so we can get some kind of consistency going and some kind of rhythm with the offense.

"But who that guy is remains to be seen, I guess."

Sacca played the last few minutes against Rutgers and completed 1 of 3 passes for 14 yards in a mop-up role. By the time of his entrance, only about 25,000 of the 92,000 announced crowd remained, but they greeted him with applause and encouragement.

All both quarterbacks could do was wait until Paterno's decision for the next week.

"I'm just gonna try to do the things I did in the past and in the game today, and try to keep it going," Collins said. "That's my priority now. If I don't do it, I know any one of the quarterbacks can come in and do the job."

To Collins, that meant doing the job even though there would always be someone there looking over your shoulder.

"It's tough because John's a good quarterback," Collins said. "I don't like to say I have to look over my shoulder, but I certainly know that he's behind me."

Little did Collins, or anyone else on the Penn State football squad know, but it wouldn't be long before the quarterback situation would resolve itself without hardly any grueling decisions by the coaching staff.

OCTOBER 2, COLLEGE PARK, MD — The best thing the Penn State players could do in the 37th matchup in school history against the Maryland Terrapins was forget about the first 36 games. If they thought about those, they might take the Terrapins too lightly. After all, things like that can happen when a series is as lopsided as 34-1-1 in your favor.

This was to be the last meeting (mercifully for Maryland) indefinitely between the two schools because of Penn State's move to the Big Ten and with the Lions heading into the meat of their conference schedule, they felt great importance in coming away from Maryland's Byrd Stadium victorious.

The Terps were 0-4 and sputtering under the rusted engines of their run-and-shoot offense, which had shot mostly blanks for most of the season. When the Nittany Lions arrived for the 7 p.m. start, the players casually strolled out to the field to get a feel for the playing surface as is the normal pre-game custom.

As the players dressed inside the locker room, Joe Paterno sat quietly in the cramped coaches quarters afforded the visiting team. As is his own pregame custom, Paterno unwrapped the first of two hot dogs brought to him before every game by one of Penn State's student managers. "Can you get me a Coke with that?" he asks.

"Do you ever eat the pregame meal with the players?" he is asked.

"No, not usually," he replies. "I just like doing it like this."

"You always eat a couple of hot dogs before the game?"

"Just about always."

"Is it some sort of superstitious thing you have going with yourself?" the brave questioner continues.

"No," the legendary coach answers. "It's mostly because I'm hungry."

With that, Paterno takes a sip of his soft drink and continues with his dinner. When that is through, he takes a list of last-minute reminders from his pocket. The list might include a couple of "what-to-do-in-certain-situations" type things, or it might contain reminders of things he wants to discuss with his players before the game.

Most of the assistant coaches are already dressed and waiting for the first unit of special teams players to hit the field. Defensive coordinator Jerry Sandusky sits quietly on the bench and ponders every last-minute detail.

"It doesn't make a difference that they're 0-4 and we're 4-0," he had said earlier at the team's hotel. "If they get ahead of us with that run-and-shoot, we could find ourselves in a lot of trouble."

Sandusky is widely regarded as one of the best assistant coaches in the country. He is a 1966 Penn State graduate and was in his 26th season of coaching with the Nittany Lions. He grew up in the heart of the steel mill industry in western Pennsylvania. His mother and father ran a recreation center in Washington, Pennslyvania, and that was where this only child learned about life's constant difficulties.

Sandusky had parents who loved him to no end, but most of the kids he came in contact with at the Brownson House Rec Center had no such love to speak of. Art and Evie Sandusky were mother and father; grandmother and grandfather to all the kids they came in contact. But most of all, they were their friends. Jerry saw them share the love that he experienced with them every day, and he could feel how important it was to the kids that might otherwise have nowhere else to go.

He was fortunate to learn sports from his father and he became a three-sport star at Washington High. He made several visits when it came time to choose a college, but fell in love with Penn State when he traveled with his dad to State College. "Somehow I knew that's where I would end up," Sandusky would say many years later.

His is a unique story because he never forgot the lessons his parents conveyed to him when he was just a kid who happened to have a whole gymnasium to play in right in the very next room. He spent his life learning football and joined Joe Paterno's coaching staff on a full-time basis in 1968. He and his wife Dottie adopted five children and yet still found time for others over the years.

It was Sandusky's dream for a long time to have the ability to help several less fortunate children at one time. In 1977, he founded The Second Mile, a charitable organization that was designed to address the welfare of young people. It started with heart and love, and grew to the construction of a house for the organization in State College. House parents were hired and the first four children came through its doors the very next year.

"[Starting The Second Mile] was always a case of wanting to do more," Sandusky said. "Our oldest son, Ray, was a foster child and we saw what happened in his life in terms of the direction he was headed. He was able to adjust and change academically and get a degree from Penn State. Then we figured there are thousands of Rays out there. There are kids with the potential, but they don't necessarily have the right structure or avenue to get where they want to go.

"You want to help them all, but you can only do so much. So we decided to extend our home and have a foster home. One thing has led to another, then another. Then it led to eight different programs. I never envisioned it to grow as much as it did."

From those first four children, The Second Mile has grown to an organization that has touched 80,000 children through eight various programs. Sandusky has enjoyed the success of watching The Second Mile grow as much as he has enjoyed seeing the growing process of kids who have touched his life in one way or another. Kids whose parents write him letters, thanking him for giving their child hope. Kids who write him years later and tell him how college, or the service, or a new job has kept them going long after their first contact with The Second Mile.

Sandusky loves the stories of success he comes across and he bleeds with the stories of kids who didn't quite make it, or couldn't quite cope with the hazards of everyday life. "Unfortunately, not all of the stories end on a positive note," he said.

A bright spot to the entire Sandusky family over the past couple of years has been a growing relationship with a young man named Matt, whom Sandusky first came in contact with when Matt was eight or nine years old. Many of the kids tag along with Sandusky to Saturday home football games and help out in various ways on the Penn State sideline.

"Matt lived nearby and I met him at The Second Mile," Sandusky said. "I took him to some of the football games like I did with the other kids and he didn't seem to fool around as much as they did."

The kids Sandusky came in contact with "fooled around" mostly because they had a good teacher. Whether it is touch football, volleyball, or just running with Stosh, the Sandusky's golden retriever, Jerry, is often one of the biggest kids playing.

"Matt used to just stand in the background and never get too involved," Sandusky continued. "He was very quiet and introverted to a point."

The Penn State football program, in one way or another, has always been there to help Sandusky with The Second Mile. Since the organization's existence, current football players have acted as big brothers to the kids and given them guidance in their otherwise lost worlds.

"I give a lot of credit to Penn State football in Matt's case," Sandusky said. "I think he was looking for something and the attention from Penn State football was there. By being around a lot of the players, he was able to see what it takes both academically and athletically to be the best person you can be."

The relationship between Matt and Jerry has not always been smooth. There was often frustration on both sides, and perhaps some high expectations.

"I got upset with Matt at various times last year because he didn't seem to be responding," Sandusky said. "And then he'd get frustrated with me. He came over to our house more often and we always had a good time. As I got more involved with his life, I saw that he wasn't doing very well academically and I became disappointed because it seemed like he had let me down."

Despite the frustration sometimes on both sides, however, Sandusky knew that Matt was reaching out for someone to believe in him.

"I think he wanted someone to get involved with him," he said. "He wanted someone to care enough to give him guidance and direction. I think he wanted to do something with his life and he just needed a little push or nudge here or there to get headed in that direction. Otherwise he would have never made the commitment that he did last summer [1993] to study and work out and become a part of our family the way he did."

Matt, who came from a broken home, stayed with the Sandusky family for practically the entire summer. He was about to enter his freshman year at State College High School and Jerry made sure he was prepared to give his best effort possible in the classroom. He and Matt also spent time working out together in Penn State's weight room, where Matt was getting in shape to play freshman football.

Theirs is a special relationship that has survived through all the peaks and valleys, and still seems headed for a positive future. An ideal setting will someday have Matt wearing the blue and white Penn State uniform, with his coach and good friend Jerry hollering at him from the sideline.

Sometimes a kid needs someone who cares. As Sandusky pointed out, everything in dealing with a child is timing. "If they've come from a disrupted family and you come into their lives at the right time, when they're looking for something, then you can make an impact," he said. "If it's the wrong time, then it can be very difficult."

For Matt, timing was everything. And the Sandusky family picked up on that very easily.

"As I got to know him, I felt he had some needs that maybe we could help him with," Sandusky said. "And the more we got to know him, the more we wanted to help him because we saw the potential for a great young man. He began to spend a lot more time with us and he kind of opened up and let himself go. He became closer to our family situation and when he did that, he became a little more vulnerable and we became a little more wrapped up in his life."

From Sandusky's experiences with Matt, there was little doubt that the young man needed someone like Jerry in his life.

"I never really expected him to change the way he did," Sandusky said. "I never expected him to be into football like he is. I never expected him to be into his studies. Something has ignited him."

It's not really so difficult to discover what that "something" might be.

As Jerry Sandusky relaxed on the bench an hour or so before kickoff against Maryland, Matt stood on the field near the 50-yard line, tossing a football with one of the Penn State student equipment managers. Thoughts of stopping the run-and-shoot probably still dashed through his mind, but Sandusky was able to crack a smile when someone joked with him to the effect that Matt was probably a whole lot tougher on the field than he was.

Penn State was about to play its last non-conference game of the season and it wanted no slip-ups to interfere with its perfect 4-0 record. Kerry Collins would get his second straight start at quarterback for the Nittany Lions and if the game was going to be anywhere near the high-scoring affair most fans expected, Collins would need to have one of the best games of his career.

Maryland more closely resembled its basketball team through the first month of the season as its totals included 42 points against North Carolina and 37 against West Virginia. The only problem was the Terrapin defense, which gave up more points on both occasions — and two others. In all, the Maryland offense came into the game averaging 42 points and more than 500 yards of offense per game. The Terrapins' quarterback, Scott Milanovich, came into the game rated No. 1 in the nation in total offense with a per game average of 402.5 yards.

What would Penn State's response be to all those staggering numbers?

The Nittany Lion defense held Milanovich to just 158 yards on 19 of 32 passing. The 6-foot-4, 220-pound sophomore was intercepted three times and sacked five times by a hounding defensive rush for losses totaling 47 yards. He even had one of his seven punts blocked by the never-ending army of white jerseys that invaded his backfield.

It was a wipeout from beginning to end. Final score: Penn State 70, Maryland 7. The kind of finish that gives everyone on the winning side the ability to think positive thoughts.

"We did a great job tonight," Penn State defensive end Eric Ravotti said. "We set out to put some pressure on the quarterback so maybe he'd make a few mistakes, and I think we did that."

"Jerry [Sandusky] put in a good defensive plan," hero back Derek Bochna said. "We knew they would be a little confused, which they were. We knew if they never figured it out we'd be able to contain them pretty well, and it happened that way. They got down, they started forcing things and everything worked out real well."

Penn State played to near perfection on defense, but even more of a pleasant surprise to the Penn State coaching staff was another complete performance from the Nittany Lions' offense. Penn State used power and speed almost equally as it amassed 526 yards on the ground for a 9.2 yards per carry average.

Tailback Ki-Jana Carter had his fourth 100-yard game of the season (159 yards on 13 carries, three touchdowns), while another tailback, Mike Archie, accounted for 120 yards on 11 carries and had one score. Fullbacks Brian O'Neal, Brian Milne and Jon Witman combined for 174 yards against the beleaguered Maryland defense.

"Our offensive line has dominated everyone through the first five games," said Carter, who saw little playing time in the second half after collecting 133 of his yards in the first. "I don't think they've had any problems with anyone so far. I'm just reading their blocks and hitting the holes as fast as I can. A lot of times I'm getting so many yards I don't need to play in the third or fourth quarters."

Penn State scored on its first three possessions to put the game away in a hurry. Carter's 63-yard touchdown run on the third play from scrimmage set the tone for the rest of the game. It was a great block by O'Neal that sent Carter on his way.

"It was a sweep and when I got the ball I saw the fullback take out two guys," Carter said. "After that, I just saw nothing but green, so I took off."

Penn State led 25-0 before Maryland got on the scoreboard in the second quarter, but a 36-yard touchdown run by Carter sandwiched by touchdown catches of 10 and 16 yards by Bobby Engram gave the Nittany Lions a commanding 46-7 lead at halftime.

Freshman Brett Conway kicked the first field goal of his career (a 28-yarder) to start the second half for Penn State and

Archie, O'Neal and Milne scored on runs of 1, 1 and 10 yards, respectively, to account for the final score.

"I don't like games like this," Joe Paterno said afterward. "I would have preferred a closer game. A game like this doesn't prove anything."

In one sense, all the game did was make just about every player look good on the final stat sheet. Carter raised his season rushing total to 609 yards. Engram set a school record for sophomore receivers with his seventh touchdown of the season. Milne had a season-high 65 yards on just five carries.

The Nittany Lion defense was playing better than expected with 19 sacks and 14 interceptions through five games, and had allowed opposing offenses to convert just 25 percent of their third-down conversions. The Lions were also holding their opponents to less than 75 yards rushing per game.

"I think the defensive coaches did a good job [against Maryland]," Paterno said. "I thought the kids played with intelligence and were able to disguise a lot of things real well.

"But it was the people up front that made it happen. Milanovich didn't have time to really read what was going on down field because the guys up front kept a lot of pressure on him. We rushed with four men, and we went with five frequently, but not a lot in the sense of as many plays as they had. I just think with our pressure up front and the fact we were changing a lot of zones, they didn't have a chance to adjust the way they like. They didn't have a chance to go to the second and third receiver."

"This was a big game for us," Bochna said. "We feel like we're playing our best football right now and we're at the point where we want to be going into the game against Michigan."

Oh yeah, those guys. It would get to this point eventually. When Penn State and the Big Ten Conference announced their joint venture a little over three years before, it was a matchup like this that all parties involved in the decision had in mind. The Michigan Wolverines, perennial conference favorites, year after year, against the new guys, who knew a thing or two about football themselves.

As the seconds wound down to the final gun against Maryland, Keith Conlin, a 6-foot-7, 290-pound reserve offensive lineman for Penn State, sat on one of the aluminum benches on the sideline and quietly uttered one word to himself over and over. "Michigan, Michigan, Michigan."

Michigan would probably be the first team in the Big Ten to take Penn State's involvement as an intrusion, instead of a means of conference enhancement. This was a school that had made the Rose Bowl an annual fixture on its postseason schedule a few years back and seemed on the verge of doing so again. The Michigan players and coaches knew the Big Ten's new addition was no cream puff on the schedule and that Penn State had the kind of team that would consistently contend for the Rose Bowl championship for many years to come.

Michigan's coach, Gary Moeller, even opposed the Nittany Lions' admission to the Big Ten because it would make his job more difficult. "I'll admit I'm not thrilled," he said at the beginning of the season.

If the Big Ten was looking to knock Penn State down a few pegs, Michigan might just be the right team to place in the middle of the Nittany Lions' schedule.

10

MICHIGAN:
79 Yards, 24 Inches

Penn State was 5-0 and ranked No. 7 in the CNN/*USA Today* Top 25 poll as it prepared for its much-anticipated matchup against Michigan. Following the total annihilation the Nittany Lions put on Maryland, the team would have to wait an extra week before taking on the Wolverines. It was the first of two bye weeks on the Lions' schedule. Two weeks to prepare for the biggest game of the season so far.

"Big" wasn't even the proper word for Michigan. "Desperate" would have been a better way to describe the Wolverines, who after losing a non-conference game to Notre Dame in the second game of the season, dropped to 2-1 in the conference after losing at Michigan State just a week before coming to State College. The Wolverines were on the verge of dropping out of the Rose Bowl picture before the season was even half completed.

If the hype of the game wasn't enough for Penn State to practice through, the timing of the latest controversy could not have been worse. John Sacca, the starting quarterback at the beginning of the season who threatened to quit the team after being yanked against Iowa, apparently carried out on his threat a couple of days after the Maryland game.

Sacca, who had completed just 7 of 23 passes since his 18-for-32, 274-yard, four-touchdown performance in the Lions' opener against Minnesota, saw minimal reserve duty in his last two games as a Nittany Lion. Kerry Collins appeared to have won the job based on his performances against Rutgers and Maryland, and Sacca could not accept the role of backup.

When Sacca didn't report to practices, however, Joe Paterno and his coaching staff soon discovered that he had also left the university and had not been in touch with his parents for the last three or four days. He didn't show up for any team meetings or practices throughout the week and that prompted his father to file a missing persons report with university police.

John Sacca, Sr., who had talked his son out of quitting a couple of weeks ago, said he had not spoken with the younger Sacca since the Tuesday following the Maryland game and wasn't aware until a couple of days later that his son had left the university. "John has left the team," John Sr. said that Wednesday night. "Other than that, I'm not sure what's going on. I don't know what his plans are."

On his October 7 radio call-in show, Paterno confirmed the news that Sacca had quit the team, but wasn't certain if his academic career was over at Penn State.

"For all intents and purposes he's given up football at Penn State," Paterno said of Sacca. "but it's not just because of football. He's not deserting his teammates or anything like that. He's had some other problems. Academically, he really fell behind.

"I would not want people out there to think he just decided, 'hey, to heck with football, I don't care about anybody, I don't care about the team.' That wasn't it at all."

Paterno received a lot of questions as to who would back up Collins now that Sacca was gone and sophomore Wally Richardson was being saved for a possible redshirt. "Wally right now is the backup and will play this year," the head coach answered.

Paterno also hinted that he may not have handled the Sacca situation in the most correct of manners.

"He was a young man who worked awfully hard and was looking forward to having a great year," Paterno said. "His expectations were high, then all of a sudden he was jolted, fairly or unfairly. I may not have treated him fairly, I don't know. That's one of the hard parts of this job, making those kinds of decisions."

It wasn't until the next day, Friday, that Sacca's where-abouts were discovered. He had driven to Phoenix, his mother reported, to be with his brother Tony, who was a backup quarter-back with the NFL's Phoenix Cardinals.

Some, like his father, felt John Sacca endured a tremendous amount of pressure from the media that covered the Penn State football team on a day-to-day basis.

"He's gotten butchered by a lot of the people in the media, especially up there [in State College]" the elder Sacca told the *Philadelphia Inquirer*. "And he's been getting abuse from a lot of other people up there . . . except from the players on the football team."

Amid all of the controversy, the furor over one player starting over another, one young man was able to stay quiet. That was Kerry Collins' plan all along. He accepted the coach's deci-sion in preseason, whether he believed in it or not, and figured his opportunity would come, and that would be the time to make the most of it. Of course, even he didn't expect things to develop like this.

"It was hard to hold back," Collins said weeks later. "It got frustrating, but I wanted to wait for my chance. There were times when I thought about my own future and where I wanted to be. But I knew that shooting my mouth off wouldn't have helped."

Instead, Collins worked in the green jersey in practice, and followed the weekly game plan as though it could be his to operate at any given moment. That moment came against Iowa.

"I was a little surprised," he said. "Joe had only told me that I would see playing time at some point, but I don't remember him saying it would be in that particular game. All of a sudden he was telling me I was in on the next series. I worried about it a little at first, but once I was out there it felt good to get back into a game situation."

Collins described his relationship with John Sacca as a working relationship and there really wasn't much of a friend-ship involved. "It was probably just a personality thing," Collins said. "I mean, we would talk about things all the time relating to football, and help each other out. But we just basically worked together."

As the season's events turned more and more in his favor, Collins could see the frustration in his fellow quarterback's eyes.

"I wasn't surprised that John had those feelings [after the Iowa game]," Collins said. "I was just surprised that he did it through the press. He just reacted on gut emotions and when that happens, I guess anything can come out."

It is always wrong, but so often easy, for a player to let his ill feelings be known through the media. Especially when he knows that same media contingent will probably scoot right over to the coach to get his reaction to what was just said.

In Sacca's case, the words were derived more from frustration rather than trying to get a message across to his coach. Paterno recognized that and refused, at any time, to criticize his departed quarterback.

"John's a good kid who reacted in the way he felt best," Paterno said near the end of the season. "I'm disappointed that he didn't stick it out, but we had an understanding that he had to be in the games mentally. All the quarterbacks do, or they're gonna come out. I don't feel he was into the game against Iowa the way I would have liked and that's why I pulled him."

Was Paterno ever worried that the controversy and Sacca's resulting departure would affect the team's positive attitude heading into the bulk of its Big Ten schedule?

"I think it was more unfortunate for John," Paterno said. "It may have disturbed some of his friends, but I didn't think it would affect the team. In all fairness to John, he just wasn't comfortable with things. If he was he would have been able to handle it better.

"I feel bad for him that he felt he had to leave. It would be easy for people to say he's a quitter, he's no good and all that kind of nonsense. But he had a very difficult decision and he did it."

"I think Joe [Paterno] handled it very well," Penn State quarterback coach Dick Anderson said. "Our biggest concern was for John. We all felt he made a mistake and I don't know how he feels today, but I suspect he may say he made a mistake as well."

Collins also felt Sacca made a mistake and was somewhat surprised at the way everything was handled in the end.

"He just threw in the towel," Collins said. "The competition was so intense, maybe someone had to give. I can understand his reasons, but I thought he should have stuck it out."

"He [Sacca], nor anyone else on this football team, should make a decision or even say things on the spur of the moment," Anderson said. "He shouldn't be hasty, especially in an emotional situation after a football game. There is a responsibility to yourself, the rest of the football team and the university when something like that happens. Sometimes it takes a little maturity, and I'm sure if John had some things to do or say again, he would do it in a different manner. But it was done and everyone had to move on."

Collins knew he would have to take charge of the situation because of the nature of the quarterback position. The team was on a roll and he did not want anyone to worry about distractions such as this.

"As a team, we wanted to be aware of our roles," he said. "It was kind of like a double-edged sword, because even though there was controversy and tension, the pressure of the position seemed to have been lifted."

But the timing of Sacca's departure couldn't have been worse.

"Yeah, it was a little bit of bad timing, right before the Michigan game," Collins said.

"I think the pressure probably increased on Kerry because there would be more attention given to him," Anderson said. "But I'm not sure he wouldn't relish in that attention. Anybody who's in a position where they will get a lot of exposure will probably welcome those kind of circumstances. I think that's what it's really all about, to be in positions that are difficult, where you can make a difference and everyone's looking at you."

With two of the biggest games in Penn State football history coming back to back, Collins was about to get all the attention — and face all the pressure — he could possibly ask for.

OCTOBER 16, UNIVERSITY PARK, PA — It was probably trash talk more than anything, but the Michigan Wolverines had opened a few Penn State eyes during the days leading up to the big game. Penn State had rushed for 1,488 yards through its first five games, utilizing three premier tailbacks, while its defense had registered 18 sacks for 160 yards lost and 14 interceptions. Yet, some of the Michigan players were asking, "Who are they?"

"We're not allowed to say 'Penn State,'" said Michigan freshman fullback Jon Ritchie, who is from nearby Mechanicsburg, Pa. "We have to say, 'the other team' or 'the 11th school.'"

"It's a matter of respect," Penn State defensive tackle Lou Benfatti said. "I don't think we're going to get any respect from teams in the Big Ten like we did from the independents."

To the Michigan players, Penn State's past accomplishments didn't matter a whole lot. The Nittany Lions came to the Big Ten Conference with a rich tradition. They had beaten just about anyone and everyone over the years at least once and came into this game with two Big Ten wins already under their belts. Michigan was clinging to a 3-2 record and facing sure elimination from the Rose Bowl picture if it happened to fall to the Nittany Lions. But that phrase — Rose Bowl — was one of the very things that grabbed the Wolverines' ire.

"I think where the lack of respect comes from," Michigan star running back Tyrone Wheatley said, "is that this is their first year in the Big Ten, and they're already hollering Rose Bowl and Big Ten championship."

Michigan's sophomore defensive back, Ty Law, another Pennsylvania recruit that got away from Penn State, agreed with his teammate.

"From history, everyone knows Penn State has a great team," he said. "But you have to prove yourself in the Big Ten. Penn State, they've made their own schedule, and they've had a lot of flashy teams. The Big Ten Conference is usually hard-nosed, hit-type teams. And Penn State is going to have to come in and prove to everybody that they're a worthy team."

Law must not have checked the record books, which would show that although Penn State and Michigan had never met on the football field, Joe Paterno had accumulated a 9-6 overall record against Big Ten teams during his career and Penn State had also been rather successful against the majority of other teams on its past schedules — flashy or not flashy —including Notre Dame, whom the Wolverines had lost to earlier in the season and have had limited success against over the past several years.

It was talk that could be posted on the locker room bulletin board, but Penn State just dismissed it as trash talking. "Do you believe this guy?" Penn State special teams coach Tom Bradley asked to no one in particular when he read Law's remarks about the Nittany Lions. "Ty Law's really got his mouth going now."

In Benfatti's mind, the words really didn't mean a whole lot. He knew what mattered would be what happened on the field.

"A lot of what [other] teams say is in the heat of things," Benfatti said. "They cheap-shot you, saying things you ordinarily wouldn't hear. Things in the media. But hey, what can we do? We'll just go in there and do our best.

"I don't think many teams respect us the way independents do, and I think what we're going to have to do is go out and gain the respect back."

A record crowd of 96,719 filled Beaver Stadium to watch Penn State's 1,000th game in school history, but first ever against the Michigan Wolverines. Inside the Penn State locker room, freshmen were feeling the true excitement for the very first time.

"This is why I came to Penn State," one freshman said when he saw the packed stadium. "I can't wait to get out there."

"I just hope I make it through pregame," another one said, somewhat nervous.

Freshman kicker Brett Conway, who came to Penn State from Atlanta, had only seen it on television before, but the excitement was well worth his anticipation. "If you can't get excited about this, you don't belong here," he said.

Michigan would provide a definite opportunity for the Nittany Lions to gain respect in their new conference. They had beaten a pass-happy Minnesota team and an undermanned Iowa squad in the conference so far, and despite the Wolverines' 2-1 league record, Penn State could figure on having a difficult time.

Michigan had been to the Rose Bowl four out of the past five years and coach Gary Moeller wanted nothing more than to get there again. "It's the only bowl we shoot for and the only one we want to play in," said Moeller, whose team hadn't lost a conference game in three years before losing at Michigan State a week earlier.

That was a sentiment that Penn State seemed to have a little trouble getting used to. It had been widely noted in years past that Big Ten teams generally aim for the conference championship first and the national championship second.

"I always wondered how they could look at things like that," Penn State defensive end Tyoka Jackson said. "That conference championship means everything to these schools and although that's what we want too, we want to keep winning and have a shot at the national championship."

Penn State came out against Michigan like it still had the national title in mind. The Nittany Lions jumped to a 10-0 lead almost too easily as Craig Fayak booted a 40-yard field goal late in the first quarter and Kerry Collins hit wideout Bobby Engram for a 37-yard touchdown pass midway through the second.

The lead was nice, but the Lions were making errors that teams can't usually afford against the likes of Michigan. One case in point was Penn State's very first possession. Collins came out and took charge with his offense by moving it to a first-and-goal at the Michigan 8-yard line. On second-and-goal from the 3, Penn State was called for procedure that moved it back. Two pass plays fell incomplete and the drive totally fizzled when Fayak missed a 25-yard field goal. Even when Fayak hit his 40-yarder, a motion penalty wiped out the drive at the Michigan 17.

Bobby Engram, PSU's leading receiver through the first five games, came off the field at one point near the end of the first quarter and banged his helmet on the aluminum bench in frustration over the Nittany Lions' simple mistakes that were resulting in stalled drives.

Receivers coach Kenny Jackson, a former All-American receiver at Penn State himself, calmed Engram's nerves, and tried to settle those around him. "You're trying for too much too fast," Jackson told his players. "You want it all right now, but you got to give it time. Relax, there's still three quarters to go."

Still, Penn State was playing just well enough on defense to corral Michigan's star running back Tyrone Wheatley, who had been held to just 33 yards rushing in the Wolverines' loss to Michigan State. The first of two crucial — and costly — mistakes crept up on the Nittany Lions with five minutes and 14 seconds left in the second quarter.

Penn State's punt coverage had been excellent all season long to this point, but when Michigan's Derrick Alexander, a 6-2, 190-pound speedy wide receiver, handled a Penn State punt at the Nittany Lion 48-yard line, he started straight ahead and quickly darted to his left.

"I was coming up the middle and then I didn't see him till he broke around me," Penn State linebacker Brian Gelzheiser said.

That was the last anyone saw of Alexander until he raised his arms in the end zone with the Wolverines' first touchdown of the game. Penn State was stunned momentarily, but still managed to secure a 10-7 lead at halftime.

The teams traded possessions through the first part of the third quarter, neither one putting out much of a threat. Anything might turn the tide of the game. A turnover could be costly. A mental mistake could be deadly. Penn State could have been the beneficiary of one, but instead, it was a victim of the other.

Michigan quarterback Todd Collins had driven his team to a third-and-five at the Penn State 23-yard line. He dropped back to pass, but was hit from behind by Lion defensive end Eric Ravotti. The ball fell free and was scooped up by Penn State's Lou Benfatti, who rumbled all the way to the Wolverines' 30-yard line. As the crowd celebrated the turnover, the Penn State sideline stood in silence when it saw one of the officials pointing at the ground at the original line of scrimmage. The play was ruled an incomplete pass as the official said Collins' arm was in motion at the time of Ravotti's tackle.

"I didn't like that call at all," Tyoka Jackson said. "There was no way he got rid of that ball before Eric got to him. It was a fumble, but what are we gonna do? That play wasn't the difference in the game."

Instead of a Penn State first down in Michigan territory, the Wolverines would have an opportunity for a field goal. Their kicker, Peter Elezovic, had missed one from 32 yards earlier in the game and the Nittany Lions were eager to get a rush on him in hopes of disrupting the 40-yard attempt. Perhaps they were a bit too eager.

The kick sailed wide left and Penn State appeared to have dodged a bullet — until the yellow flags went flying. Penn State's Shelly Hammonds, normally a defensive back, lined up tight on the left side of the line and jumped offside just a second before the ball was snapped.

The penalty gave Michigan new life and a first down at the Nittany Lions' 18-yard line. As the crowd booed, still in disagreement with the non-fumble call, Collins wasted little time in capitalizing on Hammonds' huge mistake. The 6-5 senior threw a 16-yard strike that was hauled in for a touchdown by wide receiver Mercury Hayes. Elezovic's extra point kick made it 14-

10, Michigan, and the Nittany Lions trailed in a ball game for the first time all season.

Then came the drive that covered 79 yards and 24 inches. Those last 12 inches would go down as one of the most agonizing measurements in Penn State history.

Ki-Jana Carter, who led the Nittany Lions with 127 yards rushing, worked with fellow tailback Mike Archie to move the Lions into Michigan territory. Kerry Collins mixed his plays up well as Penn State did its best to respond to the team's first deficit all year. He hit Archie for eight yards and tight end Kyle Brady for 18 more.

Penn State was also aided by a pair of pass interference calls against Michigan defensive back Ty Law, and when Archie carried three straight times to the Michigan 1-yard line, the Nittany Lions appeared poised to regain the lead.

The official distance the Lions needed for a touchdown was one yard, but the nose of the ball was resting right in front of the goal line. This was Big Ten football about to unfold. Two monstrous lines facing each other, each with the idea of putting the other on its collective back side. Gary Moeller had won 31 games as a coach in the Big Ten with this style of play, and although Joe Paterno was new to the conference, he hailed from the old school that just wouldn't have it any other way.

The Penn State linemen looked across to Michigan as if to say, "We're comin' your way," while the Wolverines glared back and seemed to say, "Give it your best shot."

Paterno played it simple on first down. He asked his line to clear a path just wide enough to let his 6-foot-5 quarterback fall into. Instead, Collins fell into the arms of Michigan middle guard Tony Henderson. No gain. The play didn't sound like much in the logic department, but it still should work. Paterno had so much confidence in fact, that he tried it again. Nothing doing. Henderson met Collins as though he had just come from the Penn State huddle.

On third down, Penn State fooled no one by going up the middle again. This time it was Ki-Jana Carter who tried to hurdle the center of the line, but was met head on by Michigan defensive tackle Ninef Agkakhan. The last few seconds of the third quarter perished from the clock and Collins had a chance to talk over the fourth-down play with his coach.

Paterno figured Michigan would look for something outside from Penn State after three straight inside plays. That was why he decided to go inside one more time and let the chips fall where they may.

"They're awfully good on the goal line," Paterno would say later. "They have a clever little scheme where they pinch and then loop out. If you run the sweep — and we were debating doing that — and they loop out, then you're in trouble. So you have to guess against them.

"It was my decision, my call and I guessed that they would loop out, expecting something like a bootleg pass. And I thought we would run right at them."

The funny thing is, Michigan *was* expecting something to the outside.

"We thought they would go wide," said Henderson, who was responsible for two of the stops on this stand so far. "We thought it would be some kind of a roll-out pass."

Instead, Paterno called Carter's number again and even the fullback who tried to lead him into the end zone was stopped short of the goal line. Henderson was again there to make the play for Michigan, along with linebacker Jarrett Irons. "I saw the ball coming my way and I just stepped up," Irons said.

The goal-line stand was reminiscent of Penn State's futile attempt to score in the 1978 Sugar Bowl against Alabama, but the Nittany Lions were only stopped twice from the 1-yard line on that drive. This time, they couldn't move the ball *four times* from inside the 1.

"On the goal line, when you need a yard, you either get it or you don't," said Kerry Collins, when asked if he ever considered calling an audible.

"Everybody in the place was thinking we're going to go outside, including the Michigan coach," Paterno said. "We guessed right, we just didn't execute it well enough. We got the play we wanted against the defense we wanted on fourth down. It took more guts to run up the gut than to run outside."

"You can second-guess every play that was ever called if they don't work," Michigan coach Gary Moeller said in defense of Paterno.

Penn State was dealt a crushing blow, but it had to remember there was still the whole fourth quarter to play. A non-score in that situation would be even more painful to the Nittany Lions if the defense elected to hang its head and allow the Wolverines to march 99 yards, 24 inches in the other direction.

Fortunately, the defense held and Penn State's offense got another chance. The Lions drove to the Michigan 8-yard line, where another drive stalled, but Fayak kicked a 25-yard field goal to pull his team to within one, 14-13.

All Penn State needed to do was hold the Wolverines once more on defense and get the ball back. A field goal could win it, and the 12-inch failure could perhaps be forgotten.

But Penn State still had a little business to contend with named Tyrone Wheatley. The Lions had contained the 6-1, 226-pound running back for much of the afternoon, but with the game growing old, Wheatley was just stepping into his prime.

The Wolverines took possession of their final drive on their own 35-yard line. Wheatley carried for nine yards on the first play and four more on the second. By now, Moeller had decided it was time for Wheatley to make his presence better known. The junior tailback lost a yard on the next play, but when he found the daylight on second-and-11, Penn State's first loss of 1993 was about to materialize.

Wheatley cut left, and then cut left again as he cruised down the Michigan sideline before being dragged down at the Nittany Lions' 6-yard line. The drive accounted for 59 of his game-high 192 yards on the ground as Wheatley did his part to welcome the Nittany Lions to the Big Ten. Todd Collins lofted a three-yard TD pass to fullback Che Foster as Michigan held on for a 21-13 victory in the first-ever matchup of two of college football's greatest powers.

"A couple of times we thought we were going to put them away, but they stayed with us," Paterno said. "They came back and started running Wheatley inside."

Michigan had racked up 230 yards rushing against a defense that had allowed an average of only 76.8 in its first five games. Most of those yards were gained by the man who did most of the talking in the Michigan locker room afterward.

"You have to pay your dues," said Wheatley, who outrushed Penn State single-handedly, 192-179. "It's like a freshman coming in boasting and bragging. You have to show them you have to be here a while."

Penn State didn't worry so much about the talking Michigan did after the game. Wheatley wasn't the only Wolverine player to offer a friendly, but sarcastic welcome to Penn State in the conference. The Nittany Lions were resigned to the fact that every team would show them the same kind of unwanted courtesy until they stepped up and did something about it. Disappointedly, they didn't do it this time.

As the first wave of players entered the Penn State locker room immediately after the game, Lou Benfatti and Eric Ravotti were the first among them. "No one hangs their heads," Benfatti yelled repeatedly.

One player bashed his helmet into a side door, but was quickly reprimanded by Benfatti. "We're not gonna do that kind of stuff," Benfatti told the player. "We pick it up and we go on from here."

"Nothing's over," Ravotti echoed. "Nothing at all. We got a lot of games left. Pick your heads up and let's go back to work on Monday."

"The only team that can beat us is ourselves," Ravotti said to the media moments later.

Paterno wouldn't go that far himself because he said that's "taking away from Michigan," but he had to be thinking back to the loss to Miami in 1992 after a 5-0 start.

"If you look back over the last couple of years, the same thing that's beat us beat us today," Tyoka Jackson said. "We shot ourselves in the foot."

The players all believed — and pledged so — that there would be no disastrous finish like 1992.

"This year's team is different," Ravotti said. "There is a lot of character in that locker room and nobody will give up. There's a lot more to play for."

That was basically the message Paterno wanted to deliver in his locker room address after the game.

"Hey, I don't want you guys hanging your heads," Paterno said. "We were going along real good and sometimes these things happen. We played a good game. The mistakes just caught up to us. They're [Michigan] a big-league team and they'll take advantage of things like that.

"I made some of the mistakes today. A lot of us did. This is what Big Ten football is gonna be like. Remember it. Store it away for future reference. We're not out of this thing by a long shot. That's what conferences are for. The lesson here is move on and get the next one."

In the end, Michigan would not figure in the Big Ten's Rose Bowl plans after all. Illinois would dash those hopes the very next week in Ann Arbor with an improbable rally that resulted in a last-second touchdown pass, and an upset over the Wolverines. But those 12 third-quarter inches. Oh, how they would come back to haunt Penn State.

11

OHIO STATE: A Rose Bowl Contender

Another miserable bye week. Nobody really liked these weeks off in between games, except maybe the Penn State training staff because it gave a couple of injured players another week to heal without missing any game time. But the players and coaches for the most part, would rather keep right on playing, without any interruptions to the season. It is a quirk in the scheduling that all Division I teams must endure because of the season's early start — sometimes August 31 — and the limited number of games they are permitted to play. For Penn State, the bye weeks just happened to come in the middle of the season, which can be a blessing if your team is struggling, but a hindrance if you're riding a nice wave. Penn State was doing the latter when its first bye week came about.

"I hate the bye weeks," Nittany Lion tight end Kyle Brady said. "I know it's a part of the scheduling process, but it really throws off your normal routine as a player. We usually begin a Monday practice with the idea of preparing for a game that weekend. Like now, with Ohio State, we had to work all last week with no game to play and now this is our game week. It was the same way for the Michigan game."

In Penn State's case, the Big Ten schedule-makers went to a highly unusual format of scheduling Penn State for a week off after its first five games, then came Michigan, another week off, and then Ohio State. With their rhythm slightly ajar, the Lions played their two toughest opponents over a four-week lull. No other Big Ten team had such a schedule where it had one week off, played the next week and then followed with another week off.

"I'm never excited about [bye weeks]," Penn State quarterback coach Dick Anderson said. "Every team at that point in time is probably different. If there happens to be a couple of key players who are injured and could use the time off, then it could be positive. But that's really the only time I think it's beneficial. You could be healthy and playing well, and the week off might mess up your rhythm."

No one blamed the loss to Michigan on the previous week's respite, but Penn State's cylinders were all running in high gear at the time. While the Nittany Lions watched football on television the Saturday before Michigan, the Wolverines were in the process of losing to cross-state rival Michigan State.

Putting injuries aside, the way the time off is dealt with is probably the best way to determine if it is beneficial or not. Penn State had an extra week to stew over its biggest game of the year. Practice began in almost normal fashion — the Monday after the Maryland game — and Penn State spent hours and hours talking about Michigan. The coaches dissected film. The players studied their assignments.

"It was like we spent too much time preparing for Michigan," Brady said.

So, the Nittany Lions went for a different approach against Ohio State. For starters, there was no practice until the Wednesday after Michigan. That gave the players three days to themselves (besides classes and treatments for injuries). The team went to a light workout that first day and practiced only three times that week.

"We're getting into the seventh game and ninth week for us," Paterno said. "We'd ordinarily be playing our ninth game when we get to Ohio State. We'd be winding down our season and yet we've got a lot of football ahead of us. I've got to be very careful we don't go for the overkill. We have to be careful we don't work them too hard."

"Everyone seemed much more relaxed, like there wasn't such a heavy burden because we lost to Michigan," Brady said.

"We used the time off to think about our position and we realized Joe was right. We weren't out of the Rose Bowl picture, so the best thing we could do was stay focused."

Coming in against Penn State, Ohio State was functioning as a focused unit as well. The Buckeyes were picked to finish either second or third in the Big Ten in most preseason polls, but had thus far exceeded those expectations. They were 7-0, 4-0 in the Big Ten and ranked No. 3 in the country behind Florida State and Notre Dame, and were somehow finding ways to win.

Michigan State, which had defeated Michigan on October 9, traveled to Columbus the following week and forced five Ohio State turnovers. The Spartans had numerous chances inside Ohio State territory, but came away 28-21 losers. Other games, including a 21-12 defeat of Washington in the second game of the season, proved hazardous for the Buckeyes, but they somehow came away victorious.

People in Columbus were suddenly talking Rose Bowl again as Ohio State was off to its best start since 1979. The last time any Big Ten team had won a national championship was in 1968 when the Buckeyes capped a perfect 11-0 season with a 27-16 Rose Bowl win over Southern California. The 1993 Buckeyes literally wore that season on their sleeves as the players' jerseys had the small black numbers printed over the gray and white stripes on their home uniforms, just as they were 25 years before.

"If you would have told me that we would beat Michigan State with five turnovers, I would have said you were crazy," said Ohio State coach John Cooper, whose job had once dangled by a thread but now seemed much more secure. "There is definitely something special about this team. Up to this point, no matter the circumstances, this team seems to find a way to win.

"I know we allowed Michigan State to move the ball 12 straight times into our end of the field, but it seemed we always found a way to make the big play on defense when it had to be made."

Another memorable Ohio State win to this point was its 20-12 decision at Illinois. The Buckeyes' longest scoring drive covered 11 yards when quarterback Bobby Hoying hit star wide receiver Joey Galloway for a touchdown two plays after the Ohio State defense recovered an Illinos fumble at the Illini 11. Ohio State's only other TD came on a second-quarter fumble recovery in the end zone. Opportunistic to say the least.

Galloway was a driving force behind the Buckeyes' success with a team-leading 27 receptions for 562 yards and eight touchdowns going into the game against Penn State. Tailback Raymont Harris had rushed for 632 yards, including 311 in the last three games for Ohio State. While Hoying, a sophomore, was the Buckeyes' regular starter at quarterback, Bret Powers had established himself as one of the best backups in the nation. The senior transfer from Arizona State had completed 22 of 34 passes for 392 yards and four touchdowns through Ohio State's first six games.

"Galloway is in a class with the kids we've played from Southern Cal, Florida State and Miami," Paterno cautioned.

Two weeks before, Penn State appeared to have suffered a great letdown in its bid to make the Rose Bowl in its first year of conference existence. But the Lions were given new life when Michigan, the team that had apparently snuffed those hopes, lost in the closing seconds to Illinois. Now the setting was much clearer for the Nittany Lions. The Rose Bowl would be theirs if they could simply win the rest of the games on their schedule.

Joe Paterno didn't want to think that far down the road.

"We look at Ohio State and we know we have our hands full," Paterno said. "I think our guys have just really zeroed in on Ohio State."

Head-to-head competition was the first tie-breaker in the Big Ten's system, and if Penn State won out, it would have defeated everyone on its schedule except Michigan, who would have at least two losses. Another surprise team in the Big Ten was Wisconsin, which was quietly sneaking along with a 3-1 conference record. If the Badgers and Nittany Lions would finish in a tie for the conference lead, Penn State would get the nod for the Rose Bowl because the Big Ten's second determining factor is the team that hasn't been there over a longer period of time. Wisconsin hadn't been to the Rose Bowl since 1962, but Penn State hadn't been there since 1923 and that was before it was ever a member of the Big Ten.

The possibilities were dizzying, but as Paterno would often tell his players, that's the fun of being in a conference. Now was the time to play football and Penn State had an opportunity to prove it was better than it showed against Michigan a couple of weeks before. Ohio State, meanwhile, took the same attitude as the rest of the teams in the league.

"We will try to welcome them to the Big Ten with a loss," said Ohio State defensive tackle Dan Wilkinson, whose 6-foot-5, 310-pound frame had earned him the nickname Big Daddy. "We want to let them know the Big Ten is for real."

"We want to show them and the nation what Ohio State is capable of," tailback Raymont Harris said. "We believe we're a team to be reckoned with."

By now, Penn State was getting used to all the talk. The sentiment was pretty clear that the new guys weren't supposed to come in and walk away with a conference title.

"Coach [Paterno] told us this is the biggest game we've played in the last two, three years," Penn State fullback Brian O'Neal said. "We're in a perfect position now, even coming off the loss to Michigan."

"We're definitely thinking about the Rose Bowl," offensive guard Jeff Hartings said. "And I'm sure they don't want us to go to the Rose Bowl."

"It's put up or shut up time," Wilkinson proclaimed. "Let's get it on and see what happens."

Penn State was all for that.

OCTOBER 30, COLUMBUS, OH — As the Penn State motorcade wound its way through the snarled interstates and crowded city streets, a cold, wet snow continued to fall as it had since the early morning hours. Signs were posted everywhere, not so much to support the Buckeyes, but to further wish the Nittany Lions good luck, with just the right touch of sarcasm.

"NO MORE CUPCAKES, JOE. WELCOME TO THE BIG TEN!" was the greeting on the marquee of a downtown fitness center.

Finally, the buses reached Ohio Stadium and the team was able to make its way to the visitors' locker room amid, of course, a continuing chorus of fans clad in scarlet and gray offering every unkind greeting the Nittany Lions could have thought of.

"You got 18 minutes till the first group," Paterno reminded his squad. That meant 18 minutes until quarterbacks and special teams players were to take the field for warmups. That was the pregame method for Penn State. Times for each group were posted on some locker room chalk board and Paterno would take a glance at his own watch and then search for a clock on the wall to see if it matched his time.

The mood was quiet, as expected, and head equipment manager Tim Shope and his crew were prepared to answer all the requests for long sleeve under jerseys and tight leg warmers for those in the skill positions. It was going to be that kind of day. Cold, wet, sloppy. A Big Ten kind of day.

In front of the largest crowd ever to watch them on the road (95,060), the Nittany Lions took the opening drive right at the Buckeyes and moved 53 yards in 13 plays. Tailback Ki-Jana Carter ran for 28 yards during the drive and quarterback Kerry Collins hit two big third down passes — one to tight end Kyle Brady for 12 yards and the other to Brian O'Neal for eight. The drive stalled at the Ohio State 12 when another third-down pass from Collins fell incomplete.

Kicker Craig Fayak, who needed four points to become Penn State's all-time leading scorer, got three of them when his 29-yard field goal attempt just skipped inside the left upright to give the Lions a 3-0 lead.

Ohio State had scored on the first possession in each of its first seven games and soon made it eight in a row. The drive began when Hoying spotted fullback Jeff Cothran with a 29-yard play-action pass and ended seven plays later when Raymont Harris took a pitch to his left and made it standing up to the end zone. Penn State had a chance to snap the Buckeyes' opening series streak, but hero back Derek Bochna dropped a sure interception inside his own 20-yard line.

Penn State moved the ball effectively again on its second drive as Carter ran for 16 yards and Brady caught a 12-yarder along the left sideline. The Nittany Lions got no farther than the Ohio State 34, however, and Fayak pulled his team to within one as he connected on a 49-yard field goal that just made it over the crossbar.

The Penn State defense had played spectacularly through much of the season, but it suffered a great mental lapse on the Buckeyes' next drive that seemed to turn the tide for the entire game. On one occasion, Hoying hit flanker Chris Sanders for a first down on third-and-9 to keep the drive alive, but the big blow came a few plays later.

Ohio State was flagged for an offensive foul that created a third-and-23 situation at the Penn State 42-yard line. Hoying dropped back and immediately faced the Lions' pass rush that had registered 18 sacks to that point. Hoying eluded one tackle, then another, and spotted Sanders alone for a 32-yard completion and a first down at the Penn State 10.

The Buckeyes drove to the Nittany Lions' 2-yard line before the drive fizzled and they had to settle for a 10-6 lead after kicker Tim Williams' 22-yard field goal on the first play of the second quarter.

Collins threw the first of his four interceptions on the Nittany Lions' next series and Ohio State wasted little time in taking advantage. The Buckeyes changed quarterbacks — which was not unusual in their scheme of things — but the result was pretty much the same.

Bret Powers took his turn under center for Ohio State and promptly drove his team to the Penn State 25-yard line in seven plays. Harris had been gaining success up the middle against the Penn State defensive line and when the Lions stacked against the run, Powers offered a fake handoff, rolled to his right and floated a touchdown pass to Galloway on a perfectly-timed crossing pattern that had frozen the Nittany Lion linebackers and left cornerback Shelly Hammonds flat-footed.

"That was just a blown coverage," Hammonds said. "The safety was supposed to be back there in two-deep coverage, but he bit on the play-action."

Penn State was down 17-6 at halftime, but the fault did not lie entirely on its defense. The Nittany Lions couldn't sustain a drive on offense and had to settle for a field goal on their only foray inside the Buckeyes' 20-yard line. The only statistic Penn State led in at the halfway point was rushing yards (89-82), but that total was amassed entirely by Carter.

Inside the Penn State locker room there was still a tremendous amount of optimism at halftime. Joe Paterno went from the offensive side of the room to the defensive side making sure no one threw in the towel.

"No one gives up!" was the battle cry from several corners of the room. Defensive tackle Lou Benfatti, ever the vocal leader, had his say. "Now we're ready!" he said repeatedly. "Now we're ready!"

"When we were in that locker room at halftime, I really thought we were going to win," guard Mike Malinoski said. "I thought we were finally going to bounce back and win one. We were all jacked up and still had a lot of confidence."

Then came the back breaker.

Ohio State took the second half kickoff at its own 32-yard line and began a march that many thought would lead the Buckeyes straight to Pasadena. Nine plays; 68 yards; zero passes. The Buckeyes went straight at the Nittany Lions and opened holes for Harris to gain 57 of his game-high 151 rushing yards. Fullback Butler By'not'e accounted for the last four yards to give the Buckeyes a 24-6 lead and at the same time douse all hopes of a Penn State comeback.

"They held the ball for like five minutes," Malinoski said. "It was really tough. It might have taken us out of our game plan."

"The first drive of the second half really put the icing on the cake," Ohio State coach John Cooper said. "But a lot of credit goes to our defensive football staff and team. Any time you can hold a football team like Penn State to two field goals, obviously you have to be very, very happy about that."

"We came out of the locker room fired up, and they came out and made a statement," Paterno said.

Penn State could have had more than six points, but a late drive to the Ohio State 6-yard line resulted in a Stephen Pitts' fumble that erased any further chances of a Nittany Lion score. The Lions crossed midfield four other times, but were turned away by mistakes. Kerry Collins was a mere 23 of 39 for 122 yards. He refused to say he wasn't ready because he was still learning his role after backing up John Sacca through the first part of the season. "If I'm not ready now, I'll never be ready," the junior redshirt quarterback said.

"The biggest disappointment about this football game is that we lost," defensive tackle Tyoka Jackson said. "They [Ohio State] played great football and we played terrible football. That was probably the worst game I ever played. They ran right at me and kicked my butt."

"There's no excuses," Paterno offered. "They're an awfully good team. Their offensive line is stronger than we are. They just kicked our butts."

The line play over the last two games left the Penn State coaches looking at the one gray area that seemed to be haunting the Nittany Lions in their new surroundings. Ohio State averaged 292.2 pounds on its offensive line, which was only slightly more than Michigan had up front two weeks before. Penn State's defensive unit went into its two biggest games of the season with 18 sacks. When the two games were completed, that total remained the same.

Defensive tackle Eric Clair was one of those that was physically manhandled by the Ohio State offensive line.

"They kicked us all over the field," Clair said. "They were well coached and they did things the way you're supposed to do them and we didn't."

Lou Benfatti tried to sound upbeat about the defensive line's play, but soon corrected himself. "We came out strong," he said. Then he stopped and looked to the ground dejectedly. "I don't know how strong we came out."

Penn State, which dropped to 5-2 overall and 2-2 in the conference, would have to face the reality that its 24-6 loss would not only erase just about any hopes of an inaugural trip to the Rose Bowl, but it would breed further allegations that the Nittany Lions could no longer win the big games.

"That's something we'll have to live with for now," Kerry Collins said. "You lie in the bed that you make."

One columnist wrote that Penn State would not represent the Big Ten well whether it played in the Rose Bowl, Citrus Bowl, or the Poulan Weedeater Bowl. But the players wanted to hear none of that.

"I'm not worried about these two losses," said tailback Ki-Jana Carter, who rushed for 123 yards, his sixth 100-yard effort of the season. "We'll see what our team is really all about. It's disappointing because we wanted to come in here and hopefully get a win and get back into the Big Ten race. I played my hardest. I think the rest of the team did. We just came up short."

"We made enough mistakes in the last two games to last a whole season," Shelly Hammonds said. "Joe is upset and everyone on the team is upset."

It is rare to see Joe Paterno upset after a game. Upset, as in disappointed with a loss, sometimes. But then he only hangs his head and does his best to answer the media's questions as to what happened. Defeat with effort is something Paterno can accept. Quitting in defeat is something the 67-year-old coach has never tolerated. As the players left the Ohio Stadium field that soggy Saturday afternoon, Paterno felt it was time to take hold of the situation.

One by one, the Nittany Lions filed into their locker room. Some appeared stunned in front of their lockers. Others carried a sullen frown. A few more wiped away the dirt from their brows and began to undress in the quiet, funereal-like atmosphere. But the silence lasted for just a very short time.

The outer doors to the locker room opened with a bang and in walked Paterno carrying the towel he had been using to keep his thick glasses from steaming up. He seemed, for a second, like he didn't know how to feel. His head turned one way, then another. Finally, he stormed into the center of the room and ordered his players to gather around him. A few took their time and the coach wasted little time in letting them know he was serious.

"GET OVER HERE!" he screamed to those who dared to drag their feet. One player let out an obscenity — not directed toward Paterno, but in remorse over the outcome of the game. Paterno was quick to let him know he didn't appreciate such language.

"That kinda crap is not gonna help us," he said to the player. Then he slammed his fist on a nearby table. "I'm mad," he continued, looking around the room. "I'm mad because we stunk up the joint. I'm mad 'cause I know we're better than both of those teams we lost to. I *know* we're a better team. But we killed ourselves and never gave ourselves a chance.

"You guys gotta set your goals straight right now. Do you think I'm gonna let what happened last year happen again? Like hell I am. We're gonna win the rest of our games starting next week. I'm not gonna let last year happen all over again. I'm *not* gonna do it. You have to decide whether you want to take some pride in yourselves."

Just as quickly, Paterno walked out of the picture and left his players to ponder their short-term futures. Amid that quiet, something positive seemed to arise after all. Maybe the players finally believed that their coach was in it for the long haul. Perhaps they should join him.

Slowly but surely, the quiet turned to normal conversation. Only the reporters who went about their business of meeting deadlines reminded the players that Penn State's Rose Bowl hopes seemed to border on the impossible at this point. But the players reminded those scribes that the beauty of conference play is the thrill of the competition. There were other goals to shoot for and, yes, even the Rose Bowl still wasn't out of their grasp.

"We weren't going to quit," Kerry Collins said. "You could see from that point on that there was a challenge given to us. We had a long way to go and we wanted to find out what we were made of."

"There's no doubt about it," Kyle Brady said. "We're going to see what we're made of right now. We're going to see if we're a bunch of losers that will fall by the wayside, or if we'll suck it up and prove to everyone we belong."

Penn State had four weeks left to prove that very point.

12

INDIANA:
Season at
the Crossroads

The fork in the road came in the Nittany Lions' eighth game of the season. It had come to the point where all the old cliches could be pulled out of the closet and dusted off for review. "Put up or shut up;" "do or die situation." You name it, the players could say it. And it all seemed to revert back to a season ago.

"When we lost to Miami last season, it tore into everybody," Penn State defensive end Eric Ravotti said. "One person came into the locker room after we lost and said, 'Well, not much to play for now.' Everybody's attitude just went down hill from there."

Penn State was 5-0 when its bubble was burst by Miami in 1992. A whole week was spent discussing what happened in the loss, and why it happened. The only problem was Boston College, a team which the Nittany Lions kind of forgot to think about and the Eagles made them pay with a 35-32 upset. Those two losses, back-to-back, triggered a 2-5 skid for Penn State, and the Lions limped home to a disappointing 7-5 finish.

How eerie the circumstances had become. A 5-0 start in 1992 followed by two disappointing losses. A year later, five wins in a row to start the season. The biggest game of the season to follow on national television. Another disappointing Penn State loss. Two weeks later, the Lions are 5-2 and searching for answers.

"We just had to find ourselves," Ravotti said after his team's second loss of 1993. "I didn't worry about last year too much. The questions came up a lot, but I felt this team had too much character to let such a thing happen again."

Penn State has always been a football institution that finds itself in the spotlight. Its storied coach has a lot to do with that, but so does the consistency that follows this football team year after year. The downer of a season that plagued the Nittany Lions in 1992 had suddenly become a national topic. It could conceivably happen again, but Joe Paterno was bound and determined to see that it didn't.

"We kind of had a letdown in our last season as an independent," Paterno said of the '92 season. "This first season in the Big Ten was going to be very critical for us because we would have the opportunity to immediately establish ourselves as one of the best in the league. Or. . . ."

It was difficult for Paterno to think of the "or," but it was there in black and white. Penn State could either reestablish itself in a hurry with a successful Big Ten debut, or it could slip to mediocrity and lose the slightest amount of respect that any of the other schools in its new conference may have harbored.

How much of a factor could it be to start out so-so in your first season in a new conference? The psyche can sometimes be severely damaged when a team finds those special ways to lose in spooky, repeated fashion. The minds that once said, "We're gonna win this thing," are suddenly asking, "How did we lose another one?"

Losing breeds lack of confidence, and the cycle begins to form. Fan appreciation begins to dwindle when the losses outweigh the wins, and the top recruits are inclined to give less thought to a team that may be on its way down.

"We had to play scared for a while," Paterno said. "The prospects were there for us to totally crumble. Those last four games would be some of the most critical that Penn State had ever played."

Penn State's now critical game against Indiana did not seem as crucial at the beginning of the season. Like several others in the conference, the Hoosiers (7-1 overall, 4-1 in the conference) had found themselves in the middle of the Rose Bowl hunt — a place they had not been since their last Big Ten championship in 1967.

Penn State had fallen to 19th in the national rankings, while Indiana had climbed to 17th. The Hoosiers made that climb by highlighting defense. They were third in the nation in scoring defense, having allowed just 9.3 points per game, and were sixth in total defense (266.9 yards per game, including 114 against the run).

What's more, Penn State suddenly had several reasons to think it might not be as good as its 5-0 start had indicated. The season started with optimism because of the way Penn State's passing game had clicked on all cylinders in a 38-20 win over Big Ten foe Minnesota. Since then, however, the Nittany Lions' passing game had dropped to 10th in the league.

The Nittany Lions gained a measure of revenge in their 21-20 victory over USC in Game 2, but they had to make a stand on a two-point conversion attempt against a team that had lost to North Carolina, Notre Dame and Arizona by a combined score of 100-29.

A victory at Iowa looked good at the time for Penn State, but the Hawkeyes kept right on losing over the next four weeks and were outscored in those games, 113-30. Rutgers and Maryland were as hapless as their scores had indicated against Penn State, and were never much of a challenge.

Penn State lost to Michigan, which is never usually a tragedy, but the Wolverines then lost to Illinois and Wisconsin and dropped out of sight in the conference standings. Ohio State pounced on the Lions' shortcomings and exploited their weaknesses for all of a nationwide audience to see.

All of the above details would be studied and scrutinized even more if Penn State dropped its third straight game to Indiana. The Nittany Lions needed a win in the worst way possible.

"You lose two around here and it's rough, because we're not used to losing," defensive end Tyoka Jackson said. "It was time for a gut-check for every single member of this football team."

NOVEMBER 6, UNIVERSITY PARK, PA — As good as Indiana's defense was, its offense was supposed to be equally as bad. It appeared the estimated 91,000 fans who showed up for Penn State's annual homecoming weekend would be in for a defensive battle — artistic or not. The game would have its artistic moments, but at times, the defenses on both sides decided to take a rest.

Indiana took an early 3-0 lead when freshman kicker Bill Manolopoulos connected from 44 yards out with 9:38 remaining in the first quarter to cap a 12-play, 57-yard drive.

Penn State answered just over four minutes later when tailback Ki-Jana Carter completed a 10-play, 70-yard drive with a three-yard touchdown run. Carter, who broke four tackles to get in the end zone, started the drive with a 14-yard carry on Penn State's first play from scrimmage. Craig Fayak added a 31-yard field goal later in the first quarter, and when linebacker Brian Gelzheiser recovered an Indiana fumble, Carter helped the Nittany Lions convert the turnover into points bulling his way to a 22-yard touchdown run with only 43 seconds left in the quarter.

Indiana had allowed only two opponents to score 17 points in an entire game all season, but it trailed after one quarter against Penn State, 17-3. Quarterback John Paci, however, never lost faith in his team's ability to rally.

"We believe we are a great passing team," Paci said. "Our stats don't show that, but we just needed to get on track. Today, I think we did that."

Not only did Paci get his passing game going in the second quarter, he put it into high gear.

Following Carter's second TD, Paci completed four straight passes —three of them to junior wide receiver Thomas Lewis, who was just beginning his record-setting day. Paci and Lewis combined on a 42-yard bomb to put the Hoosiers inside the Penn State 10-yard line and two plays later, the pair hooked up for a seven-yard touchdown in the right corner of the end zone.

Penn State set up for a 32-yard field goal attempt on its next drive, but holder Chip LaBarca tried a fake, only to be dropped for a four-yard loss by the Indiana defense. Paci then guided the Hoosiers 74 yards in 10 plays, the last one a two-yard touchdown pass to tight end Ross Hales.

The score was tied at halftime, 17-17, and according to Paterno, a good third quarter loomed very large if Penn State was to come out on top.

"We have some kids I think that have been doubting themselves a little bit," Paterno said. "They had to come in at halftime — when the other guy was on the move with some momentum — they had to pick themselves up and turn it up a notch."

Penn State took charge from the second-half kickoff as Collins led the offense 84 yards in 11 plays. Fullback Brian Milne carried the final two yards for the score and Fayak's point after touchdown made it 24-17, Penn State, with 10:38 to go in the third quarter.

Ki-Jana Carter had suffered a hip pointer midway through the second quarter and although he played sparingly through the rest of the game, the Nittany Lions' leading rusher still finished with 138 yards on 23 carries. Carter piled up 31 yards on Penn State's late scoring drive in the third quarter, including 25 on a breakaway to the Indiana 24-yard line.

"I was surprised," Carter said of his performance against the Hoosiers. "I thought I might be close to 100 yards, but it didn't seem like I had that many long runs."

Collins completed the 53-yard drive with a 10-yard touchdown pass to wideout Bobby Engram to help the Nittany Lions grab a 31-17 lead with 1:58 remaining in the third quarter. Collins bounced back from his dreadful performance at Ohio State with an 18-for-29 performance against Indiana. The redshirt junior threw for 215 yards, two touchdowns and no interceptions.

"I think the kids got a little feel for him today," Paterno said of Collins. "He needed a game where he was under pressure and he had to keep bringing them back."

Yes, Penn State would have to rally again. The Nittany Lions had blown one 14-point lead and were soon about to let another one slip away. As much as the third quarter belonged to Penn State, Indiana made its mark in the fourth. Down by 14, Paci got his Hoosiers rolling in a most unusual way.

Penn State appeared to be in great position when punter V.J. Muscillo pinned the Hoosiers at their own 1-yard line just one minute into the fourth quarter. But the complexion changed on the very next play. Paci faked a handoff up the middle on first down and let go of a bullet to Thomas Lewis at the Indiana 37-yard line.

Lewis, who had faced single coverage all day from the Nittany Lions, caught the ball in full stride, and hung onto it even though cornerback Shelly Hammonds got a fingertip on it.

"I just tried to make a play on the ball," Hammonds said. "Maybe I should have just tackled him, but I thought I could get to the ball. I tipped it to him and he made a great play."

Lewis' play was so great, he took the pass 99 yards for a touchdown and Indiana was down by only seven. The 6-foot-2 wideout graciously accepted the Nittany Lions' single coverage all afternoon by catching 12 passes for two touchdowns and a league-record 285 yards. His 99-yard touchdown also tied a conference record.

"I got more single coverage [here] than I ever got in my whole entire life," Lewis said afterward.

Six minutes later, Paci had his team driving again and the Hoosiers erased their second 14-point deficit when the quarterback scored on a fourth-down option from the 1-yard line with 7:42 remaining in the game.

If Collins was ever going to pick a time to be at his best, this was it. His team had just squandered another two-touchdown lead and the fans were looking for someone to break the Nittany Lions out of their two-game slump. First, the Lions took advantage of a short kickoff by gaining possession at their own 42-yard line. Then Collins went to work.

He spotted Engram for a completion over the middle to the Indiana 45. Two plays later, Collins rolled to his right and hit Engram again cutting across the middle. The play was designed to pick up 20, maybe 25 yards, but when the redshirt sophomore receiver turned the corner, it became a foot race that Engram would not lose. The 45-yard touchdown play gave the Nittany Lions a 38-31 lead with six minutes and 25 seconds remaining in the game.

"This is a really big day for me," Collins told reporters after the game. "A lot of people were questioning what I was doing, and there were a lot of critics out there. There were some tough circumstances, but I feel good that I came in and did a good job."

Since this prospective battle of defenses had somehow turned into an offensive showcase, it was only fitting that the outcome would be decided on the game's last offensive drive.

Paci, who came into the contest rated as the second-lowest quarterback in the conference, threw for 379 yards and three touchdowns. He had his team on the march again when he let go of his only mistake of the game. Indiana converted two third downs and a fourth down to reach the Penn State 37-yard line with less than two minutes remaining in the game.

On first down, Paci's pass was too long for split end Eric Baety. He missed tight end Dan Thompson on second down, and on third down, Paci eluded a heavy rush from blitzing linebacker Rob Holmberg, scrambled to his left and let go of a pass to the sure-handed Lewis.

The pass was thrown in desperation and Penn State's defensive back, Tony Pittman, intercepted it at his own 7-yard line. His 29-yard return allowed Collins some running room, with which he converted a first down and was then able to run out the clock.

"We were in man coverage and as I turned, the guy made a post move," Pittman said of his game-saving interception. "I saw the quarterback in trouble because he was under a lot of pressure. It wasn't a very difficult play to make, I just happened to be in the right place at the right time."

"It was every kid's dream," Paci said of Indiana's final drive. "Playing at Penn State in front of 96,000 people. We came down. I threw the interception and I stopped the drive. It's disappointing."

"You think you've got it and then you haven't got it," was how Paterno described the back-and-forth scoring. "I didn't think we could get that many points against them. We played much better offensively than I thought we would."

"To be honest with you, there were more points on the board than I thought there would be, too," Indiana head coach Bill Mallory agreed.

In recent years, the Nittany Lions were being chastised for not having what it takes to win the big games. Lack of imagination on offense. No heart on defense. The critics said it all. But in many of the players' eyes, there was no bigger game than the one they had just played against Indiana.

"This game was very pivotal," Collins said. "It appeared to a lot of people that we were about to do the same thing we did last year. But we knew otherwise and we weren't ready to fold our tents just yet. We still have a long way to go, but this is the kind of game we needed, against a very good team, to restore our confidence."

"I think the second was about as important a second half as we've had around here in a long time," Paterno said. "I thought the kids went out that second half and played really hard football, particularly in the third quarter. I thought that was a big, big quarter for them. I think they found out a little bit about themselves."

One of the biggest spokesmen for the Nittany Lions over the past couple of weeks had been defensive end Eric Ravotti. A three-time letterman, Ravotti chose to sit out the 1992 season so he'd have a better opportunity as a regular on Penn State's first Big Ten defensive unit. He had registered 8.5 sacks over his three previous seasons and was expected to be a major force for the Nittany Lions in 1993.

Ravotti had lived up to those expectations by helping the defense register 20 sacks for 166 yards lost through the first eight games. His total of four sacks was second highest on the team, and it was Ravotti who forced an Iowa fumble that led to a Penn State touchdown in the Lions' 31-0 shutout over the Hawkeyes. He also caused a fumble against Michigan that was later ruled an incomplete pass. The Wolverines turned the questionable call into a touchdown that eventually propelled their victory over the Nittany Lions.

As Penn State struggled to maintain its 14-point lead midway through the second quarter against Indiana, Ravotti began feeling light-headed while standing on the sideline. He sat down on the bench and suddenly lost consciousness. Dr. Wayne Sebastianelli, Penn State's director of athletic medicine, immediately came to Ravotti's aid and said the player had remained unconscious for "about six or seven minutes."

"He slipped into what is called a grand mal seizure," Sebastianelli told the media later. "That is a condition in which the muscles of the body involuntarily contract."

Ravotti was taken from the field on a cart, and admitted to nearby Centre Community Hospital for tests. He was described as alert and talking at the hospital, the most important thing on his mind being whether Penn State won the game or not. He had no history of seizures before, according to Sebastianelli, and had no history of blood sugar problems such as diabetes. The doctor said a recent viral infection "may have lowered his seizure threshold."

Sebastianelli said such an episode didn't necessarily indicate a major problem, but doctors at the hospital felt it was serious enough to warrant further testing. A CAT scan performed at the hospital found nothing wrong, and Ravotti was to undergo a battery of neurological tests at the beginning of the new week to determine what may have caused the seizure.

"A neurologist will need to study the electrical activity in his head to see if there is any abnormal activity," Sebastianelli told the press. "In layman's terms, a 'short circuit.' Sometimes that can jump start the brain and cause a seizure. But without a [medical] history and without a major head injury, we really can't say that it's something permanent for him. Clearly, we have to work it up before we let him participate again."

Sebastianelli also ruled out the possibility that the seizure was caused by contact during the game that might have caused head trauma.

"We just want him to take it slow and make sure he's going to be OK," the doctor cautioned.

It appeared Ravotti would miss at least the first of three remaining games on the Nittany Lions' schedule. These would seem to provide all the challenges Penn State could afford to take on. Illinois was next for the Lions at Beaver Stadium, and the team was well aware of the Illini's upset over Michigan only a couple of weeks before — at Michigan. Then, the Nittany Lions would hit the road for their last two games.

They would travel to Northwestern, which was winless, but seemingly didn't lack the animosity toward Penn State that other schools in the Big Ten shared. Finally, a fledgling rivalry with Michigan State would begin in Lansing. This was another school that upset the Michigan Wolverines, and also gave Ohio State all the fits it could handle before bowing to defeat.

These games would provide a further barometer toward the Nittany Lions' success in their first year in the Big Ten just as much as the losses to Michigan and Ohio State did. Maybe even more so because, just like it did in the Indiana game, Penn State had to find out just what kind of fortitude it had inside its system. Indiana was only the first step in finding out whether 1992 could be totally forgotten.

"The Indiana game was a big one for us," hero back Derek Bochna said. "Losing that one would have set our program way back. In fact, that was a game we probably would have lost last year."

Instead, Penn State responded to its mid-season shortcomings with a win. It would take a continued effort to gain back the respect it had lost, but bit by bit, that effort was about to come forth.

13

The Pressure's Still On

One thing about the Big Ten Conference in Penn State's first season of football competition, there were no sure bets. Nothing came easy to any of the 11 teams in the conference. While Penn State was doing everything possible to hang on in its victory over Indiana; the league's only undefeated team, Ohio State, was fighting for its Rose Bowl hopes at Wisconsin. The Badgers were a team none of the experts reckoned with at the beginning of the 1993 season, but at 4-1 in the conference, they suddenly found themselves with just as much right as any team to think they could capture the conference title.

Penn State was right in the middle of the pack and needed some divine intervention to keep alive its bid for the Rose Bowl. The Nittany Lions needed a Wisconsin win over Ohio State, plus another loss or two from the Buckeyes just to have a chance. Anything else just wouldn't cut it. The Badgers were doing their part as they held a 14-7 lead with about five minutes left in the game.

Ohio State was in further trouble as it started a drive from its own 1-yard line, but it took just four plays for star receiver Joey Galloway to haul in a 26-yard touchdown pass to pull the Buckeyes to within one. Ohio State coach John Cooper didn't hesitate in going for the extra point instead of a two-point conversion with 3:48 remaining, as he figured his team was playing well enough to get the ball back.

Wisconsin used its ball-control offense and the running of conference-leading tailback Brent Moss to move to the Buckeyes' 15-yard line. Freshman kicker Rick Schnetzky lined up to kick the game-winning field goal, but Ohio State's Marlon Kerner broke through the line and blocked the kick with seven seconds left to preserve the tie for the Buckeyes and their conference lead.

Even Northwestern, which was 0-6 in the conference, supplied excitement in the Big Ten that day as the Wildcats took Michigan State down to the wire before falling, 31-29.

That's the way the Big Ten had shaped up all season. Upsets, upsets everywhere; but not a clear-cut leader to spare. Actually, Ohio State was that leader for much of the season, but there was still a chance the Buckeyes could fall from the good graces of the Columbus faithful.

If Ohio State would happen to tumble from its No. 1 position in the conference, Illinois was one of the teams that was within earshot of taking over. In fact, the Illini looked like a carbon copy of the Indiana team Penn State had faced just a week before — only a little bit better, perhaps. Indiana came into University Park with one of the nation's top ten defenses, Penn State solved it. Illinois came in with the No. 3 defense in the country, which had allowed opponents only 85.4 yards per game on the ground.

The Illini defense was led by a trio of linebackers that had even the Penn State fans wondering about in awe. The Nittany Lion football program is well documented for its ability to produce great linebackers, so the appearance of John Holocek, Dana Howard and Simeon Rice would surely give the Penn State fans an opportunity to compare these Illinois stars to some of the heroes from Penn State history.

Howard and Holocek, both juniors, came into the game with 100 and 86 tackles, respectively, while Rice, a sophomore whose official position listing was "rush" linebacker, was credited with 64 tackles and a team-leading eight sacks.

"If there is a better rush linebacker in the country, I haven't seen him," Illinois coach Lou Tepper said. "When we need a big play, he makes it."

Illinois' fourth linebacker, sophomore Kevin Hardy, didn't gain as much press as the others, but his 63 tackles — including

13 in the Illini's 24-21 upset over Michigan — and two sacks did the talking for him. The matchup of Illinois' linebackers and Penn State's running game would be something to watch, considering the Lions were averaging 253 yards on the ground.

"Defensively, they're outstanding," Penn State coach Joe Paterno said of Illinois. "There isn't anybody in the country playing better defense than Illinois is right now. They hustle and hit and fly to the ball. People who like defensive football will enjoy watching these kids play.

"Their linebackers are super. The outside guys are so quick and the inside guys are aggressive. I haven't seen four better linebackers in a long, long time. It's hard to believe they've lost four games."

Paterno went on to say that Illinois was a couple of unfortunate plays away from being 7-2 instead of 5-4, and that its defense was even better than Indiana's.

Tepper was quick to remember Paterno's penchant for throwing accolades at everyone but himself, especially the competition.

"You've got to remember that Joe praises everybody's defense," Tepper said in the week leading up to the game. "My feet were off the ground when he said that about our team. But actually, Indiana's statistics are better than ours."

Although the Illini were 5-4, they had a 5-1 conference record and still raised legitimate hopes of making their own plans to spend New Year's Day in Pasadena. The game was pivotal for both teams because Penn State, at 3-2 in the conference, was still looking for conference respect and could gain a decent position in the final bowl standings with a win.

Even though John Sacca had long since departed Penn State, the quarterback situation continued to plague Joe Paterno. Kerry Collins was his man as the starter, there was no doubt about that. But Paterno also knew he was walking on eggshells with the backup situation. The head coach wanted very badly to save sophomore Wally Richardson's eligibility by redshirting him this season.

There were three games, plus a possible bowl game, left and Paterno was continually asked the question of who would replace Collins in the event of an injury. Richardson had been listed on all the depth charts as Collins' backup ever since Sacca's departure, but with each passing game, Paterno felt a little bit closer to saving Richardson for the extra year of eligibility.

That left a true freshman as the only other quarterback listed on Penn State's roster. Mike McQueary was a big, strong quarterback, who hailed from nearby State College High School. He seemed capable of playing in a backup role, but fans, perhaps more than visiting reporters, knew of Paterno's disdain for playing freshmen. And this time, the fans were right on the money.

"Playing McQueary at about that time never crossed my mind," Paterno said. "I don't think it would've been fair to throw him into a game under those types of conditions. If at all possible, we wanted to let him get as much observation time in as possible. Even if it took the whole year. I didn't think we were in such a sticky situation that we had to put in a freshman."

Wait a minute. Your original choice for starting quarterback quits the team, you're one blind-sided tackle away from having to fritter away a kid's year of eligibility with just a couple of games remaining, and you're not in a sticky situation?

"We talk about [the quarterback situation] every Monday," Paterno said. "Is there somebody on the squad we ought to work out at quarterback? If something happened early against Illinois, then what do you do? Do you go to Wally? I haven't even talked to Wally about it."

Paterno talked often about not knowing what his contingency plan would be. But the coaches did strike up one possibility and, as ridiculous as it may have sounded, there was some profound logic to its background.

The Penn State coaches had a quarterback waiting in the wings after all. And they only had to go as far as the kicking field to get him. Craig Fayak was recruited as a kicker at Penn State. He had a career total of 20 field goals at Belle Vernon High School in Pittsburgh, and in his last two seasons he scored 226 points. Only 140 of those points, however, were from his powerful and accurate right leg. The others came from the 21 touchdowns he was accountable for either on the ground or through the air as Belle Vernon's starting quarterback.

"Right now, Fayak could go in and play, and do a good job," Paterno said. "He's pretty good as a quarterback. Things change every week, but basically, if the situation came up, Fayak would probably play."

The possibility was there a week before, too, as Fayak practiced all week at running Penn State's offense and he apparently would have gone in if an emergency developed against Indiana.

While Penn State explored the possibility of playing its kicker at quarterback, it also had to accept that one of its defensive ends would not be playing at all against Illinois. Eric Ravotti, who had suffered the seizure in the second quarter of the Nittany Lions' game against Indiana, was advised by doctors to sit out one more game. It was disappointing for the senior to miss his final home game in a Penn State uniform, but the Lions introduced him with his parents and the rest of the senior players.

"The neurologist gave me the okay to resume lifting and running," Ravotti said. "I tried to get them to clear me for this week, but they told me it's not in my best interests."

Ravotti was to take an anti-seizure medication for the rest of the season "for precautionary reasons," but was cleared for the following week's game at Northwestern and was assured there would be no danger in playing again. "The chances of it happening again are slim," Ravotti said.

He had been running a fever before the Indiana game, but didn't feel the illness would slow him down on the field. It was in the second quarter when he collapsed on the bench due to what was later diagnosed as a low blood sugar count caused by a virus.

"I didn't feel it until I sat down on the bench," he said. "That's when my head started to spin."

Ravotti began convulsing as he fell to the ground and his family jumped the Beaver Stadium railing when they noticed what was happening. When he bit his tongue, their panic was even more intensified.

"They were an emotional wreck," Ravotti said a few days after the incident. "Even a lot of the guys on the team were scared. I guess it was a pretty violent scene with people trying to hold me down."

Whatever he wasn't told, Ravotti could only guess the rest because he had no memory of the actual events after the seizure.

"I didn't remember anything until I woke up an hour or so later in the hospital," he said. What he found out — by his own request — was that Penn State was ahead 31-17 at the time and had later won the game, 38-31. He wasn't told the part about

Indiana's rally that tied it at 31-31 midway through the fourth quarter.

"In my weakened state, I don't know if I could have taken that," Ravotti chuckled.

So, Penn State would have to go on without its own expert "rush" specialist, and with a kicker who could throw an occasional pass or two. It sounded like a baseball team that was using its utility man to pitch in a blowout, but the Nittany Lions were in a battle for respect and dignity, and were serious about every step they were taking.

NOVEMBER 13, UNIVERSITY PARK, PA — Illinois was a team that had averaged only eight points in its first three games — all non-conference losses. Coach Lou Tepper went with his own quarterback change and the Illini upped their points per game average to 26. Sophomore Johnny Johnson took over during the fourth game of the season — and first conference game — and led the Illini to a win at Purdue. Turnovers hurt in a loss to Ohio State, but Johnson excited the Illinois fans with four straight wins, including a last-second touchdown to lift his team past Michigan and a 14-point second-half comeback against Minnesota.

Once again, Penn State had a hot team to deal with, but both teams would have to deal with the cold, rainy weather. It was a late afternoon start to accommodate ABC television and that only gave the field more time to absorb the moisture from an all-day rain. At times it was a torrential downpour as both teams would find the traction less than adequate.

Hanging onto the ball is another difficult task when the rain is coming down in sheets. Illinois found that out on its very first series as the Illini's leading rusher, Ty Douthard, fumbled at his own 40-yard line. Penn State defensive back Marlon Forbes picked up the loose ball and returned it to the Illini 32.

Penn State defensive tackle Lou Benfatti made the big hit on the play after smelling out the trap play as he smothered Douthard before the play gained any momentum.

"Lou did most of the work on that one," linebacker Brian Gelzheiser said. "He got off his block really quick and just stripped the ball."

It was the first of many big plays for a Nittany Lion defense that was a bit embarrassed after allowing Indiana to rally from a 14-point deficit the week before not once, but twice.

Penn State was eager to see what it could do offensively against Illinois' much talked about defense and it wasted little time in making something happen. Tailback Mike Archie took a handoff from quarterback Kerry Collins, found a hole through the line and carried 22 yards to the Illinois goal line. Archie's carry covered the entire 22 yards Penn State needed for the touchdown, but as he hit the goal line, he was stripped of the ball by Illinois strong safety Mike Russell. An alert Chip LaBarca stole it away from defensive tackle Chad Copher in the end zone for the touchdown, which meant the senior wide receiver was credited with a rushing touchdown of zero yards. Craig Fayak added the extra point and it was 7-0, Lions.

The Illini took a page from the Minnesota game plan against Penn State during their next series. In that game way back at the beginning of the season, Gophers' coach Jim Wacker called for a fake punt in the fourth quarter that failed miserably and ultimately led to a Penn State score.

Illinois faced a fourth-and-five at its own 41-yard line when coach Lou Tepper decided now would be a good time for the same play. He may have fooled the Nittany Lion defense for a split second, but it appeared that tight end Dave Olson was also fooled on the play. The punter-turned-quarterback, Forry Wells, took the snap and threw a pass in the driving rain that sailed high and wide of Olson, who turned around too late to see where the ball had gone.

"Who was the dummy who called that one?" Tepper asked in jest. "It was me. It was something I thought we could have, so I went with the call."

"For a split second our defense was fooled by the fake," Gelzheiser said. "But we reacted fast and our guys were able to get all over their receivers."

Now Penn State had a first down on the Illini 41 and it took six plays for the Nittany Lions to cover the distance. Archie again covered most of the ground work as he chewed up 29 yards on four carries. A key eight-yard completion from Collins to LaBarca set up fullback Brian Milne's four-yard touchdown run with 4:15 remaining in the first quarter to give the Lions a 14-0 lead.

The Nittany Lions lost a key performer in the series as regular tailback Ki-Jana Carter pulled a calf muscle and was forced to miss the rest of the game. The redshirt sophomore had rushed for over 100 yards in seven of Penn State's first eight games, but today's spotlight belonged to Archie.

Penn State's defense did its impression of a stone wall again on the Illini's next drive as it held on three plays and forced another special teams gaffe. Illinois kicked the ball away, but Penn State's Bobby Engram fielded the low punt at his own 39-yard line, found a couple of holes and raced 46 yards to the Illinois 15. To that point, Illinois had allowed opposing punt returners a grand total of 44 yards all season.

"That punt return was a big play," Tepper said.

It took Archie one play to carry the Lions into the end zone as he received a huge block from guard Jeff Hartings that opened the path to the goal line. LaBarca didn't have to recover this one and Fayak's kick made it 21-0 with just over three minutes still remaining in the first quarter.

The defense wasn't finished as it came up big on yet another Illinois possession. Reserve defensive end Jeff Perry, subbing for Eric Ravotti, sacked Illini quarterback Johnny Johnson at the Penn State 43-yard line, causing a fumble.

In the pouring rain, it appeared no one wanted to get a handle on the ball as a couple of Penn State players got their hands on it in the backfield. Finally, linebacker Terry Killens picked it up in full stride at mid-field. Killens looked as though he was on his way to a touchdown when he suddenly tripped himself up around the 30-yard line. He lost his balance and was finally brought down at the Illinois 24.

"Jeff got to their quarterback before he really got a chance to set up," Gelzheiser said. "We weren't in a blitz, we just got to him with a tough four-man rush. At that point, our defense was on a roll."

The offense was doing its job to capitalize on the Illinois misfortunes as Archie carried five straight times — the last one for nine yards and a TD — to give the Nittany Lions a 28-0 lead against a stunned Illinois defense.

"I don't have any doubts about the intensity of our defense," Tepper said. "But I don't think it played very well in the first half."

Neither did most of the 90,000 or so fans who braved the miserable weather to see Penn State's last home game of 1993. By the end of the second quarter, there was a steady stream of red tail lights along the highways leading out of Beaver Stadium as most seemed satisfied that Penn State could hang onto this one safely.

Illinois finally got something out of its offense in the last few minutes of the first half as Penn State seemed to go into football's much-maligned prevent defense that seems to only provide the opposition with a better opportunity to score. Johnson ended a six-play, 43-yard drive with a 22-yard touchdown pass to wideout Gary Voelker. It was 28-7, Lions, at halftime and the Illini would manage one more touchdown with 1:40 left in the third quarter to account for the 28-14 final score.

Two players stood tall for Penn State when faced with a challenge. Offensively, Mike Archie took the rushing load when his friend and counterpart had to watch the majority of the game from the bench. Ki-Jana Carter felt his calf muscle pull midway through the first quarter and although he returned for one more play, he figured rest would be the best cure with his team building a comfortable lead.

Archie had 86 yards in the first quarter against a defense that had allowed an average of 85 yards per game all season.

"I knew I had to step it up," said Archie, who reached the 100-yard mark early in the second quarter and finished with 134 yards on 30 carries. "I asked Ki-Jana at halftime if he could go and he said, 'No man, it's your turn now.'"

Actually, Archie had done most of his day's work by halftime as he ran for 118 yards and scored both of his touchdowns in the first 30 minutes.

"I always like to think we can run the ball, no matter who we're playing," offensive guard Mike Malinoski said. "But seeing them [Illinois] on film, I'd have to say I was really pleased with the way we were running on them early."

"I was surprised we could run that well," Joe Paterno admitted. "We did not think we could run that well. We thought we were going to have to throw a little bit more to keep them honest. As it worked out, in the first half we were able to run the ball a little bit better than I thought we could."

For Archie, who had seen his playing time cut when Carter had emerged as the Nittany Lions' leading ball carrier, it was the type of game he always knew he was capable of. Before Illinois, the 5-foot-8, 200-pound redshirt sophomore, had carried the ball just eight times in PSU's two previous games.

"I had been getting a little frustrated," he said. "But I kept my head up, because I knew that one day I'd get the call and it would be my turn to step up. That's what I did, I came through."

Penn State's offensive line came through as well, as redshirt freshman Barry Tielsch got his first start at center in place of injured Bucky Greeley and tackle Dale Harvey replaced starter Marco Rivera in the second quarter after Rivera went down with a dislocated shoulder.

"We had two second-teamers in there and I think they both played very solid," Malinoski said.

Tight end Kyle Brady did a blocking number on the much-heralded linebacking crew of Illinois. He stifled the highly-touted Simeon Rice, who had just one tackle. Fullbacks Brian O'Neal and Brian Milne took care of the linebackers and held the Illini's second leading tackler, John Holocek, to just three stops against the Nittany Lions.

"I think you'd have to say the fullbacks, the offensive line and particularly Brady did a good job," Paterno said.

Archie agreed as he answered reporter's questions in the Penn State media room.

"You've got the wrong guy talking up here," he said. "You should have the offensive line, the fullbacks and the receivers who opened the holes."

Penn State went into some kind of twilight zone with its offense in the second half as it did just enough to grind out the clock, but very little else. The offense went with most of the same plays the coaches drew up in the original game plan, but Illinois did a nice job of adjusting at halftime.

"We didn't have many running plays in our package," guard Jeff Hartings said. "Illinois made good adjustments and we didn't have anything to come back with."

"We really got out of our game plan [in the second half]," said Paterno, who figured the Lions would have to pass a bit more against Illinois' run-oriented defense. "We felt we'd have to throw a lot of play-action passes, particularly over the middle because their linebackers are so aggressive."

Instead it was Penn State which got the aggressive play from its linebacking corps, especially Brian Gelzheiser. The redshirt junior collected a career-high 16 tackles — 11 solo — to raise his season total to 91. To him, it was all in a day's work.

"I just go out and try to do my best, that's all," said Gelzheiser, who also registered a sack. "It's nothing special, someone just has to step up. It's not that I don't count, I try to make as many plays as I can.

"All you do is go out there and tough it out. If you have the will to make a play, you'll make the play. It doesn't matter how tired you are. It's what's inside you that counts."

"We felt that it was up to us to play a strong four quarters," defensive tackle Tyoka Jackson said. "We had a couple of break-downs, but we didn't let the thing get out of hand. I'm proud of our defense."

Paterno was proud of the way both Penn State units stepped up during key points in the game.

"I thought our defense played well," he said. "The offense played a great first half and the defense played a great second half."

It was another downer of an afternoon for Kerry Collins as the redshirt junior quarterback had trouble finding his receivers all day long in the poor field conditions. Collins followed up an impressive performance against Indiana a week earlier by completing only five of 18 passes for 49 yards and tossing three interceptions.

"I wasn't too good," Collins said. "but I take solace in the fact that we won."

While most of the team rejoiced over the victory, Collins sat quietly in front of his locker and thought of the negative reaction he received from what was left of the crowd in the second half.

"It's hard not to hear 95,000 people [booing]," he said, trying to force a smile. "It's not fun. I'd be lying if I said I let it bounce off me. I know it comes with the territory, and sometimes I let it get to me more than I should."

Those that booed should have noticed how Penn State didn't need to throw much in the first half and that Paterno reviewed the situation at halftime and decided he "wanted to be very careful throwing the football" and "didn't want to throw it over the middle." The rainy weather also did nothing to enhance Collins' options on the field. All but seven of his passes were thrown on third down.

"The weather affected the timing," Collins said. "People were slipping all over the place and the ball weighed about 30 pounds."

Paterno defended Collins in his post-game comments and refused to pass judgment based on his performance in a game played under such adverse conditions.

"I have a lot of confidence in Kerry," Paterno said. "He'll be fine, and in all fairness, he's not played a lot of football. We just didn't want to throw the thing over the middle. We were ahead by three scores at halftime, and you don't want to go out there and get foolish."

"[Illinois] is a tough team," Collins said. "They had us well-scouted. Unless they were guessing, they pretty much knew what was coming."

Somewhere between Penn State's offensive deluge, then shutdown, the inevitable was announced. Ohio State had defeated Indiana, 23-17, and that officially eliminated the Nittany Lions from any chance of going to the Rose Bowl in their first season of Big Ten football. When the Lions finished disposing of Illinois, the conference picture seemed to clear up even a bit further. The Illini were also eliminated from Rose Bowl contention and with just two weeks left in the regular season, it appeared the front-runners for the conference title would be either Ohio State or surprising Wisconsin.

Penn State was still out for respectability in the conference and since that wouldn't come in Pasadena, everyone on the team had to redirect their sights on second place, which would mean a trip to Orlando for the Citrus Bowl.

"We set a goal for ourselves after the loss to Ohio State," Lou Benfatti said. "We wanted to win the last four regular season games and go to the best bowl we could. We just didn't want to fall apart like we did the season before."

NOVEMBER 20, EVANSTON, IL — On the surface, it appeared Penn State would have a cake walk against the 10th week's opponent. The Nittany Lions had reached as high as seventh in the national rankings during the middle part of the season, but then plummeted to 19th after consecutive losses to

Michigan and Ohio State. Two weeks later, after back-to-back wins over Indiana and Illinois, the Lions had worked their way back to No. 14 in the Associated Press rankings.

Northwestern was a team that, for the longest time, could only dream of being ranked in the Top 25. The Wildcats' last winning season was in 1971, when they were 7-4. Since then, they have endured four winless seasons, three one-win seasons and have never won more than four games in a year.

Northwestern's second-year coach, Gary Barnett, had preached to his team at the beginning of the '93 season a simple two word phrase: "Expect victory." For a while, it appeared Northwestern's players just may have been listening.

The Big Ten Conference's perennial doormats for the past couple of decades or so opened the season by losing to Notre Dame. No big surprise there, but scoreboard watchers around the country were shocked to find that Northwestern was leading the Fighting Irish through a good portion of the game. The Wildcats expected victory in their next non-conference matchup and they got it. A 22-21 shocker over Boston College put them at .500 for the season, and expectations were raised even further when they followed the BC win with a 26-14 victory over Wake Forest.

Barnett told anyone who would listen upon his arrival that Northwestern was a sleeping giant and he believed he could someday lead the team not only back to respectability, but even greater distances — like the one that goes to Pasadena.

"I didn't leave a program like Colorado to become part of a losing program here," said Barnett, whose team went 3-8 in his rookie season. "We have an excellent opportunity at Northwestern. I would not have taken the job if I didn't think I could win here. Our school has the chance to have the best blend of academics and athletics in the conference. All we have to do is approach things in a very aggressive and positive manner."

Barnett's words of optimism were spoken at the beginning of the 1993 season, but when his team was 2-1 heading into its first conference game, he spoke with even more assuredness.

"Hopefully, this will make our players believe in themselves," Barnett said of the Wildcats' two-game winning streak. "Last year, Boston College annihilated us in Boston [49-0]. Not one of our coaches believed we were that bad of a football team.

"Ever since that loss, we were pointing to this year's [Boston College] game. I hope our fans realize how big of a game this really was for our program."

As the '93 season wore on, hard times would somehow find their way into the Northwestern program, just as had happened in all the years before. As the conference schedule was set to begin, the Wildcats began to feel the crunch of injuries. Through the next six games, 11 starters missed at least one game due to injuries, seven starters on defense missed at least two games and two players were lost for the season. The results became evident in a 51-3 loss at Ohio State and a 53-14 setback at Wisconsin.

"I'm not going to use our injuries as an excuse," Barnett said after a tough October 30 loss to Illinois. "But I'd be a fool if I said it didn't have an impact on our season."

Before meeting Penn State for the first time in school history, Northwestern had dropped its seventh straight game. This one went like the couple before it, which only meant there was improvement in the losses, but they were Northwestern losses nevertheless. Penn State was facing a team that lost its last three games by seven, two and four points. And that was the element that Joe Paterno had stressed to his players in practice all week long.

"All I know is that Northwestern has lost to the last three teams by a total of 13 points," Paterno said. "Our kids are smart enough when they look at the tapes to see that Northwestern is really going to be tough. And we don't know what the weather will be like, or how the wind will affect the kicking game. Northwestern's kicking game is outstanding."

That is Paterno's style whenever he talks about the other team. Think about their strengths, don't dwell on their weaknesses.

"Joe always points out the good parts of the team we're going to play," Penn State linebacker Willie Smith said. "We know they have a good running back and their receiver was the Big Ten Player of the Year last year."

The league's MVP of a season before, senior wide receiver Lee Gissendaner, came into the game as the conference's second leading receiver with 586 yards on 52 catches and five touchdowns.

"A great talent," Paterno said. "Not big, but quick as a cat."

"You can't stop him," Smith said. "So what we have to do is corral him, wrap him up, keep him from getting those 70-yarders."

Gissendaner may have been Northwestern's only potential threat to Penn State, but as is Paterno's custom, nothing should be taken for granted.

"They've given a lot of teams some good battles," he said. "It's all a part of the Big Ten and you can't take any one team too lightly. We're gonna have to come out and play a real solid game to win."

The trip started out in a rather ominous tone for Penn State as only 39 players made it to Evanston on the first team plane that Friday afternoon. The second plane had mechanical problems and didn't arrive until late Friday night.

All of the Penn State buses arrived on time, however, at Northwestern's Dyche Stadium and that, in the long run, proved ominous for the Wildcats. Penn State scored on its first five possessions and cruised to a 43-21 decision.

Tailback Mike Archie led the way for the second straight week with 173 yards rushing — the most by a Penn State running back all season — and two touchdowns on 27 carries. It was Archie who set the tone during Penn State's first series, as he accumulated 45 of the Lions' 80 yards during the drive, including the last five for the opening touchdown.

The Lions took a 10-0 lead early in the second quarter on Craig Fayak's 42-yard field goal, but Northwestern didn't plan on giving in that easily. The Wildcats' quarterback, Len Williams, was expected to miss his second straight game due to a rib injury, but he braved the cold, windy conditions that nearby Lake Michigan afforded the two teams and completed 14 of 27 passes for 264 yards and two touchdowns.

The artificial turf was like cement under the players' feet and Williams felt the sting of the Nittany Lions' pass rush on more than one occasion. Penn State nose guard Eric Clair drove him hard into the ground in the first quarter, but Williams recovered quickly and refused to come out. With his team down by 10, Williams led the Wildcats 71 yards in nine plays to make it a 10-7 Penn State lead. Williams covered the last two yards himself for the score.

Penn State answered with another 42-yard Fayak field goal, but Northwestern responded again. The Wildcats were first-

and-10 on their own 26-yard line when Williams hit wideout Dave Beazley across the middle. Beazley saw a mixup in the Lions' secondary and turned up field for a 74-yard touchdown to give his team a 14-10 lead. The play was Northwestern's longest from scrimmage since the 1988 season.

"I was furious about that," Joe Paterno said. "I told the kids before the ball game that this may not be a big crowd [30,355 was the announced attendance], but it's a big game. It's a big game for us, and it's a big game for Northwestern. I was hoping they were going to believe that because it was true. Everywhere we played this season was a big game for the team we were playing."

Fortunately, the Nittany Lions did believe their coach's words. It just took a while for them to sink in. Penn State responded on its next possession as fullback Brian Milne culminated an 11-play, 69-yard drive with a one-yard run to help the Lions regain their lead. Fayak's extra point was wide left, but PSU had a 16-14 advantage with 4:32 remaining in the second quarter.

Defensive back Tony Pittman intercepted Williams on the Wildcats' next drive and Penn State took over on its own 47-yard line with 46 seconds left in the first half. Kerry Collins looked like a more confident quarterback than in weeks past as he spotted Archie for 14 yards, tight end Kyle Brady for 16, and finally, wideout Bobby Engram, who made a great leaping reception at the goal line to pull in a 16-yard touchdown.

"Engram made a couple of sensational catches," Paterno said. "We've had some trouble catching the ball. We've not had people make big catches, but I think today we had some big catches and that makes a big difference."

The third quarter belonged to Penn State as fullback Brian O'Neal bulled his way into the end zone from the 1-yard line and Fayak kicked his third field goal of the afternoon from 31 yards out.

Archie made it 43-14 early in the fourth quarter when he broke loose for a 23-yard TD. Northwestern made the final outcome a bit more respectable when Williams hit wideout Chris Gamble for a 15-yard touchdown pass with 11:59 left in the game. Gamble and Gissendaner accounted for most of the Wolverines' yardage as they caught six passes each for a combined 182 yards.

Afterward, Paterno seemed in much better spirits when the subject of his team's offensive display was discussed. While the running game had its usual day at the office (291 rushing yards), Collins also found a way to silence the Nittany Lion boo birds. The redshirt junior quarterback was criticized by Nittany Lion faithful everywhere for his two poor performances against Ohio State and Illinois over the past few weeks. Collins knew that might become part of the territory with the position he played, but he couldn't deny the cross words had an effect on him.

"The fans pay their money and they want to see the quarterback throw so many touchdown passes or do everything perfect," he said. "I can understand that and I probably let the booing bother me more than it should have. I know I'm out there doing my best and I think the way our offense played against Northwestern had me feeling a whole lot better."

Collins, who set season highs in completions (19) and passing yardage (278) against the Wildcats, also had the firm support of his teammates and coaches.

"I thought the offense and the passing game got in a groove today," said Engram, who caught eight passes for 132 yards and scored his 11th touchdown of the season. "Kerry was throwing the ball real well, and the guys up front were protecting, so we had a chance to do some of the things we've been working on."

"Kerry had a great game," center Bucky Greeley said. "Our receivers caught the ball and ran well with it. Today I thought we balanced everything out well."

"Kerry gets excited sometimes when he sees wide open receivers and he tends to overthrow," quarterback coach Dick Anderson said. "But he's going to be a fine quarterback. He's shown a lot of consistency lately and he's going to get better."

Paterno was pleased with the way his offense handled Northwestern's switch to a single-coverage passing defense to bunch up against the Nittany Lions' running game.

"Today, when the running started to get tough and they started to give us a lot of single coverage, we decided to throw the ball more on first down," he said. "That's what bothers me about people criticizing our offense against Illinois. We had a big lead [in the second half], why am I gonna throw the ball on first and second down? The conditions were tough and Kerry played it the way we asked him to. Illinois adjusted to our run and that's why our offense looked like it was going nowhere in the second half."

The Penn State defense also had its usual game with five sacks, two fumble recoveries and two interceptions. The Nittany

Lions were steady on defense and platooned frequently to allow some of the backups as much playing time as possible. The secondary tightened up in the second half, allowing only 70 yards passing after being burnt for 194 in the first two quarters.

"We played really well defensively in the second half," Paterno said. "The one drive [Northwestern] got, they really earned it. They made some great plays."

During the week of practice leading up to the Lions' game against Northwestern, Fayak, the kicker, was handling about 25 percent of the offensive snaps in practice, just in case Penn State would need Fayak, the quarterback.

With two games remaining in the regular season, Paterno finally admitted that Fayak would be his backup in an emergency and the coaching staff was going ahead with its plan to redshirt sophomore Wally Richardson. In fact, Richardson didn't even make the trip to Northwestern, which seemed to assure Fayak that he was the man to go behind center if needed.

He performed his specialty at various times throughout the game. Three field goals and four extra points, to be exact. Collins was moving the offense nicely and the Penn State offensive line did an outstanding job of protecting. It appeared Fayak would get through the game without having to handle the ball with anything other than his foot.

Then, with about four-and-a-half minutes left in the game, Paterno called upon his kicker one more time. Fayak could have been surprised at his coach's call, thinking, *"Gee coach, I don't know. I have a strong leg and everything, but kicking from our own territory is kind of a little too far for my liking."*

But this series wasn't for a field goal, nor extra point, nor even a drop kick. Fayak was about to live his dream. He did the basics. Handoff left; handoff right; handoff up the middle. His final ledger read: 0-0-0-0, as in passes completed-passes attempted-yardage-touchdowns, which was okay for Fayak.

"Coach wanted me to take a couple of snaps," Penn State's all-time leading scorer said. "It was fun being out there, but I hope for Kerry's sake and the team's sake I won't *have* to go out there."

Then he joked and said, "We should have gone deep."

No one knew if Paterno would allow Fayak to go to that extreme, but he felt very confident that the Lions would be in capable hands if something did chase Collins from the game.

"If something happens [to Collins], Fayak's our quarter-back," he said. "You might be surprised at how good he is."

Penn State's win against Northwestern was a given. Cutting through all the pregame candor that coaches pour on one another, it was a game that Penn State should have won — and did win — in convincing fashion. The quest coming into the conference was not so much whether the Nittany Lions could hold up against an overmatched Northwestern, but whether it could compete on a yearly basis with the elite teams in the conference. Michigan and Ohio State are the first two teams that come to mind when speaking of that status. That was a level Penn State had achieved quite regularly as an independent, but rightfully so, it would have to do so all over again against the teams in its new conference.

The Nittany Lions came up empty in their two biggest games of 1993, but as Paterno said what seemed like ages ago in Penn State's spring workouts, the nice thing about being in a conference is that you can lose a couple of games and still be playing for something.

In the beginning, Penn State was playing for the Rose Bowl. And why not, it had just as much a chance as the rest of the teams in the conference. After seven games, the Lions were 2-2 in the conference and had all but blown their opportunity to reach the grandaddy of 'em all. But there was still second place, which was a far cry from 1992. When they lost to Miami after a 5-0 start, the Nittany Lions felt there was no reason to say, "Oh well, there's always second place."

Second place for what? There would be no national championship, which was the goal of every team in the nation. The Blockbuster Bowl was wrapped up with one more win. Deep down, the players on that team were thinking and sometimes quietly muttering, "BIG DEAL."

With their Big Ten championship hopes dashed officially after Ohio State's win over Indiana a week earlier, Penn State found out perhaps for the first time, the true meaning of playing in a conference. That regardless of the won-loss situation, there is always the conference pride and competitiveness. Each player would learn that whether the competition is Michigan or Northwestern, that team was going to come at you with full force for 60 minutes. Win or lose, they wouldn't stop hitting until the final gun.

"I prefer it this way," Paterno said when asked whether he liked going down to the last game of the season to decide Penn State's bowl future, or whether he liked knowing in advance like the Nittany Lions did in 1992. "I think playing like this has positive effects on this football team. I think they need to learn how to play under pressure, they need to play with something at stake."

Penn State had to go about its business against Northwestern. It wasn't a case of playing out the string, as the 10th game might have been had the Nittany Lions still been an independent. For, while Penn State was disposing of Northwestern that day, other games in the conference were molding the shape of the conference's final bowl structure.

Michigan, which had fallen from Rose Bowl contention soon after it had defeated Penn State, played its best game of the season in its annual rivalry with Ohio State. The Wolverines' 28-0 shutout suddenly left the Buckeyes' Rose Bowl fate in the hands of Wisconsin, which had defeated Illinois quite easily that day, 35-10.

Ohio State finished the regular season with a 6-1-1 conference record, while Wisconsin had one more conference game left against Michigan State in of all places, Tokyo, Japan. The Badgers were 5-1-1 and if they could defeat Michigan State, they would go to the Rose Bowl because they had been away from the bowl longer than Ohio State.

Penn State had one more regular season game left also. That was in East Lansing against those same Spartans of Michigan State. A Nittany Lion victory would guarantee at least third place in the conference, while a loss could have dropped them to fifth. Second place in the conference would come down to that final game in Tokyo as a Wisconsin win would send the Badgers to the Rose Bowl, Ohio State to the Citrus Bowl and Penn State to the Holiday Bowl in San Diego as the Big Ten's third place team. A Wisconsin loss would send the Buckeyes to the Rose, Penn State to the Citrus — as the second place team — and the Badgers to the Holiday.

In 1992, Penn State's 10th game of the season was for pride, but little else. The Nittany Lions lost on the last play of the game — a two-point conversion play — to Notre Dame, but a victory would not have changed their bowl plans. All season long, six wins guaranteed a bid to the Blockbuster Bowl. The university knew that back in May of that year. On paper, it would seem to be a far cry from matching up with Notre Dame when paralleled against playing Northwestern. But deep down, every player who had the opportunity to suit up for both of those games undoubtedly had a lot more fun, and a lot more to look forward to by playing Northwestern.

"We looked at these last two games [Northwestern and Michigan State] and thought of a couple things," Kerry Collins said. "We figured we could win them and go to the second place bowl game or lose them and probably not go anywhere."

The fun wasn't even finished yet.

14

MICHIGAN STATE:
The New Rivalry

The last time Joe Paterno brought a Penn State team to Michigan State was in the fall of 1966. It was his very first season as head coach and the first time he had taken the Nittany Lions on the road with the same title. It was also probably a day Paterno would just as soon forget. Michigan State won the game 42-8 in front of over 64,000 fans and laid further claim to being one of the few teams that had posted a winning record against Penn State over the years. The Lions fell to 1-8-1 against the Spartans, dating back to a series that started in 1914.

Little did anyone figure that 27 years later Michigan State would be taking the University of Pittsburgh's place as Penn State's biggest rival. For over 90 years, Penn State and Pitt played the final game of the season that caused fans from both schools to say and do things out of the ordinary. When Penn State joined the Big Ten Conference, Pitt fans were outraged that such an occurrence could be allowed to happen. Penn State fans were also unhappy with Paterno's seeming lack of sentiment toward the storied tradition of the series.

Unfortunately, Penn State had to develop a schedule to conform with that of the Big Ten, so it had to exclude Pitt from its schedule for at least the next four years. The funny thing was, while some eastern schools weren't too happy with Penn State's venture into the Big Ten, neither were some of the Big Ten schools. Most thought it was ludicrous to add another tough, physical team to a conference that prides itself on tough, physical play. Mind-bending logic, to say the least.

One coach in the Big Ten, however, opened his arms wide to the Nittany Lions when the announcement was made. George Perles was in his 11th season with the Spartans in 1993, and he remembered his reaction when Penn State was announced as the Big Ten's 11th member.

"The moment I heard that Penn State was coming to the Big Ten, I got on the phone and called Joe [Paterno] to congratulate him," Perles said. "For years we had been searching for a team in the conference to become our Michigan or Ohio State. Right after that I got on the phone to the Big Ten conference office and requested that Penn State be the last game on our schedule."

The league granted Perles' wish by designating the Penn State-Michigan State game last on both team's schedules for at least the next four years starting in '93. Both coaches were happy with the setup and both became hopeful that the game would eventually at least parallel the luster that Michigan-Ohio State creates.

"We believe that someday this game can become bigger than Michigan-Ohio State and be a permanent fixture on national television," Perles said.

"George was the first Big Ten coach that called and welcomed us into the conference," Paterno confirmed. "I've appreciated the fact that from day one he's been very, very gracious toward Penn State and very enthusiastic about Penn State joining the Big Ten. I hope that sometime in the future, this game can be as important to our fans as our games with Notre Dame, Alabama and Nebraska were in the 1980s."

Most rivals have their certain trophies or jugs or some kind of historic treasure to play for, and the two schools wanted to make sure their new rivalry wouldn't be left without some kind of traveling trophy. It would be called the "Land Grant Trophy" to honor the two schools' "unique places in history as two pioneer land-grant schools in the nation," according to press releases.

Their places in history are unique because Michigan State and Penn State were founded within 12 days of each other. Michigan State came into existence on February 10, 1855, while Penn State opened its doors on February 22 of the same year.

The Land Grant Trophy would feature pictures of the school's landmark buildings — Penn State's Old Main and Michigan State's Beaumont Tower — as well as replicas of the teams' athletic mascots.

Michigan State was 4-2 in the conference and 6-3 overall. Wins over Penn State and Wisconsin would throw the Spartans into the Citrus Bowl and knock the Nittany Lions all the way down to fourth in the conference.

Paterno said he wasn't worried about bowl implications at the moment and that it would take his team's best effort all season to have a chance against Michigan State.

"We have to play a *complete* game," he said. "Our defense will have to play by far their best game. Our offense will have to play by far their best game. Our kicking game, you can't have a mistake on the kicking game. We can't put the ball on the ground, we can't throw it up for grabs."

Paterno was concerned about every facet of Michigan State's game, especially the offensive-defensive match-ups.

"They're not fancy, they're not flashy," he said. "They just keep coming at you. On offense they're going to run right at us."

"We're not a one-dimensional team," Perles said. "We have a good-sized offensive line, so we have the potential to run the ball. And we can play two or three tailbacks, which helps to keep them fresh."

"We've had trouble with people who have done that to us," Paterno said. "People who are strong enough and have the kind of backs they have."

Perles described his offensive line as "good-sized." Maybe he was talking about a line in the NFL. The Michigan State offensive line averaged 304 pounds across the line from tackle to tackle, and would go against a Penn State defensive front four that averaged around 260.

"Penn State's really quick," Perles said of the 40-pound-per-man difference. "so it's a wash."

Somebody should have told the Nittany Lions that before their games with Michigan and Ohio State, where they were outsized by similar numbers and were able to put very little pressure on the quarterback in either game.

Penn State would again be without its three-man tailback system as Ki-Jana Carter didn't expect to play due to the pulled calf injury he suffered in the Lions' win over Illinois. Mike Archie had filled in nicely for the Nittany Lions when given the opportunity and had averaged 153.5 yards per game in the wins over Illinois and Northwestern.

Despite Penn State's No. 1 ranking in the conference in rushing yardage, Paterno was very cautious about his team's ability to perform equally as well against Michigan State's stunting defense.

"They have been very dominant, particularly against the run, which has been our forte," Paterno said. "They force you into a lot of mistakes because of Perles' scheme, the stunts they do. So it's not a good match-up for us."

Michigan State designed much of its offense in '93 around its three tailback system, which sometimes overlooked the talents of quarterback Jim Miller. The senior quarterback had thrown for 1,674 yards through the Spartans' first nine games, with six touchdowns and had completed 65.7 percent of his passes. He was rated second among Big Ten starting quarterbacks in percentage, but sixth in the conference in pass efficiency, due mostly to his seven interceptions.

Miller's favorite targets were junior wideout Mill Coleman, who led the Spartans' with 34 catches for 387 yards, and sophomore wideout Napoleon Outlaw, who was averaging 16 yards per catch. Miller also threw a lot to his fullback, Brice Abrams, who came into the Penn State game with 23 catches for 160 yards.

It appeared there would be a lot of good match-ups on both sides of the ball when Penn State and Michigan State teed it up for the first time in 27 years. The opposing coaches wanted to see the game develop a bigger rivalry than the Michigan-Ohio State game. National television year after year, the whole bit. If that were to happen, Paterno and Perles knew it would take a dazzling display in the first meeting to get the series off on the right foot.

Little did either coach know exactly how much drama this game was about to unfold, and how unforgettable the rivalry's first installment would be.

NOVEMBER 27, EAST LANSING, MI — The first play of the game appeared to be an omen for Penn State — a bad one.

Tailback Mike Archie fumbled after being drilled by Michigan State defensive back Myron Bell. Center Bucky Greely recovered for Penn State, but when another tailback, Stephen Pitts, coughed up the ball five plays later at the Michigan State 15-yard line, Bell pounced on it for the Spartans. Michigan State couldn't move the ball on its first two possessions, but Penn State refused to take advantage. Instead the Nittany Lions made mistakes, like the fumble that did nothing but push them backward.

Penn State's second miscue came on a fourth and inches at the Michigan State 31. Tackle Andre Johnson, starting his second consecutive game for the injured Marco Rivera, jumped offside forcing Craig Fayak to try a 47-yard field goal that fell short.

This time, Michigan State responded to the Nittany Lions' charity. Quarterback Jim Miller led the Spartans 70 yards in nine plays for the first touchdown of the game. Junior wideout Mill Coleman caught the 28-yard TD strike from Miller with 3:58 left in the first quarter to give the Spartans a 6-0 lead.

Penn State quarterback Kerry Collins would end the day with a career-high performance, but his only interception put the Nittany Lions into a 13-0 hole just 31 seconds into the second quarter. Collins pass over the middle was tipped by Michigan State defensive end Richard Glover and intercepted by linebacker Matt Christensen at the 50-yard line. The Spartans needed two plays to go in for the score as Miller again hooked up with Coleman, this time for 47 yards, and third-team tailback Steve Holman carried it the final three.

The Nittany Lions finally answered on their next possession as Collins completed 4 of 4 passes for 46 yards, and Archie broke free for a 24-yard touchdown run to complete a seven-play, 70-yard drive with 11:21 left in the first half.

Michigan State had an answer of its own, however, as freshman Derrick Mason returned the kickoff 34 yards and Holman carried six times for 39 of his game-high 116 yards. There were still over eight minutes left in the second quarter when Holman found his way to the end zone from six yards out to give the Spartans a 20-7 advantage.

Michigan State seemed to be moving the ball at will against an uncharacteristically disorganized Penn State defense.

"We were hurting there in the first half," said defensive end Eric Ravotti, who returned to the Penn State lineup after missing two games from suffering the seizure against Indiana. "We were getting beat up, it seemed like they were running all over us."

Even when the Penn State defense did stop the Spartans, the offense couldn't take advantage of its own chances through much of the first half. Archie returned a Michigan State punt 62 yards to set the Lions up at the Spartans' 8-yard line. Three plays netted one yard and Penn State had to settle for a 24-yard Fayak field goal.

Michigan State kicker Bill Stoyanovich drilled a 37-yard field goal with just over a minute left before halftime, and it appeared the Spartans would settle for a 23-10 lead at intermission. Penn State had other ideas, however.

The Nittany Lions started at their own 35-yard line and Collins went to work with the two-minute offense. He threw six passes during the drive and completed five, including the last one — a 16-yarder to redshirt freshman Freddie Scott that split three defenders over the middle — with just five seconds remaining in the half.

"I thought the touchdown pass was a great, great throw," Paterno said of Collins' pass.

At times, the two-minute drill Penn State successfully carried out didn't seem as precise as it looked. Paterno yelled at Collins at one point for wasting a timeout instead of grounding the ball, but the quarterback kept his poise and threaded the needle with the scoring pass to Scott.

"We knew what was going on, it just looked like we didn't," Collins joked afterward. "The two-minute drill never really goes smoothly, it's very rare if it does."

Whatever the case, Penn State hoped the Collins-to-Scott touchdown pass would provide the Lions with some momentum as the third quarter got underway with Michigan State leading 23-17. Instead, the defense couldn't find an answer to several facets of Michigan State's offense and soon began pinning blame on one another.

Holman was running through and around the Penn State front line, which was being pushed around by the Spartans' offensive line. Running back Duane Goulbourne was also on his way to a 100-yard performance (he finished with 112) and Miller was crossing the Lions up with precision passing.

Goulbourne made it 30-17 with just over eight minutes left in the third quarter when he scored from five yards out and to cap off what had turned into an embarrassing day for Penn State, the Spartans scored their final touchdown on a three-yard tackle-eligible pass from Miller to offensive lineman Bob Denton.

There were almost three minutes left in the third quarter and Penn State trailed Michigan State, 37-17. The problems had escalated in such a short time and everyone looked to someone else for an answer. The Michigan State sideline was celebrating and the Penn State players were hearing that old familiar phrase, "Welcome to the Big Ten."

"From a defensive standpoint, I don't know what happened the first three quarters," Penn State hero back Derek Bochna said. "We were fighting amongst ourselves, we were arguing, we weren't doing what we were supposed to do."

"There were a lot of missed tackles, and because of those missed tackles we had one guy blaming another guy," Ravotti said. "Then the blame started to pass around the huddle. The defensive backs were blaming the linebackers who were blaming the defensive line."

"I really thought we were in pretty good shape at that point," Michigan State coach George Perles said of his team's 20-point cushion.

Michigan State's defense would hold Penn State's strong running game to 87 yards, while its own running game totaled 240. The size mismatch seemed to reflect memories of the losses to Michigan and Ohio State, but Penn State's defense suddenly decided enough was enough.

The Penn State offense went three-and-out following Denton's touchdown play and Miller figured to go after more. He figured wrong as Bochna stepped in front of the quarterback's errant pass and picked it off at the Penn State 42-yard line.

Three plays later, Collins threw deep to Bobby Engram, the conference's leading receiver, who pulled in a 40-yard bomb for the touchdown. Fayak's extra point made it a 37-24 ball game still late in the third quarter.

Goulbourne fumbled on the Spartans' next offensive series and Penn State linebacker Brian Gelzheiser recovered at the Michigan State 40-yard line. Suddenly, the mistakes and turnovers were turning in the Nittany Lions' favor. Penn State failed to get a first down, but when punter V.J. Muscillo was roughed by Michigan State's Juan Hammonds, it gave the Lions a new set of downs.

Collins then hit tight end Kyle Brady for 20 yards and a first down at the Michigan State 3-yard line and fullback Brian O'Neal carried it in to pull the Lions to within six, 37-31, with 13:02 remaining in the game.

"Before that they were talking a good game," Bochna said of the Michigan State players. "After we got within six, they didn't say a whole lot."

Michigan State took over at its own 20-yard line on the next series following a touchback. The Spartans were looking at a second and 10 when Gelzheiser blitzed for the first time all afternoon and dropped Miller for a nine-yard loss. It was the first of four Penn State sacks, but one of several huge plays for the rejuvenated Nittany Lion defense.

"We just all of a sudden started coming at them," said Bochna, who had seven tackles. "and I don't think they were ready for it."

The Spartans were also unprepared for what happened next. After failing to get a first down on third and 19, Michigan State punted the ball back to Penn State. The Nittany Lions took over on their own 48 and Collins wasted little time in going up top.

On the first play, Collins found Engram with man coverage deep along the Penn State sideline. Engram caught the ball behind Michigan State defensive back Howard Triplett at the 7-yard line and took it in for the score. Fayak's kick gave the Lions their first lead of the game, 38-37.

"We had just come off a big stop, so we knew we had to go after them early and try to hit them with a big score," said Engram, who caught three passes for 106 yards and two TDs. "Coach called my number, Kerry made a great throw and I was able to come up with the catch."

Collins seemed unstoppable in the second half, at a time when the team needed strong quarterback leadership the most. He finished with a career-high 352 yards and three touchdowns on 23 of 42 passing. More importantly, he stepped to the front at perhaps the season's most dire moment and took the rest of the offense under his wing.

"Kerry made some great throws to get us back in it," Paterno gushed. "We didn't want to throw the ball as much as we did, but after the first quarter, we couldn't run it."

"I just have to give a lot of thanks to the offense for keeping us in the game," Ravotti said. "We played a pretty bad defensive game in those first three quarters, but the offense bailed us out."

Most Nittany Lion followers would find it highly ironic that the offense would save the defense, considering the storied tradition of great defenses past at Penn State. This defensive crew certainly ranked with some of the best ever at Penn State, but in the two mid-season losses, when it ran into offenses that were able to control the line play, the Penn State offense didn't respond as it did against Michigan State.

With the Lions holding secure to their one-point lead, the defense appeared more ready for the challenge than ever. There were still about 11 minutes left when Collins-to-Engram caught the Michigan State defense by surprise. The Spartans had been bitten by the same mistakes and blunders that caused Penn State to fall behind in the first half. Now it was a question of whether the Nittany Lion defenders could stare down the challenge of the game's last few minutes.

The first drive for Michigan State got as far as the Penn State 48-yard line. A punt pinned the Lions down, but Collins engineered a few first downs and most importantly, shaved some more time off the clock before Penn State gave up the ball again.

"We realized they had 80 yards to go," Ravotti said of Michigan State's last possession. "[Defensive coordinator] Jerry Sandusky decided to let us pin our ears back and take off."

The Spartans actually started at their own 18-yard line with about six minutes remaining in the fourth quarter. Miller got one first down, but then proceeded to go backward. First, it was Ravotti who sacked him, then, reserve defensive end Todd Atkins, and finally, Ravotti again. Michigan State lost 24 yards to Penn State's fired up defense and Miller's desperation pass on fourth and 26 was way short of intended receiver Nigea Carter.

Collins and his offense took over on downs and ran off the final minute and a half to secure one of the greatest comebacks in Penn State football history.

"It's really hard to swallow when you're up by 20 points and blow it," said Miller, who completed 14 of 29 passes for 186 yards. "We just flopped when we shouldn't have."

"Needless to say, it's a tough way to lose a football game," Perles said.

The Michigan State coach may not have been as happy as he once was about having Penn State in the Big Ten, but if the two teams wanted an exciting game to stir the curiosity of the conference's fans, they succeeded.

"If they're all like that, it's gonna be a fun series," Paterno said.

Penn State's head coach of 28 years had seen a handful of games like the one he had just witnessed. Whether his team had won or lost in a rally of that sort, he is a man that still would have said, "If they're all like that, it's gonna be a fun series."

Deep down, what may have been troubling the legend the most was the perception that Penn State couldn't win the big game anymore. Even the ABC announcers brought up that subject during the game's telecast. Players hear such comments, or read them in the newspapers, and they try too hard sometimes to prove their doubters wrong. Soon the pressure builds and a glaring mistake costs the team another big game.

Fifth place; fourth place; second place. This was a big game for Penn State, and for three quarters, it appeared another big one had fallen too far from the Nittany Lions' grasp. But something called character suddenly loomed inside their hearts. And it came at the most opportune moment.

After winning three in a row against Indiana, Illinois and Northwestern, a loss to Michigan State would have planted the Nittany Lions in the middle of the conference pack. For the fans; the coaches; the players; middle of the road is unsatisfactory. Middle of the road could have created another off-season of uncertainty. Middle of the road could have entrenched the Nittany Lions into the long-term middle of the road.

A loss to Michigan State would probably have landed Penn State in the Liberty Bowl, which would be a nice reward for some teams, but would do little to raise the excitement level of a team that was used to playing on New Year's Day.

"We needed to win a big game," defensive end Tyoka Jackson said.

"This," Paterno said after his team's last regular season game, "will obviously mean a lot."

"Tons of character out there," said tight end Kyle Brady, who caught a career-best seven passes for 72 yards. "Lots of heart. Nobody gave up. If you want to see heart and character, show people this game.

"We had to prove it. Sometimes you look around and wonder why you don't win the big games, and what's going on. We're so close, yet so far. This is huge. This will do a lot for our program."

The players and coaches thought they would have to wait a week to see what the victory would do to their bowl possibilities. Michigan State was scheduled to play its final regular season game on December 4 against Wisconsin in Tokyo, Japan. Penn State's come-from-behind win ruined the Spartans' chances of going to the Citrus Bowl, which was considered the conference's second most attractive bowl game behind the Rose Bowl.

Penn State figured it would have to wait for the outcome in Tokyo because of the Rose Bowl standings. A Wisconsin win over Michigan State would send the Badgers to the Rose Bowl and lock up second place in the conference for Ohio State. A Wisconsin loss would send the Buckeyes to Pasadena and the Badgers to San Diego for the third-place Holiday Bowl with a 5-2-1 conference record, one-half game behind Penn State's 6-2 mark.

When Penn State officials took a further glance at the conference's bowl picture, however, they began to realize that the Citrus Bowl was just about in the bag for the Nittany Lions. The league's no-repeat clause would see to that. After further review, it was discovered that even a Wisconsin win over Michigan State in Tokyo would assure the Nittany Lions of a Citrus Bowl invitation because Ohio State had been to the Citrus Bowl the season before and conference rules prevent a team from going to the same bowl it participated in the season before, unless of course, that bowl is the Rose Bowl.

There was only one possible scenario for Penn State to wind up in the Holiday Bowl. A Wisconsin-Michigan State tie would have given the Badgers second place in the conference, a half-game in front of Penn State. The Citrus Bowl committee had a decision to make as far as waiting for the final Big Ten regular season game to be played out. The committee made its decision quickly.

On November 29, 1993; five days before the Big Ten's final regular season game, the official Citrus Bowl invitation was handed to Joe Paterno and his Penn State Nittany Lions. There were three reasons why the Citrus Bowl people decided not to wait for the results in Tokyo: 1) They decided the chances of a tie were very remote; 2) They figured further delays created the possibility of hindering ticket sales; 3) They wanted Penn State anyway.

"We're making the same decision now as we would be a week from now," Citrus Bowl representative Mark Whitehead said at the time of the announcement.

"This decision gives Penn State and Big Ten fans an opportunity to make their holiday arrangements a week earlier," said Chuck Rohe, who is the executive director of the Citrus Bowl.

"We're absolutely delighted," Paterno said of Penn State's Citrus Bowl announcement. "We've been to the Citrus Bowl before and had a wonderful time."

Penn State also had fun in the Fiesta Bowl just two years before. In that game, the Nittany Lions rallied from a 17-7 third-quarter deficit with a 35-point unanswered barrage to defeat Tennessee, 42-17. As he accepted the Citrus Bowl invitation, along with Penn State's soon-to-be retired athletic director Jim Tarman, Paterno learned that Penn State would once again square off against the Volunteers on New Year's Day.

"It'll be a great opportunity to play a team with a great tradition and is as good a team as Tennessee," Paterno said. "We were very fortunate against them [in the Fiesta Bowl]. Tennessee could have been up three or four touchdowns in the first half. I would say they were probably a better football team. We just got a couple of breaks and some crazy things happened."

The opponent in the Citrus Bowl really didn't matter to the Nittany Lions. Not as long as they had reached their best position possible. They had proven themselves admirably against quality Big Ten opponents and had even earned some respect in the losses to Michigan and Ohio State. Now would come a time to represent the conference. And to everyone affiliated with the team, now was the time to stand up for the conference with pride, just as they had for their own university. Independence was gone, and there was still that little matter of making believers out of the rest of the Big Ten members. A win in the Citrus Bowl would go a long way toward making that possible.

The Penn State doubters must have had a field day through the first three quarters against Michigan State, but the players and coaches never stopped believing. Because of that, the Nittany Lions secured themselves of a respectable finish in the Big Ten

Conference standings. At least third, possibly second. Not bad for a team that was supposed to give in to the rigors of the Big Ten's physical style of play.

"There were people in the [Michigan State] stands yelling to go back to the Big East, that we don't belong," Kyle Brady said. "This team is very worthy of being in this conference, and I think we'll be one of the better teams every year. We proved that today."

The first season struggle was over, and if records meant anything, it wasn't much of a struggle at all. The Lions finished the regular season at 9-2. They endured the skeptics who said they didn't have what it takes to play in the Big Ten. They survived rain storms and snow storms, even the defection of a quarterback. But the best part of the entire season — if one happened to be wearing a Penn State uniform — was the answer to the endless hostility.

Penn State traveled to four new places in the Big Ten in 1993. During each stop, the Lions were showered with choruses of boos and made to feel like unwanted stepchildren. "This is Big Ten country, go back home to the east!" they would hear, or "Welcome to the Big Ten. It's time you learned what real football's like!"

The Nittany Lions heard it endlessly during the middle part of their game against Michigan State. Down by 20 with just over 15 minutes left to play, Penn State rallied for the victory. As the players exited the playing field following their improbable 38-37 win over the Spartans, they wallowed in the silence of the slowly-emptying stadium.

For the first time, Penn State could listen to the fans say, "Welcome to the Big Ten!" and get some satisfaction in saying, "Thank you very much!"

Penn State had indeed finally won the big one.

15

CITRUS BOWL:
A Volunteer
Rematch

The Big Ten Conference fared well as far as bowl invitations were concerned in 1993. Seven teams in all were invited to post-season action, including Iowa, which was 3-5 in the conference, but 6-5 overall. The Big Ten has an arrangement for its top four finishers to get automatic bids to the Rose Bowl, Citrus Bowl, Holiday Bowl and Hall of Fame Bowl in that order. So it was a testament to the conference's strength that three additional teams seemed worthy enough by bowl scouts around the country to merit consideration.

In addition to Penn State's invitation to the Citrus Bowl, Wisconsin locked up the Rose Bowl by defeating Michigan State in the final conference game of the regular season. That sent Ohio State packing to the Holiday Bowl in San Diego December 31, and fourth-place Michigan was headed to Tampa to play in the Hall of Fame Bowl on New Year's Day. Indiana accepted an invitation to the Independence Bowl in Shreveport, Lousiana, to play against Virginia Tech, while the Liberty Bowl in Memphis matched Michigan State and Louisville, and the inaugural Alamo Bowl would pit Iowa against California.

The Rose Bowl is normally the Big Ten's marquee matchup simply because it is the game that is most synonymous with the conference. The game annually features the conference's champion against the top finisher from the Pac-10 Conference. So it should be two of the best teams in the country going head to head.

Of the bowls tied into the conference's top four finishers, the Rose Bowl had Wisconsin (9-1-1) facing Pac-10 champ UCLA (8-3); the Holiday Bowl featured Ohio State (9-1-1) versus Western Athletic Conference champ Brigham Young (6-5); and the Hall of Fame Bowl had a pair of 7-4 teams going at it in Michigan and North Carolina State.

It didn't take long for the experts — or anyone for that matter — to figure out which Big Ten team got the toughest post-season draw. Tennessee was ranked fifth in the final regular season *USA Today*/CNN coaches poll and sixth in the Associated Press writers poll. The Volunteers finished 9-1-1 during the regular season, losing to Sugar Bowl-bound Florida, 41-34, and drawing even with defending national champion, Alabama, 17-17.

Tennessee received its Citrus Bowl invitation in much the same bizarre fashion as Penn State. It was a team that perhaps merited playing in the Sugar Bowl or Cotton Bowl, but it would certainly not complain with its New Year's Day draw.

"This is a good situation for us," Tennessee coach Phillip Fulmer said. "We'll be playing a top-quality team and although I'm sure there are still a lot of people associated with this team who remember the Fiesta Bowl two years ago, we're not using that as some revenge factor. We have to worry about playing this Penn State team."

Tennessee was well respected, as was apparent by its national ranking, but in a December 9 press conference at Beaver Stadium, Joe Paterno wanted to make sure the Volunteers received the highest consideration.

"I think right now, Tennessee and Florida State are playing the best football in the country," Paterno said. "I know Don Nehlen and Tommy Osborne and some people in South Bend aren't going to like my saying that, but I really feel that way. I think that right now, Tennessee is as good a football team as anybody."

Nehlen and Osborne were coaching the nation's only two undefeated teams (West Virginia and Nebraska) heading into the New Year's Day bowl games. The Mountaineers were scheduled to meet Florida in the Sugar Bowl and the Cornhuskers were up against No. 1 Florida State in the Orange Bowl. Florida State and Notre Dame had lost one game each, but due to the bowl coalition, West Virginia and Nebraska would not have the opportunity to settle with each other on the field. Both teams, in fact, had little chance at all of even winning the national championship. The Cornhuskers were heavy underdogs against Florida State and West Virginia needed divine intervention to win the title, even if it defeated Florida.

All the talk aside, however, Paterno's comments were not so far off base as everyone might have thought. Tennessee headed into the Citrus Bowl with the best passing offense Penn State would see all year. The Volunteers threw for 2,664 yards and 31 touchdowns led by the Southeastern Conference's most valuable player, Heath Shuler, who completed 184 of 285 passes for 2,353 yards, 25 touchdowns, eight interceptions and a 64.6 completion percentage.

Shuler had one more season of eligibility after the Citrus Bowl, but many pro scouts believed he would be a certain first-round draft pick if he chose to leave Tennessee. Paterno compared the 6-foot-3, 212-pounder to a young John Elway.

"They [Tennessee] can do whatever they want to do offensively," Paterno said. "They give you two-back offense, give you the 'I,' give you single-back, give you no backs, give you the shotgun. They do a lot of things and with a kid like Shuler there who's able to handle all that stuff, they do it very, very well. I know we haven't played anybody this year with as much offense as they have, and very few teams we've played through the years would be in that class."

Fulmer wouldn't go as far as to agree on every count with Paterno, but he did acknowledge his starting quarterback to be one of the best he had ever worked with.

"I'm convinced Heath could have easily thrown for 4,000 yards this season, if that is what we wanted to accomplish with our offense," Fulmer said following his team's 62-14 season-ending win over Vanderbilt. "He's the best pure passer that I've ever been around."

"They're very potent, very destructive," Penn State defensive end Eric Ravotti said after reviewing films of Tennessee's offense in action. "I believe in my heart that Tennessee is one of the top five teams, maybe one of the top three teams, in the nation right now the way they're playing."

Two other SEC coaches had similar reviews.

"You can't stop Tennessee's offense," said Florida coach Steve Spurrier, whose team handed the Vols' their only loss, but not because of its defense. "You just have to find a way to score more points."

"Fulmer has made Tennessee's offense the best in the SEC," Alabama coach Gene Stallings said. "They're the best balanced offense I've ever had to coach against. Shutting down Shuler doesn't mean you're going to be able to shut down their offense. That's something I believe is impossible."

Stallings' assessment was correct, because if Shuler wasn't throwing over and around the competition, Tennessee's running game was probably smashing through it. The Volunteers' tailback trio finished the regular season at least as Penn State's equal, maybe a little bit better. Charlie Garner, James Stewart and Aaron Hayden combined for 1,915 yards on 273 carries and averaged more than seven yards per attempt. Garner carried the bulk of that load with 1,161 yards and a 7.3 yards per carry average.

Tennessee used its fullbacks mainly as blockers, but junior Mose Phillips was also the team's fourth-leading receiver with 21 catches. The Volunteers scored more points than any team in the SEC (42.8 per game), and totaled 60 touchdowns to go along with 12 of 13 field goal attempts. The Tennessee offensive line allowed just 11 sacks all season on 320 passing attempts and allowed Shuler enough time to convert 47 percent of the team's third-down chances.

Just in case there was too much emphasis placed on Tennessee's offense, Penn State also had to contend with the third-best defense in the SEC against the run, allowing just 117.3 yards per game on the ground. The Vols' defensive effort was spearheaded by junior linebacker Ben Talley, who led the team during the regular season with 87 tackles. Two other linebackers were instrumental in the Volunteers' success as Reggie Ingram finished second in tackles with 77 and Scott Gaylon fourth, with 54.

Tennessee applied the pressure to the opposing quarterback whenever possible and that led to 38 sacks, including a team-leading eight by defensive end Horace Morris and 7.5 by James Wilson, another defensive end. If the Volunteers had any weakness, it was in their secondary, which allowed the opposition 191.4 yards per game through the air.

As powerful as Tennessee appeared to be on paper — and on film — the Nittany Lions were looking forward to playing such a quality opponent in their first bowl game as a Big Ten representative.

"We were very lucky with the draw and the way things turned out," Ravotti said. "We get to play a top-ranked opponent and see how good we really are."

Penn State appeared up for the challenge as it headed to Florida on Dec. 19, the earliest it had ever left for a post-season New Year's Day bowl game. The Nittany Lions were ranked 12th in the coaches poll and 13th in the writers poll. Along the way, they also ran up some impressive numbers of their own.

Penn State finished first in the Big Ten and 17th nationally in scoring offense with 32.5 points per game; it was second in the conference and 14th nationally with 236.1 rushing yards per game, and second in the league in total offense with 416.6 yards per game.

Tailback Ki-Jana Carter carried the ball only four times in the Lions' last three regular season games, but still finished second in the Big Ten in rushing with 1,046 yards. Wideout Bobby Engram was fifth in the conference in receiving yardage with 873 yards on 48 catches.

Penn State would have to hope its passing game, which ranked 10th in the conference at 180.5 yards per game, could maintain the late-season success it achieved in the wins over Northwestern and Michigan State. At the same time, the Nittany Lions would have to rely on their defense to stop the high-flying Shuler and company.

"The key is the front four," Ravotti said. "It's us getting pressure on Shuler and stopping the run. We had a problem with that against Michigan and we've had a problem with that against other teams. We have to go out there with a new attitude. We need to stop the run and take away the pass, because they're very good at both."

One writer suggested keeping Tennessee's offense off the field entirely might be the Lions' best solution, which was probably true. But with that seeming to be out of the question, Penn State felt it could adequately handle the many possibilities Tennessee would undoubtedly throw at it.

The availability of Carter in the backfield would be a tremendous boost to the Nittany Lions' hopes for success. He suffered a calf injury against Illinois near the end of the regular season and missed his team's last two games against Northwestern and Michigan State. The injury at first appeared minor, but took longer to heal than was expected. Carter, who averaged 6.6 yards per carry during the season, was optimistic about his chances of playing in the Citrus Bowl, but was told by team doctors to be very cautious so as not to jeopardize his long-term health.

"Right now, I'm saying yeah, I should be playing," Carter said just before the Nittany Lions left for Florida. "We're going day-to-day, and they have me doing more stuff each day without my knee bothering me."

If Carter couldn't go, Paterno knew he could count on Mike Archie, who rushed for 134 yards against Illinois and 173 against Northwestern. His third tailback, Stephen Pitts, also proved capable as he rushed for 351 yards in a limited role throughout the season.

One thing the Lions were thinking about as they headed to Florida was erasing the memories of past trips to the Sunshine State. Penn State had lost its last seven games played in Florida, dating back to 1976. The current roster wouldn't remember that Gator Bowl victory, but they did remember the events of January 1, 1993.

That day marked the sputtering conclusion to the lifeless 1992 season of disaster. The Blockbuster Bowl provided a wonder drug for insomniacs as Penn State slept through a 24-3 setback against Stanford. There was no excitement, no life, not even a pulse in the Nittany Lions' system that day.

"I think last year a lot of people were thinking, let's get down there and get it over with," guard Mike Malinoski said. "This year it's different. Everybody's saying we have a chance to win a big ball game, get ourselves in the Top 10 and end up with 10 wins."

To do that, there would have to be some sacrifices. One in particular was Paterno's decision to head to Florida earlier than the normal routine. The Citrus Bowl committee didn't require the participating teams to arrive in Orlando until December 23, but Paterno felt a few extra days in the southern climate would do his players a world of good.

The plan called for a December 19 departure that would land the Nittany Lions in Melbourne, Florida. Practices were to be held at the Florida Institute of Technology before moving to Orlando at the required time. But those four days in Melbourne were by no means intended to be an early vacation for the Nittany Lions.

This trip was intended for players, coaches and staff only. No coach's families, no band, no cheerleaders. They would go to Orlando on their prescribed days. At first the players thought they would go through the typical early walk-throughs, without the shoulder pads and other heavy equipment. Paterno, however, had other ideas.

He remembered the last couple of trips to Florida. The snoozer from a year before, and the 1988 Citrus Bowl, when Penn State was waxed by Clemson, 35-10, in a game that was as lifeless as the score indicated. He wanted to do everything possible to keep that from happening again.

Sometimes, coaches use bowl practices to get a head start on the next season. Senior players get a little less work, while the guys who will be filling their roles come next season get closer looks from the coaching staff. Paterno had no such intentions as he prepared his team against Tennessee.

"Our whole focus is on winning the game," he said. "Tennessee is too good for that. We owe it to the seniors, the fans, everybody."

Paterno asked his players in a team meeting if they were up to the task of spending their holiday away from their families in Florida and his answer was a unanimous yes.

"I think it's going to work out well," kicker Craig Fayak said. "We'll get used to the warmer weather, get used to the climate and the whole situation. It's a tough job, but somebody's got to do it. I guess we'll volunteer to suffer and go down to Florida."

Fayak smiled when he spoke of suffering, but little did he know what the coaching staff had in mind for the players once they arrived at their practice camp in Melbourne. Players who make bowl trips consistently, like they do at Penn State, get used to the commotion of having to be here and there. There are photo sessions, media conferences, and still more photo opportunities. Sometimes those things can become more of a distraction than an attraction for players.

Paterno knew he couldn't tie his players down completely, but did stress his hopes to see a little more self-control in their off-field activities. He just wanted to maintain his bowl philosophy of having fun, but not getting carried away.

"I'd like a little less activity," he said. "You're always worried about their legs, and they're running around. But that's all part of it. I was young once and probably would have enjoyed running around to all those places myself, getting to meet new people, particularly of the other sex."

Why would a 9-2 team go back to the basics? Because it was a new approach. Something out of the ordinary to put the spark into a team that may not have even needed one. Football practices in Melbourne could also have been called, Pre-Season II. That's because Paterno had his troops on the field almost at the crack of dawn for a morning practice session for the next three days. After that it was lunch, then an afternoon session. None of the light stuff either. Pads were an essential, as the players went through some of the most rigorous practices they had seen all year.

The players may have been surprised at Paterno's unusual approach, but none were upset. There was no moaning or back-biting. Everyone took the regimen as a challenge.

"We're serious about this game," center Bucky Greeley said. "We want to practice hard, we want to do the hard work that it takes to win the ball game. Let's face it, bowl games are only fun if you win them."

That was a far cry from, "Let's get down there and get this thing over with."

Joe Paterno gave his team just the right amount of slack in terms of free time once the Lions had settled in Orlando. The two-a-days were over, and the players were able to get into the normal game-week situation. The Citrus Bowl committee had done its part to see that both teams were well entertained. There were the usual functions or luncheons that brought both teams together for an afternoon or evening, a trip to Sea World, and what vacation in Orlando would be complete without the customary visit to Disney World? The players had their fun and obeyed all the curfews, which made it a more enjoyable trip for the assistant coaches, who are often assigned to monitor the nightly curfew checks.

One of the requirements of both teams at any bowl game is the media day session. Players dress in their game uniforms for easier identification and mill about on the stadium turf for the media contingent to poke and prod with seemingly endless questions. Questions about the regular season pop up. Personal statistics are discussed. Favorite movies, favorite colors. You name it, a reporter has probably asked it.

On one section of the Citrus Bowl Stadium field, a young man wearing the white pants and dark blue No. 12 Penn State jersey watches a circle of cameras and microphones slowly form around him. His blond hair glistens in the sun as he answers the questions, one after the other, of the circumstances that lifted him to his current status. For the entire season, Kerry Collins kept his thoughts and feelings to himself. Occasionally, the harshest response anyone could get out of him was how unfortunate it was that John Sacca decided to quit the Penn State football team in the middle of the season.

Collins, a redshirt junior, accepted Paterno's decision to start Sacca when the season opened September 4 against Minnesota. He figured it was best to keep his mouth shut and be prepared in case his services were needed somewhere down the road. That opportunity came in the Nittany Lions' third game at Iowa when Paterno tired of Sacca's poor decision making and inserted Collins in the middle of the second quarter.

Sacca never started another game and threw only seven more passes as a Nittany Lion. He threatened to leave Penn State immediately after the Iowa game, but was talked into staying by friends and members of his family. Two weeks later, Sacca made good on his threat. Relegated to mop-up duty, the junior quarterback withdrew from school and left campus in his Chevy Blazer. For days, no one, not even his parents, knew of his whereabouts. Finally, Sacca turned up in Arizona, where his older brother, Tony, was playing for the Phoenix Cardinals. It wasn't until weeks later that Sacca returned to his home and revealed his reasons for defection to a reporter from the *New York Times*.

"I wasn't running away from anything," Sacca was quoted as saying. "It takes more guts to do what I did than to stay there [at Penn State] and be a puppet."

Kerry Collins can only smile when he considers such a comment. It is amusing to surmise that all of Joe Paterno's players are puppets in Sacca's eyes, while he did the brave thing by walking out on his teammates when the going reached its toughest point. Collins stayed behind to face the criticism that every Penn State quarterback endures. When he spent the rest of the season as the Nittany Lions' starter, the words Collins heard most often were, "Put in Richardson."

Such is the life as Penn State's starting quarterback. You're only as popular as your backup status. Even when Sacca was gone, Collins publicly wished him well and repeatedly said it was an unfortunate situation. But the national story that labeled Penn State's players as puppets didn't sit right with too many people, especially Collins.

"I don't think it takes too much guts to quit," Collins said. "If anything, it takes a lot of guts to stay here. I've put up with a lot of crap from the fans and the media, and to be honest with you, it's tough playing under Joe as a quarterback. I certainly think that it takes more guts to stay than it does to quit, to throw in the towel and give it up like John did."

When Sacca quit the team after the Maryland game, Penn State was heading into the meat of its Big Ten schedule and about to play two key matchups with Michigan and Ohio State. Many questioned the timing of Sacca's decision and wondered whether it would create a distraction to the team. The players quickly insisted it would not. "Joe had a handle on the situation," defensive tackle Lou Benfatti said. "He told us just to concentrate on the games we had coming up and don't dwell on it."

Collins was a little bit rusty when he stepped in against Iowa, but looked sharp in his next two starts against Rutgers and Maryland. At that time, the skeptics said, "Yeah, but look at the teams he was playing against." Collins had his team at the goal line in the loss to Michigan, but couldn't punch it in. He was unimpressive in the Lions' downfall at Ohio State. The critics came out of the woodwork after that one.

The 6-foot-5, 235-pound quarterback answered them by leading his team to four straight wins and a 9-2 finish. Penn State played in near monsoon conditions at home against Illinois. The final score was 28-14, but most of the Lions' yardage came on the ground and all of their points were scored in the first half. Collins was a mere five of 18 for 49 yards, but the fans who booed him knew nothing of Penn State's conservative second-half approach that included just seven passes.

When he put up some impressive numbers at Northwestern the following week, the critics' answer was, "So what, everybody puts up those kind of numbers against Northwestern." The field at Michigan State was like an ice rink in the early going due to a combination of rain and snow that hit the East Lansing area the night before. Furthermore, Michigan State shut down Penn State's No. 1 rushing offense and forced the Lions to throw when it built a 20-point lead in the third quarter. Collins rallied his team to the one-point victory and finally seemed to gain some points in confidence.

"Writers and fans question my talent level, do I really have what it takes to be a Division I quarterback, that kind of thing," Collins said. "I think it's unfair criticism because of the conditions and because we were playing some tough teams. People were saying, 'Why don't you put Wally in, why don't you do this, you're lucky Sacca isn't here.'"

It was after the win over Illinois that Collins seemed to let the fans get to him for the first time.

"Everybody was booing me, telling me I was the worst quarterback that ever went to Penn State," he said. "At that point, it just got ridiculous."

So Collins did the only thing he could do. He ignored everything — the criticism, the fans, the booing. He decided to use whatever was left of the Nittany Lions' season and give it everything he had to prove he belonged behind the center at Penn State.

"I had a lot more confidence," Collins said of those final two regular season games. "It actually started with the Indiana game [a 38-31 Penn State win]. To me, Illinois was pretty much a fluke. I felt a lot better as the season went on, and I think it was from getting that kind of experience.

"I don't do anything to please other people. I don't do anything with other people in mind, aside from my teammates and family and friends. It was a matter of personal pride for myself because even though there were tough conditions, statistically, I didn't do well. If I had to prove it to anybody, I had to prove it to my teammates. But I really didn't do it for the people who were saying this or that. I did it for myself."

After the Michigan State game, Paterno commented on Collins' steady improvement and said he felt "Collins seemed to be getting a feel for the game." The teammates he so wanted to impress also stood up and took notice.

"Kerry being a quarterback, he's going to shoulder most of the blame," said Bobby Engram, who with 48 receptions during the regular season, became any Penn State quarterback's favorite receiver. "He shouldn't take all that because part of it was the receivers, part of it was the line. Kerry had some bad games, but if the offense isn't clicking, if it's not precise and consistent, it isn't going to work. Obviously, the quarterback is the one who's blamed."

Collins never whined or complained about the criticism — warranted or not — during the regular season. He just did his job with the knowledge that one day this turmoil would be behind him and he would be able to settle into the starting quarterback position comfortably, without having to look over his own shoulder.

His regular season statistics weren't really indicative of a poor quarterbacking performance. Collins played very little in the Lions' first two games, but finished the season with 1,605 yards passing, which was the ninth-best single-season total in school history, and completed 50.1 percent of his passes.

Collins hung around to accept the blame for Penn State's inability to win the Big Ten Conference championship in its first year. Paterno stressed to the media in his preseason analysis that he didn't think this Penn State team would be ready to challenge for the conference crown.

"It's just too difficult when you're facing eight or nine new teams," Paterno said at the time. "I think we can do okay, but it'll take a lot to win the conference in the first year. I'm not expecting that at all."

After the losses to Michigan and Ohio State that almost assuredly knocked the Nittany Lions out of the running for the Rose Bowl, Paterno simply reiterated those remarks.

When Collins looks back on the season and recalls how Sacca used the term "puppet," it is apparent he is still unhappy with the question whether it takes more guts to stay at Penn State or just pack up and leave.

"Of course he [Sacca] is going to try to make himself look as good as possible," Collins said. "But I don't think he thought that one out before he said it. It's easy to quit. Anyone can quit. I can quit and not have to put up with the media or the fans giving me crap. It's easy to walk away. It takes a heck of a lot more guts to stay here and become a better person. John Sacca didn't become a better person by quitting. He would have become a better person if he had stayed, but that's the option he chose and he has to live with it."

Collins ended the regular season ninth on Penn State's list of all-time passing leaders with 2,615 career yards. With each game, he felt a little more comfortable, despite the booing, and his confidence level rose ever so slowly, but surely.

"Overall I think I came along well," Collins said. "I had three or four really good games, and those games were telltale of what I can do on a consistent basis if needed. Let's face it, our offense is geared toward the run. But at the same time, we're opening things up. We have some really nice things in this year as far as the passing game goes. I think the continuity between myself and the receivers is going to get better and I expect good things to happen.

"I think going into next year I'll feel confident that I had games that were rough sometimes, and because I stuck it out, I'll know I can do it every game."

It would have suited Paterno if Collins were ready to start his resurgence of confidence against Tennessee in the Citrus Bowl. Collins heard all the pre-bowl talk about the Volunteers' highly-touted quarterback, Heath Shuler, who was supposed to run Tennessee's powerful offense all over Penn State.

"I know I'm not going to throw for the same kind of yardage that Heath Shuler is going to throw for because we've got a different offense," Collins said. "He's a great quarterback, and if he comes out this year, he's going to be a top NFL pick. But I don't want him to steal the show from me."

So much for not having the confidence to do the job.

JANUARY 1, 1994, ORLANDO, FL — Penn State was a heavy underdog to Tennessee — anywhere from nine to 10 points in the eyes of most oddsmakers — and it was a common feeling among many of the experts that the Nittany Lions received the toughest draw of any Big Ten team in postseason play. The Lions' defense could not hold up against the flashy, quick Volunteer offense, or so it was felt. Heath Shuler, the All-Everything quarterback for Tennessee, had reporters and photographers hounding him everywhere he went, wondering if the Heisman Trophy runnerup would turn pro after the Citrus Bowl. Penn State enjoyed the scenery and all the pregame festivities, but the only attention it seemed to receive were the questions of how tough would it be to play against a guy like Shuler. From an offensive standpoint, quarterback Kerry Collins heard just about every question but, "Do you want to be like Heath Shuler when you get older?"

"I'd be lying if I said it didn't bother me," Collins said about all the quarterback comparisons he was subjected to. "It seems like neither myself or Penn State is getting any respect in this thing. All we can do is go out and give it our best."

That is what the major theme was in the Penn State camp. Give it your best. There was no battle cry, or 'us against them' approach.

On the other hand, Tennessee was doing its best to remember the Fiesta Bowl massacre Penn State put on the Volunteers two years before. That's why the Vols came out firing after receiving the opening kickoff. Tennessee moved 54 yards in nine plays, but had to settle for a 46-yard field goal from kicker John Becksvoort and a 3-0 lead with 11:54 remaining in the first quarter. The drive was stalled by a false start penalty, which was a small indication of things to come for the Volunteers.

Penn State went nowhere on its first possession as Collins was sacked on third down. The Lions punted to Tennessee and Shuler then orchestrated the first number on what was supposed to be Tennessee's waltz through a New Year's Day concert. The scoring drive, which was highlighted by wide receiver Billy Williams' 38-yard reverse, covered 55 yards in four plays. Shuler hit another wideout, Cory Fleming, for a 19-yard scoring pass and a 10-0 Tennessee lead with still over nine minutes left in the opening quarter.

It seemed like the rout was on as the Volunteers used two quick scores to remind everyone why they had outscored their last four 1993 opponents by an average margin of more than 45 points. Fortunately, Penn State had other thoughts in mind.

The Penn State offense has often been called conservative, which is most often a major understatement. Tennessee, meanwhile, came out with some major gimmicks in its first two possessions, most notably, Williams' big gainer on the reverse. After seeing that, Joe Paterno decided to pull out his own bag of tricks.

The Lions started from their own 30-yard line knowing they would have to get some points on the scoreboard or it could turn into that long afternoon most seemed to fear. Collins moved his offense methodically to start the drive, and then the floodgates opened.

Crucial third-down play; Penn State didn't want to give the ball back to the Volunteers again so soon. Keep the ball out of the Tennessee offense's hands. That was the game plan, wasn't it? Collins drops back to pass, looks for a second down field, and spots wideout Bobby Engram coming across the middle — *behind* the line of scrimmage.

The seldom-used center screen pass from Penn State's play book turned into a 36-yard completion as Engram got past the Volunteers' front coverage. A few plays later, tailback Ki-Jana Carter ran over from three yards out and Craig Fayak's extra point reduced Penn State's deficit to 10-7 at the end of the first quarter.

It was that one electrifying play from Collins to Engram that seemed to loosen things up on the Nittany Lions' sideline and hopefully serve notice for the rest of the afternoon.

"That play helped us set a tone," Engram said. "They saw we had some speed after all, and you could just see it in their eyes they weren't sure they could stop us."

Penn State's defense started measuring up to Tennessee as well and shut the door on the Volunteers' next possession. Fayak tied the game with a short 19-yard field goal, but it was Engram who again put the Lions in position.

The six-play, 57-yard drive started with Engram's 16-yard punt return. He then caught a 16-yard completion from Collins and later eluded three tacklers on his way to a 35-yard run on a reverse play to the Tennessee 7-yard line.

"I still can't believe some of the things he does," Carter said of Engram. "He can do anything — catch the ball, run with it, block. He has the total package. I'm excited to be playing with him."

Carter provided a bit of excitement for Penn State football fans throughout the season as well, and just being able to play in this game after the calf injury he suffered against Illinois was a welcome sight. But he was about to provide maybe the biggest play of the game.

After Beckvoort kicked a 50-yard field goal with just over a minute to play in the first half, Tennessee found itself carrying a 13-10 lead into the locker room at the intermission, or so it thought. In preparing for the Nittany Lions, the Tennessee coaches may have noticed their opposition's cunning ability to manipulate the two-minute offense in the last two wins over Northwestern and Michigan State. In both games, Penn State drove for a touchdown in the closing seconds of the first half. After Beckvoort's field goal, Paterno and company had a minute and five seconds to work with.

Collins, starting from his own 35-yard line, worked quickly and kept the Nittany Lions poised the whole way down the field. Tailback Mike Archie ran for 12 yards, Engram caught a pass for 18 more. And fullback Brian O'Neal turned a shovel pass into a 12-yard gain to move the Lions deep into Tennessee territory.

Finally, Penn State faced a second and 10 at the Volunteers' 14-yard line with 10 seconds left before halftime. Paterno and offensive coordinator Fran Ganter used a timeout to discuss the strategy that practically every person in the stadium figured on. "Throw a pass toward the back of the end zone. If our guy can't catch it, make sure theirs can't either," would have been the likely logic for Collins to follow.

"We knew we had another timeout," Paterno said, "so we decided, let's go for it."

It was, by far, the gutsiest call of the game. His team was down by three before halftime. Paterno wanted the lead. He called for a counter draw to Carter that would hopefully fool the Tennessee defense enough to allow the touchdown. It did. Tackle Derick Pickett and Engram (who else?) threw tremendous blocks and Carter broke another tackle himself to fall into the end zone for the first lead of the afternoon for the Nittany Lions.

"We had [wide receiver] Freddie Scott stationed along the sideline next to the official in case we didn't get in the end zone," Paterno said. "If he doesn't make it, we still have enough time for the timeout and kick the field goal. But we thought the play could work and decided to go for it. Fortunately, it did."

"I think most people in the stadium thought they were going to throw the football," Tennessee coach Phillip Fulmer said. "It was a gutsy call."

"It wouldn't have been such a great call if he [Carter] hadn't broken that tackle around the goal line," Paterno answered with a smile.

Scoring before the end of the first half, as Penn State had found in the last couple of regular season games, was a tremendous boost to any team's confidence. It can also do a lot to damage the opposition's psyche. Tennessee was rattled as it took the field for the second half. Penn State won the coin toss to start the game and deferred the kickoff to the second half. The Nittany Lions took advantage of the situation by moving 60 yards in 11 plays with the second-half kickoff to go ahead 24-13.

Archie carried three times for 26 yards during the drive and Penn State converted three of three third-down opportunities. In the Lions' Fiesta Bowl victory two years before over Tennessee, tight end Kyle Brady scored on the misdirection play that he soon became a master at performing. It is the play that has everyone on offense move in one direction while the tight end sort of slowly ambles to the other side. If it works right, the quarterback then turns to that side and lofts a pass to the open area where only the tight end has wandered.

It was first-and-goal at the Tennessee 7-yard line when Collins rolled to his left, turned and lofted a pass across the field to a wide open Brady in the right side of the end zone. Same play.

"It was amazing, I didn't think they'd fall for it again," said Brady, whose touchdown came with 10 minutes left in the third quarter. "My eyes lit up, and so did Kerry's. We couldn't believe how wide open I was."

"We thought it was very important in the first five minutes of the second half that we regain momentum," Fulmer said. "But really, it went from bad to worse."

Penn State's 11-point lead stood until the fourth quarter when it only grew bigger. The Nittany Lion defense did its part to control the game by sacking Shuler three times and limiting the Volunteers to negative rushing yardage in the second half. Tennessee tailback Charlie Garner rushed for 82 yards on 12 carries in the first half, but was held to just seven yards on four carries in the second.

"We just kept going," said senior defensive tackle Lou Benfatti, who registered five tackles. "That was our whole mentality the whole time we were down here. Just to go 100 percent on every play."

Penn State's offense believed in the 100 percent mentality also and delivered the knockout blow early in the fourth quarter when Collins concluded a seven-play, 49-yard drive with a 15-yard TD pass to Engram. Collins was 3-for-4 on the drive for 36 yards, including a 12-yarder to Engram right before the touchdown pass.

Paterno then allowed as many players as possible who were dressed, to get into the game. Not that he hadn't been doing so already. The idea was not to get worn out, so the coaching staff, especially defensively, rotated players in and out of the game all afternoon. The results were especially absorbing along the line of scrimmage as Penn State controlled an offensive line that had allowed only 11 sacks all year.

"We felt in a game like this, where you're going against a team with outstanding speed, you better have fresh kids in there," Paterno said. "We played a lot of down guys, we changed linebackers frequently, and I thought the young kids in the secondary played really well."

Dropped passes haunted the Volunteers throughout the game, but Fulmer and the rest of the team knew that wasn't Tennessee's major problem.

"They did some things they did on film, some things they did two years ago [in the Fiesta Bowl], some new things, and they disguised their coverages real well," Fulmer said of Penn State's defense. "But if we catch the football and protect the quarterback, we should have those things taken care of. Penn State did a good job of giving us enough rope to hang ourselves, and we did."

There were many stars for Penn State. Engram earned the game's Most Valuable Player award as he caught seven passes for 104 yards and a touchdown. The redshirt sophomore had the 35-yard reverse and returned three punts for 42 additional yards.

"I came in *thinking* he was a good football player," Fulmer said of Engram, who totaled 184 all-purpose yards. "Now I *know* he is."

Engram, who led the Big Ten with 13 regular season touchdown receptions, was one of nine Penn State players to earn All-

Conference and was the only player who was named first-team All-Big Ten by both the coaches and media.

"Never in my wildest dreams did I imagine I could have a season like this," the soft-spoken Engram told reporters after the Citrus Bowl.

"I think Bobby's as good a pure receiver as O.J. [McDuffie]," Collins said. "When you have a guy like Bobby, you want to get him the ball as much as possible."

Collins also earned some respect in the Nittany Lions' victory. While the pregame talk focused largely on Heath Shuler, Collins quietly went about his business of preparing for the game. The redshirt junior completed a modest 15 of 24 passes for 162 yards and two touchdowns, but it was his consummate professionalism under fire that made him stand apart from the much more publicized Shuler.

"Everything was 'Tennessee this and Tennessee that,'" said Collins, who just wanted the Lions to earn a little respect. "They hadn't been in a big ball game in I don't know how many weeks. In the Big Ten, we're in a big ball game every week.

"There was a lot of talk about Heath Shuler, about them blowing people out. A lot of people underestimated us. In a lot of ways, we felt we were a better team. All we had to do was go out and prove it, regardless of what writers and TV people and Tennessee people and Tennessee players have said."

So Collins decided to keep his mouth shut, along with the rest of his teammates, and simply play the game.

"I didn't want to make it a situation like, 'If I don't do as well as Heath Shuler, I fail,' kind of thing," Collins said. "I just stayed with our game plan. Nothing spectacular, just make good, solid plays.

"We were so prepared for this game. We gave it our best. We thought we were going to win going away, and that's exactly what happened."

Shuler basically got his yardage, but not the kind he was used to. Penn State held him to 205 yards on 22 of 42 passing, which produced a season-low 52 percent. Tennessee's 13 points was its lowest output since a 17-10 loss to Alabama in 1992.

"After a couple of series, we realized they weren't that great," Penn State nose guard Eric Clair said. "We got a couple of turnovers, and our offense started moving the ball. We knew we could play with them. The papers said we were heavy under-dogs, but that just motivated us more."

"I thought our kids played a great game in every aspect," said Paterno, who tied Bear Bryant's all-time record for bowl victories at 15. "It was a big game and I'm proud we won it. I think we won it because we were consistent in all aspects of the game."

Shuler found that out the hard way.

"That's part of the game," Shuler said. "On any given day, anybody can win, and any team can stop another. But things switched for us really fast and once it did, we couldn't stop it.

"We were up in the beginning, and everything seemed to be going our way with a 10-0 lead. But then they came back and scored a few times to take the lead and we never really got back into it. Penn State deserves a lot of credit, they played really well, but they didn't do anything we didn't expect."

Seldom does Penn State ever do anything out of the ordi-nary. Paterno believes in the simple, hard work theory and his players follow the game plan to a "t". The Nittany Lions re-sponded with timely execution and an overpowering display along both sides of the line of scrimmage.

"Penn State had a good line," Tennessee defensive tackle Paul Yatkowski said. "They were physical and they played well against us. I don't think they really came out and overpowered us. We just didn't execute very well against whatever they did. They had a good game plan and executed it.

"They were especially successful on the ground. They caught us off guard on the draw, especially the one [Carter's 14-yard touchdown] at the end of the first half. That was a killer. That really turned the game around. Then they scored on the opening drive of the second half, and really turned it up a notch on both sides of the ball. We didn't do too much after that."

"They kicked our butts like they did two years ago," Tennessee linebacker Reggie Ingram said. "I've never been hit so hard in my life. They hit us, ran the ball, tricked us. Just Penn State football."

Penn State's defensive performance was so well rounded that six different players recorded at least five tackles, including defensive back Cliff Dingle's six. Clair, Eric Ravotti, Jeff Perry and Brian Gelzheiser each recorded a second half sack, while Benfatti had a tackle behind the line of scrimmage and defensive end Tyoka Jackson tipped a pass that was intercepted by the game's outstanding defensive performer, free safety Lee Rubin, who was one of the players with five tackles.

There were many heroes to note in Penn State's convincing Citrus Bowl win over Tennessee. There was Collins' coolness under fire; Engram's steady, but usually sensational performance; Carter and Archie rushing for 93 and 69 yards, respectively. The offensive and defensive lines' manhandling efforts and the coaching coordinators' abilities to open things up and let the game play itself out.

But one man's contribution held more than just 28 years of coaching experience. Joe Paterno proved to be the great tactician once again by using an off-the-field element to fire his team up.

"I'm surprised it isn't more to be totally honest with you," Paterno said when asked his feelings about Penn State being a 9-1/2-point underdog to Tennessee in the weeks leading up to the Citrus Bowl. "They've got a great football team and we're gonna have a hard time staying with them."

Don't think for a minute he said the same things to his players as they labored through two-a-day practices under the hot Florida sun for three-and-a-half days. "No one is giving us a chance," Paterno would preach to his team. "They don't think we deserve to be here and those guys on the other side of the field think they're gonna have their way with you."

Paterno showed them pregame predictions, one for example, forecasting a 48-14 Tennessee landslide. Soon his players took the bait. They listened to their coach as he told them about the lack of respect they were receiving. Then they read his comments in the papers to the effect that Tennessee deserved all the accolades it was receiving and was a much better football team than Penn State. The players knew what Paterno was doing.

By the time both teams settled into the action comfortably, it appeared the pregame analysis would be proven accurate. Tennessee had built a 10-0 lead and seemed to be having its way with Penn State. But that was the cue the Lions needed.

"As a Penn State player, I go into every game thinking we're going to win," Lee Rubin said. "Whatever the media says, whatever the polls say, that's beside the point."

"Nobody puts us as a nine-and-a-half-point underdog," Penn State defensive back Shelly Hammonds said. "Tennessee's a good team, but we're pretty good, too. They took us for granted, but we came here to play."

The Nittany Lions followed their coach's lead and lauded the Volunteers with equal flair right up until game time. After that, though, the Penn State players only wanted to hear about Penn State, and that sentiment carried over long after the final outcome.

"Tennessee was talking all week about how good they were," Clair said. "They were looking at the line in the paper and the predictions people were making, and we stayed with Penn State tradition and kept our mouths shut. We knew what we had to do. We went out and proved to everyone that Penn State is for real."

"They thought we were a doormat and were just going to roll over and play dead," Kyle Brady said. "They were favored by a ridiculous amount."

"I don't know who those people [oddsmakers and critics] thought we were, but I have never seen these guys as ready to play as they were today," Hammonds added.

Even Paterno, who stirred the fire under his players' feet, felt afterward that the oddsmakers had done a bit of an injustice toward Penn State.

"That was kind of interesting," Paterno said. "I really felt a little annoyed that we would come down here and be nine-and-a-half, ten-point underdogs. We're not a great team, but that's a lot of points. I'm sure that rankled some of the kids. I don't think we ever felt we were an underdog, quite frankly. We felt were as good a football team as Tennessee."

Paterno, the coach, did his job on the field, and Paterno, the motivator, performed magic off the field. He used the best method he knew of to overcome the talented Tennessee offense, and equally strong defense. Mind games. He used psychology to psyche up his own players, and maybe to psyche out the opposition.

As the clock wound down on Penn State's Citrus Bowl victory, thoughts began to turn already to next season. But Paterno wanted to think about the importance of this latest win. The satisfaction was evident on everyone's faces around the locker room as Paterno reflected on the importance of winning the Big Ten's second-most lucrative bowl in the Nittany Lions' first season in the conference.

"The only way to see what this game will mean for next year depends on how these kids take it. If they take it with the idea they could be a real good football team and work as hard as this team in the winter program, spring practice and in the summer, it will mean a lot. If they feel like this is something beyond the fact that we won a big bowl game, then it doesn't do much for you."

Only time would tell what the future held for the Nittany Lions, but judging from the determination that overcame mid-season adversity, there wasn't a player among those returning for 1994 that didn't believe there were bigger and better things ahead.

16

Getting Things Right

The Penn State Nittany Lions learned a lot about themselves in the fall of 1993. Not so much about winning on a major college level. No matter who the players were, they had always been able to do that. Instead, they learned about competition on a slightly different level. Penn State had known no other style of football other than playing as an independent. It had done so for the past 106 seasons. But along came 1993, and the Nittany Lions had to adjust to a different style.

The Big Ten Conference was a whole new ball game for Penn State, but Joe Paterno took it as a major challenge. There were eight new teams on the Nittany Lions' schedule, teams that hadn't appeared on a Penn State calendar in at least 10 years, but would become an annual fixture in the seasons to come.

Penn State handled its new setting fairly well, especially considering the down year it suffered in 1992. Not only did Paterno have to contend with rallying his team from a 7-5 downer in '92, he was facing that task as head coach of the Big Ten's 11th member.

"It was certainly challenging," Paterno said at the conclusion of Penn State's successful 10-2 inaugural season in the Big Ten. "I spent more time examining tapes and making sure our plans were okay because I really wasn't quite comfortable that I knew enough about the new teams we were playing."

One thing Paterno knew going into the season was that the physical style of the Big Ten was incredible. Week in and week out, there would be hitting like his players had never seen. But the benefits of the Big Ten would far outweigh any adversity that would come along. Paterno told the fans how the Big Ten would offer excitement with each game, and even a loss did not mean the end of a season, as seemed to be the case when Penn State lost to Miami in the sixth game of the '92 season.

That statement proved true in the middle of the first ever Big Ten season for Penn State in 1993 when, despite back-to-back losses to Michigan and Ohio State, the Nittany Lions still had an outside chance of playing in the Rose Bowl. As an independent, a mid-season loss seriously damages your hopes for a major bowl bid and just about erases any thoughts of a national championship.

"Going into the conference was just about as I thought it would be," said Paterno, whose team finished seventh in the final USA Today/CNN coaches poll and eighth in the Associated Press poll. "I thought it would add something to our season and it did. Even though we lost a couple of games, we still had something to shoot for and there were always goals to realize. Now that the fans are more aware of the options to our team in the conference, the coming years should be very exciting."

Paterno has spoken for the last couple of years of his intention to keep coaching until he is 70 years old. He was 67 when he ended the 1993 season and at that point, his intentions apparently had not wavered.

"I'd still like to think of it that way," he said. "One very important factor would be the state of the team at that time. I really want to leave the team to the next person on a positive note. I don't want to jump ship with things in disarray because I don't think it would be fair to the next person."

If he does stick around past 70, who could blame him? Coaching in a big-time atmosphere for one of the greatest college football teams ever would be an enjoyable experience for just about anyone. But Paterno also knows how much pressure can be involved if that finely tuned machine seems to sputter just a bit.

That could have been the case after Penn State's second consecutive 5-0 start in 1993. The year before, the Lions lost five of their last seven and seemed very disinterested. When Michigan and Ohio State won two games from Penn State in the middle of 1993, fans weren't the only ones concerned about a reprise of 1992.

"I was worried, obviously, about another letdown [in 1993]," Paterno said. "but I think the circumstances were different. A year ago, we had our bowl bid all locked up. We played just terrible in some of those losses. This year, we had to play some pretty good football teams in Ohio State and Indiana. That one was really a pivotal game for us and [quarterback] Kerry Collins responded when he had to."

Paterno heard all the sarcastic remarks directed at his team wherever it visited, but to him, it was actually kind of fun. That is the beauty of college football, the fan involvement, and Paterno was delighted to see the people responding to Penn State in one form or another.

"It was a lot of fun going to the different places," he said. "The fans were very enthusiastic about welcoming us for the most part. They teased us about finding out how good we were, and those sorts of things, but we expected that. We were the hot shots from the east and those schools were showing a lot of pride."

What Paterno will remember most about fan involvement in 1993 were the fans around the Big Ten who came to State College for the first time.

"The people showed the natural resentment toward Penn State because we are the new team, but they were really impressed with the football setting that we have here in State College," he said. "You don't know how many letters I got from fans in other Big Ten locations saying things like, 'State College was a beautiful place to visit and Beaver Stadium is an excellent football facility. We were treated great by people wherever we went. Good luck in the Big Ten.' Those kind of things really meant a lot to me."

Penn State surprised many people in its first year in the conference and with a year under his belt, Paterno hopes things will only get better for his team in future seasons.

"It should be a little bit easier to prepare for 1994," Paterno said. "We've gotten our feet wet and we'll know a little bit more about the teams we're playing now that we've been through it once. I don't think we'll have to spend so much time dissecting film to pick up certain coaches' tendencies and things like that. We should have a better feel for that because we've already been through it once."

Paterno also senses that his players may be less subjected to the harsh criticisms and wise-cracking remarks from fans and players of other teams in the coming years. Even the coaches and athletic directors who seemed less than thrilled to have Penn State in the conference in '93 may warm up if Paterno is figuring right.

"I think things will get better," he said. "Really, they did as the season went on. And we had a Big Ten coaches meeting in New York before the bowl games, and I got the feeling that it wasn't 10-and-1 anymore. It seemed like we were all Big Ten now.

"I think we had to go through that first year. Many of the coaches in the conference have been very supportive, and really knocked themselves out to make us feel more comfortable. But I would think that at one time there were some in the conference who didn't want us in it, didn't think we belonged in it. And I don't get that sense anymore."

One thing players and coaches both noticed about the Big Ten was the increased intensity level. "You'd see it week in and week out," defensive tackle Lou Benfatti said. "Those teams were out there hitting. They'd come after you with every play, and I think that was something we had to become accustomed to in a big hurry."

"There is a natural intensity level in conference competition every week," Paterno said. "And I think it was even more so this season because every one of those teams was determined to not be a team that let Penn State beat them. I think the caliber of play was better than I thought it would be, probably better than a lot of people thought it would be. A lot of the teams were young and very well coached. I thought the league would be tough and with seven teams in bowl games, I think that shows that it was."

Penn State, like everyone else in the Big Ten Conference, played 11 grueling football games to complete its 1993 regular season schedule. On a 100-yard field, it's hard to believe that a conference championship could be decided by 12 inches. That was it. One foot of measurement kept Penn State from playing in the Rose Bowl in its first year of Big Ten competition. What an accomplishment that would have been. It is difficult for Joe Paterno to find anything disappointing about a 9-2 regular season and a convincing win over one of the top five teams in the country in a bowl game. But if one thing sticks in his memory during the lapse between seasons, it may be the Lions' inability to push the ball those final 12 inches for a score against Michigan.

"You know," Paterno said. "You can look back and say, well, why did you do this on the goal line against Michigan, and things like that. And fortunately, I would probably do the same thing against Michigan if I were in the same situation prior to the game."

Believe it or not, the Penn State coaching staff is prepared for such situations as the goal line series against Michigan in October of 1993. The staff scripts out a series of offensive plays for nearly every possible situation during the week before each game, considering such factors as the down, the distance and field position. When the plays were run against Michigan — two quarterback sneaks and two tries up the middle by the tailback — Paterno had his reasons for making the calls.

"We had an idea how to get the ball in the end zone," Paterno said. "We just didn't execute it right. When you think about it being that close, then yeah, it could have been a little bit disappointing."

Penn State's offensive coordinator, Fran Ganter, said the Michigan game was one that still has him thinking from time to time, but he agreed that poor execution was the ultimate factor in Penn State's ineffectiveness at that time.

"We got away from the script a little bit during that series," Ganter said. "We didn't go with the original plan, but we were pretty confident they were going to do one thing and they didn't. So we said, well, they're gonna do it this time, and they didn't. Then, on the fourth-down play, they finally did what we thought they would do and we didn't execute. There was no indecision. Joe knew what we were gonna do, and that's what we were gonna do."

What does it mean to be a member of the Penn State football team? Everyone is special in that unit. Everyone from players, managers, trainers and coaches. For every person who would describe their Penn State football experience as four years of hell, there would be a thousand more to contradict that theory. The requirements are simple. You must work hard, you must keep up your grades, and you must be loyal to the person working beside you. It is a common bond like no other, where the difference between winning and losing can make all the difference in the world.

"At the end of last year we weren't having fun," senior defensive back Derek Bochna said before the Lions' 1994 Citrus Bowl appearance. "Coming into the last game this year, it's going to be sad to get it over with because I was having so much fun."

The end of the 1993 season could just as easily have turned into another lost season if Penn State had listened to the so-called experts after losing its second game in a row at Ohio State. "Now that the Big Ten's powerhouses had stepped into the picture, Penn State proved it wasn't on the same level," was the way one scribe had put it.

The Nittany Lions may not have won the two featured matchups on their Big Ten schedule, but the losses were in no way an indication that the team didn't belong in the Big Ten. Character says a lot about a team's performance, as well. Penn State responded to the mid-season slump by winning its last four regular season games and the Citrus Bowl against Tennessee, one of the better teams in the country at the time.

Michigan finished 4-4 in the conference and lost to Illinois and eventual conference champ, Wisconsin. Ohio State played for a tie instead of chancing a two-point conversion late in its game against Wisconsin. That decision probably cost the Buckeyes the Rose Bowl.

If anything, the Big Ten probably added to Penn State's already proud character. The Lions learned how to deal with the everyday pressures of conference play, and discovered some new rivalries in the league, whether those teams would like to think so or not.

The 1993 senior football class lived a piece of Penn State history it will never forget. It was a part of the changeover that is sure to be only the springboard to even greater things at Beaver

Stadium, or any other Big Ten campus that hosts the new guys on the block in the generic blue and white uniforms.

Looking into the eyes of the senior Penn State players, one could see the envy directed toward the underclassmen. It was time to move on, but the elders could feel the electricity that was only beginning.

"I'll never forget that I was here for the beginning of all this," senior defensive end Eric Ravotti said. "There is no doubt in my mind that Penn State belongs here, and they'll get their chance to go to the Rose Bowl very soon."

"It was a great experience," defensive back Shelly Hammonds said. "You kind of don't know what to expect until it happens, but once it does, it turns into the thrill of a lifetime. I'll never forget it."

It is now up to the underclassmen to carry on the torch that was passed by those senior members of what will go down as a historical team. It was a team effort that refused to give up when others gave up on them, but it took seniors like Ravotti, Hammonds, Bochna, Lou Benfatti, Tyoka Jackson, Mike Malinoski, Craig Fayak, and so many others to step up and convince the rest of the country that Penn State truly belonged in the Big Ten Conference.

"There is no better feeling in the world," said Tyoka Jackson, one of 19 seniors who played in his final game for Penn State in the Citrus Bowl. "This is the reason I came to Penn State. Part of me would love to come back next year, but I know it's time to move on. I have a feeling this team is gonna do something very special."

It'll be difficult to top the special season that was 1993, Penn State's first ever in the Big Ten.

Epilogue

When I went through the college football recruiting phase in 1982, I received a lot of exposure to the conference scene. The ACC recruited me heavily, as did the Big Ten and others. I grew up in Forestville, Maryland, and often found myself wondering if I should stay in state and attend the University of Maryland. But Maryland never had what I was looking for.

The truth is, I never even visited Maryland's campus in the recruiting phase, because they didn't have the comfort zone I was seeking. The comfort zone was finding a school where I knew the tradition wouldn't be questioned, where academics wouldn't be a question, where honesty and integrity wouldn't be questioned. Maryland had those things, but it didn't have the stability that was part of that comfort zone. They were in the midst of a coaching change and I didn't want to go through the possibility of changing coaches every year or two.

I found more and more that I wanted to play for an independent, because I knew in conference play, from being a football fan for a long time, that if you achieved the goal of your conference every year—to win the conference championship—you would go to the same bowl game every year. Win the Big Ten, go to the Rose Bowl. Win the Pac-10, go to the Rose Bowl. Win the WAC championship, go to the Holiday Bowl. At that time, if you won the ACC, you went to the Citrus Bowl.

I figured if I go to a conference, I may have success and win the conference every year, but I felt I'd be cheating myself by going to the same bowl every year. I liked the idea of going to an independent school that might contend for a national title every year, play in a different bowl game, travel and see the country while not being bound by league play; playing the same teams over and over. That, to me, was very attractive, and that was why I chose to attend Penn State.

Another thing about football when I came out was the fact that conference teams weren't winning the national championship. Then, schools like Miami, Notre Dame and Penn State were dominating college football. The word "independent" really summed it up. They were able to play the best teams and go to the best bowls without being bound.

Talks of joining the Big Ten hadn't started yet at Penn State when I was considering college, so it wasn't something they hid from me in recruiting me. Initially, the announcement disappointed me. I was in my sophomore year, and I realized we'd be going into the Big Ten by the time my last season came around. At the time, I thought, "Wow, I'm glad I only have to play one year in the conference." When I thought more about it, I realized it would still be the situation I had wanted all along, but maybe better. We would be playing new teams in my last year and we'd have a chance to go to the Rose Bowl. That was how I resolved it.

I started out looking at the 1993 season as my last year at Penn State University, and it was necessary that I played well. Then as I had more time to think about it, and to see all the preparation, I said to myself, "This thing's bigger than I thought it would be." I realized this is a team that could go down in history as Penn State's first season in the Big Ten. I realized I'd be a senior, and a leader on the team. It would be something I could remember for the rest of my life, something I could feel special about.

Once I started realizing all the potential the season had for being special, I started taking a lot more pride in being a part of it. I don't know how all the other players made their decisions to attend Penn State, but I know they shared my sentiments as the season drew closer. By the time opening day came around, I think we all shared a lot of pride in playing for Penn State as part of the Big Ten.

The one thing that stood out about the season was the competition level. If you are a football player and a true competitor, if you enjoy playing against the best week in and week out, there will be competition. What I had not anticipated was the intensity on the field during conference play. It didn't matter who we played, from No. 1 in the standings to the last place team. When you play them, it's a totally different ballgame than playing an out-of-conference team. And it even gets more intensified at the away games. When you go on the road in the Big Ten, it's a tough, tough haul. That's something I'll always remember about Big Ten conference play.

Athletics is one of those things where you can control most of what you do and how you do it. But there's one little part of it that you can't control. That is, what happens through the level of competition. You can try to play your best and play at the highest level you possibly can, but there's always one more level that you can't get to without excellent competition. That's what I thought we already had before we entered the Big Ten, but once we got in the conference, I realized there was another level we could go to as a team.

And as for me, an individual football player, I'd like to think we added another level to the Big Ten by bringing in our competition at Penn State. After all the sour grapes, and the articles saying the rest of the Big Ten didn't want us, I think we're happy to be a part of the Big Ten and I hope in a couple of years the rest of the conference will be happy to have us.

I remember after the last game at Michigan State, when we rallied from 20 points down to win, I was sitting in the locker room thinking to myself, "We fell a little bit short of our goal of playing in the Rose Bowl. I wish we would have started Big Ten play my junior year." I didn't wish for another year at Penn State, I'll be honest about that. Four years was enough for me to get what I needed to get out of school, and enough for what the school could get out of me. But I did think about wishing we'd have entered my junior year because we'd have been a little more prepared my senior year, and maybe we could have won that thing.

That's another thing: these teams' biggest goal has always been to go to the Rose Bowl. Why not a national title? They feel, and now I understand it, if you can get to the Rose Bowl, a national title is not far behind. Because of the nature of Big Ten play if a team ever goes undefeated in this conference, the national championship should be right there, hanging in the balance.

As I said, I didn't want an extra year, but I just wished we would have gotten there one year earlier. I want one more crack at Ohio State. And Michigan— I want two more cracks at them. The competition of the players and coaches left me hungry for a little bit more. It looks like Penn State will be in the Big Ten for a long, long time, and I hope the players who follow me will find that same hunger and desire that we all did in our first year in the league.

I realize now I was fortunate enough to be a part of something very special at a place I'll never forget. I'll always be happy about that.

Tyoka Jackson
Senior defensive end